*Rediscovering the Holy Spirit
from Creation through Today.*

SPIRIT +
TRUTH

DAVID TOKAJER

D1527058

Spirit + Truth

(Second Edition)

David Tokajer
10526 County Road 64
Daphne, AL 36526
ISBN: 9781711912554

Published by:
David Tokajer: 10526 County Road 64 Daphne, AL 36526

Cover design: Image from pngtree.com

Scott + Laura,

I pray this book is a blessing. Especially considering Laura has known me since High School and still bought it.

Dut 31:6

Dedicated to my wife, Danielle, who has put up with me through all the crazy ups and downs, who has challenged me to chase after God's calling and dreams for our life, and who has walked hand-in-hand with me through it all for 18 years and counting.

INTRODUCTION

I am a fervent believer in the Power of God. I don't mean people showing off like certain televangelists that seem to drive people away from God rather than closer to Him. I'm talking about the kind of Power of God that Moses had radiating on his face after he encountered the *Shechinah* (Divine Glory) of God in Exodus. The kind of Power of God that changes hearts and lives, that reorients peoples' directions, that causes hearts to make *T'shuvah* (repentance).

There has been a strong conviction on my heart these past few years, likely longer than that, and it's taken me this long to wake up to the reality, that the Body of Messiah has been a poor template of the Power of God. It is my hope, desire, and prayer that this changes and soon. The *Besorah* (Good News) of Messiah needs us to better portray Adonai's presence than we have been doing recently.

We live in a time that I like to call the "Post-Truth Era." You may find yourself asking, "what does this mean…?" I didn't coin the terminology of course, nor was it originally intended in this particular context, but the weight and reality are just the same. It was originally used in reference to political discourse, in which talking points at emotional responses rather than factually based truths are common. The idea is simple though, we live in an era that supposes what is truth for me may not be truth for the next guy. In other words, most people would say there is no "absolute truth." Absolute truth is a philosophical concept that can be defined as inflexible reality: fixed, invariable, unalterable facts.

This presents a major problem for Believers, seeing as how we believe that certain things are absolute truths and inflexible realities. Such as:

- The death, burial, and resurrection of *Yeshua HaMashiach* (Jesus the Messiah)
- The young nation of Israel stood at the base of Mount Sinai and heard the audible voice of God speak forth
- That God spoke the *Aseret HaDibrot* (Ten Words/ Commandments) to Israel at Mount Sinai
- We believe that to be saved one must accept the blood atonement of Messiah Yeshua
- We believe in heaven and hell
- A seven-day creation
- That Adam and Eve were the first humans
- That the *Ruach HaKodesh* (Holy Spirit) was poured out in Acts 2
- The virgin birth of Yeshua
- Yeshua's ability to heal the blind, the deaf, the lame, even raise the dead to life
- That Yeshua ascended into heaven from the Mount of Olives
- That the events of Acts 2 occurred literally

But, for the most part, those with whom we might find ourselves sharing the Gospel with today likely do not accept the possibility that there is an absolute truth at all.

All of these things, along with the thousands of other vitally important biblical narratives that either point to or flow from the plan of Salvation are simply viewed by most outside the Body of Messiah (and in today's world, likely some within) as folklore and fairy tale. In their eyes, anyone who believes in such narratives is simply naive, close-minded, or too ignorant and uneducated to know any better. In today's society, especially in western society, anyone who is a Believer is viewed as an idiot, a simpleton, someone who is just blinded to the rapidly changing world around us by the archaic tales of long ago. They even go so far as to attack the very book we find our faith in—the Bible. We believe it to be infallible and authoritative, but society would have us believe that because it was written by human hands over centuries upon centuries and then translated and retranslated throughout millennia that it can't possibly be anything other than tainted.

Not to be left unmentioned is the reality that leading up to this "Post-Truth Era" the Body of Messiah hasn't really done much to help our case. Think about the failed televangelists, the many, many ministers who have fallen prey to sexual deviance, the mass amounts of overly obvious hypocrisies seen easily from the outside. It is easy to talk the talk... But, so few actually attempt to walk the walk... Even more horrendous is that the outside world sees this for what it really is, a total mess and realistically a shame on the Body of Messiah.

So, this begs the question, how is a Believer to share the Gospel in such a despairing and depressing world as we now find ourselves in? Matthew 28:19-20 says,

"Go therefore and make disciples of all nations, immersing them in the name of the Father and the Son and the Ruach HaKodesh, teaching them to observe all I have commanded you. And remember! I am with you always, even to the end of the age."

This is, in my opinion, one of the most important statements in all of the Bible. It is a directive for all believers, not just pastors, rabbis, missionaries, evangelists, etc., it is for ALL believers. But, if that is the case and this "Post-Truth Era" is where we find ourselves, how do we share the Gospel when most people we'd likely come into contact with would find such faith a waste of time and energy?

I pose the answer is found in the dynamic presence of the Power of God—the Ruach HaKodesh. I have realized that no amount of evangelism, apologetics, missions work, preaching, altar calls, or anything else will amount to much today without there being a dramatic shift to a reliance on the Power of God first and foremost. We can preach until our faces turn blue, but if we are not truly transformed by the Ruach then the world around us will see and they will not buy into a word we have to say. They must see Him in us before they hear us say anything about Him, they must see Him in us before they see us at all.

What would the effect of our faith look like on the world around us if we truly walked in the fire of the Holy Spirit as we see all over the pages of the Book of Acts, the Gospels, or even the life of Elijah and Elisha? What if people saw the radiant Glory of God in our lives before they ever heard us speak the first word of the Gospel? What if they saw the Presence of God in His bride in such a way that they couldn't help but be drawn to the reality of the hope they need most in their lives? But, what would this even look like?

I will attempt to respond to each one of these questions moving forward. The core purpose of my writing this book (as will be discussed in greater detail in the first chapter) is that I believe (as many Messianic Jewish rabbis before me have postulated) that we are on the cusp of an end-time revival, the latter-day rains, the realization of the promise of life from the dead from Romans 11:15. I believe the Messianic Jewish movement is an end-time revival movement that will ignite a wildfire of the Ruach that will impact the great Body of Messiah as a whole. So, if this is the case, if there is a revival coming, what do we do with all of the varied and contradicting opinions, doctrines and theologies on the Holy Spirit? This book takes an in-depth look at the Ruach HaKodesh from creation through the *Brit Chadashah* (New Testament) and into today with the goal of developing a groundwork for a more biblical approach to understanding the empowering of the Holy Spirit.

So let's jump right into it...

CHAPTER 1

I believe fervently that we are in the days of the latter rains. Scripture talks about the latter outpouring in Joel 2, as Peter references in Acts 2, I believe that these days are upon us. I believe we are going to see an increase in signs, wonders, and miracles through the Ruach HaKodesh in our lives, in our congregations, and in the Body of Messiah. It is through these things that we will see the most impact in the lives of those who are in need of and hungry for Salvation and they will see the Lord and find Salvation because of His Presence in their midst.

As such, I also realize that we all come from different backgrounds, and in Messianic Judaism that is most certainly the case. In our synagogue in Daphne, AL we have those that come from a traditional Jewish background, those that come from a more Pentecostal background, those from Christian backgrounds that believe in Cessationism (that the gifts of the Spirit have ceased) and everything in between. So, as a congregation, where we see the Ruach moving in a powerful and mighty way and we see the Lord moving among us, it is important to have a biblically solid foundation of what the move of the Ruach HaKodesh looks like. That is where this book is birthed from, a look at the Ruach HaKodesh from Creation through the modern-day and how we are to operate in it.

So, we begin looking at this discussion at the very beginning, *Bereshit*, Genesis chapter one. But first, I want to set up a discussion on why humanity was created in the first place. I know it may be hard to believe, but in the grand scheme of things, history shows us that God didn't need us to muck things up for Him. So, obviously, there was a grander picture He was looking at in creating humanity.

When we look at the overall context of Scripture I think we find the reason He created us is very clear, to love us. God is love. As a matter of fact, the sum foundation of all of the commandments, of all of Scripture is *LOVE*…

When Yeshua is approached in Matthew 22 with a tricky question by the Torah scholars and scribes asking what the most important commandment in all the Torah was, He quoted directly from Deuteronomy 6:5 and Leviticus 19:18. These words are not just powerful within Scripture, but they are also an integral part of Jewish liturgical prayer every single day. Yeshua's response in Matthew 22 was, ***37 And He said to him, "'You shall love Adonai your God with all your heart, and with all your soul, and with all your mind.' 38 This is the first and greatest commandment. 38 And the second is like it, 'You shall love your neighbor as yourself.' The entire Torah and the Prophets hang on these two commandments."***

He created us to love us and to receive our love. He created us to be in His Presence. His Presence is a tangible reality and He created us to be in His Presence, in His Shechinah. He created us to experience His Presence in our lives day in and day out.

Notice after Adam and Eve sinned the Bible says the Lord came to walk in the Garden in the middle of the day. It does not say that they were at all surprised that He came to do this. We have no idea how long they lived in the Garden before they ate of the fruit, the Bible doesn't give us a time frame here. They were there for some time, they ate of the fruit and sinned and they were kicked out of the Garden. But, we have no idea how much time passed. And it is safe to presume that the reason they weren't shocked when the Lord came to walk with them in the middle of the day was that this was something that happened every day, that the Lord came to meet with His creation every day.

Although we were kicked out of the Garden I do not believe that Adonai's desire for interaction with His creation ever changed. This is the foundation for the importance of the Ruach HaKodesh today, and why as believers we need to have a good understanding of the Ruach throughout Scripture. Unfortunately for most of the Body of Messiah, the only context in which the Holy Spirit is considered is within the New Testament alone. However, we know Scripturally that the Holy Spirit existed long before the events of Acts 2, as a matter of fact, we read about the Ruach throughout the *Tanakh* (Torah, Nevi'im and Ketuvim/Torah, Prophets and Writings/Old Testament)

Genesis 1 tells us the narration of Creation itself, the first six days, and the seventh day, the day of *Shabbat* (Sabbath). We see the discussion of how God created everything and from day three on He says, "and He saw… it is good." That includes mankind…

As we look at John 1 we get a deeper understanding of Genesis 1, what was going on at the foundation of time, at the foundations of creation itself.

John 1 begins, *1 In the beginning was the Word. The Word was with God, and the Word was God. 2 He was with God in the beginning. 3 All things were made through Him, and apart from Him nothing was made that has come into being. 4 In Him was life, and the life was the light of men. 5 The light shines in the darkness, and the darkness has not overpowered it... 10 He was in the world, and the world was made through Him; but the world did not know Him. 11 He came to His own, but His own did not receive Him. 12 But whoever did receive Him, those trusting in His name, to these He gave the right to become children of God. 13 They were born not of a bloodline, nor of human desire, nor of man's will, but of God. 14 And the Word became flesh and tabernacled among us. We looked upon His glory, the glory of the one and only from the Father, full of grace and truth.*

It's important that we understand "In the beginning was the Word. The Word was with God and the Word was God." In the beginning was the Word… The Word is Yeshua! Yeshua didn't just magically appear on the scene in the book of Matthew, no more than the Ruach magically appeared in Acts 2. Yeshua didn't suddenly come into the picture in the grand nativity scene people love to put up at Christmas. Yeshua didn't come into the scene when *Miriam* (Mary) the virgin became miraculously pregnant. Yeshua has always been. All creation was created through Him. Yeshua wasn't something new. Colossians 1:15 tells us, *"He is the image of the invisible God, the firstborn of all creation."* Adonai has always existed, thus meaning His visible image has always existed. There's no way to get around this reality.

So, John 1 gives us this correlation to Genesis 1, a correlation to Creation, and it gives us a foundation. You've got to remember, the Torah was given to explain to us how the people of God are to live, how are we to walk, how are we to worship, and so on. The Brit Chadashah, well, honestly the entirety of the rest of the Bible from Joshua through the Brit Chadashah, was given to us to better understand how to do so. I often say that the Torah is the Word of God and the rest of the Bible is God's commentary on the Word of God. So, the Gospels and the remainder of the Brit Chadashah are meant to give us a better understanding of God's Word and here in John 1 we see this important foundation, this tangible expression of creation as something that was through Yeshua. Not that Yeshua was an afterthought, as in God suddenly realized His creation had sinned and He had to rush to make a plan B to make things right.

18

In Matthew 3:16 we see Yeshua being immersed by Yochanan HaMatbil (John the Immerser). Beginning with verse 16 we read, *16 After being immersed, Yeshua rose up out of the water; and behold, the heavens were opened to Him, and He saw the Ruach Elohim descending like a dove and coming upon Him. 17 And behold, a voice from the heavens said, "This is My Son, whom I love; with Him I am well pleased!"*

What a lot of people don't realize is that Matthew 3, and the same narration in Luke 3, are a mirroring image of creation at the beginning of Yeshua's ministry. In creation, Genesis 1 tells us that God spoke and all things came to be and His Spirit hovered over the depths of the sea. *1 In the beginning God created the heavens and the earth. 2 Now the earth was chaos and waste, darkness was on the surface of the deep, and the Ruach Elohim was hovering upon the surface of the water.*
3 Then God said, "Let there be light!" and there was light. 4 God saw that the light was good. So God distinguished the light from the darkness. 5 God called the light "day," and the darkness He called "night." So there was evening and there was morning —one day.

So, what we see here in the narrative of Matthew 3 and Luke 3 is those with Yeshua see the sky open up and they see the Ruach come upon Yeshua appearing like a dove descending. Now, this does not mean that this was literally a dove descending on Him, but rather the author is using the most fantastic language they can to express what this scene was like, but with the expectation that the reader would understand it was something far grander than just a literal dove descending upon Yeshua's head. It talks about how there was this voice from heaven (reminiscent of creation in which the *Kol HaElohim* (Voice of God) spoke and things came into being), there was the Ruach HaKodesh which hovered over the depths of the sea and here we see the Ruach HaKodesh descend upon Yeshua and there is Yeshua, the Light Himself, the Word made flesh that tabernacled among man. So, all of the Godhead is present in this one scene, and all of creation is being recreated in this one scene in Matthew 3 and Luke 3. It's important as we dig through this that we see this powerful image. The reason we talk about this correlation here is that the Ruach descending upon Yeshua in Matthew/Luke 3 isn't the first we read about the Ruach HaKodesh. Genesis 1 is the first time we read about the Holy Spirit. In Genesis 1 it says that the Ruach, the Spirit, hovered over the depths of the sea, *"...and the Ruach Elohim was hovering upon the surface of the water."* (Genesis 1:2b) So, we see that the very foundation of creation involves the Ruach Elohim, the Spirit of God.

For us as believers to either write off the Spirit altogether because we no longer live in the days of the Apostles, or for us to completely overdo what the Spirit of God does or misunderstand how the Spirit of God works, we are not just diminishing and demolishing what the Lord is wanting to do through His body, but we are also undermining what happened at the foundation of creation. It is at that foundation that we see the fullness of the Godhead in that one incident, and it's repeated in Matthew 3 at the beginning of Yeshua's ministry.

As we continue through Genesis, we read in 2:7—*7 Then Adonai Elohim formed the man out of the dust from the ground and He breathed into his nostrils a breath of life—so the man became a living being.* In Genesis 2 we see God is creating mankind and it says He breathed the Breath of Life into him, the actual Hebrew is *Neshama Chayim*. Neshama is a word used in Hebrew for spirit/soul, so it's something greater than just our own individual soul, there's something of a divine nature to the presence of the Neshama. It's where our soul, the part of us that will never die, our eternal nature meets the eternal nature of God. Genesis talks about how God breathed the breath of life into Adam, and I believe that in His breathing this breath of life into Adam this was, in a way, an impartation of the Ruach HaKodesh into Adam, because the breath of life within him was the Presence of God within Him.

In Jewish tradition, we talk about all creation having a divine spark within it, and whenever we come together to do something for God, it is these divine sparks coming together and becoming a greater presence of the divine spark. If we can get the divine spark of all humanity together for God's purpose, then the Presence of God would be overwhelming in creation itself. Now, this is not so far removed from what we talk about Scripturally. Yeshua says, ***20 For where two or three are gathered together in My name, there I am in their midst.*** (Matthew 18:20). So we see there is actually a unique perspective here that agrees with what Scripture says. Here in Genesis 2, we read about Adam being created, God breathed the breath of life within him, that breath of life being the soul—the infinite part of humanity—in connection with the infinite Presence of God coming together in the Neshama.

CHAPTER 2

Then we come to Genesis 3 and this is where things begin to come unglued… This is where we begin to undo everything God had done for us. This is where the discussion becomes so vitally important for us to understand what is going on.

In Genesis 3 we read, *1 But the serpent was shrewder than any animal of the field that Adonai Elohim made. So it said to the woman, "Did God really say, 'You must not eat from all the trees of the garden'?" 2 The woman said to the serpent, "Of the fruit of the trees, we may eat. 3 But of the fruit of the tree which is in the middle of the garden, God said, 'You must not eat of it and you must not touch it, or you will die.'" 4 The serpent said to the woman, "You most assuredly won't die! 5 For God knows that when you eat of it, your eyes will be opened and you will be like God, knowing good and evil."*

Now, I want to take this a little further into Scripture to Isaiah 14. It reads, *12 How you have fallen from heaven, O brighstar, son of the dawn! How you are cut down to the earth, you who made the nations prostrate! 13 You said in your heart: "I will ascend to heaven, I will exalt my throne above the stars of God. I will sit upon the mount of meeting, in the uttermost parts of the north. 14 I will ascend above the high places of the clouds—I will make myself like Elyon." 15 Yet you will be brought down to Sheol, to the lowest parts of the Pit.*

This is speaking of *HaSatan* (the accuser), the evil one, and how he was cast out of heaven. Some people may look at this passage and say it is just allegory, but we can actually go forward to Luke 10:*18 And Yeshua said to them, "I was watching satan fall like lightning from heaven. 19 Behold, I have given you authority to trample upon serpents and scorpions, and over all the power of the enemy; nothing will harm you. 20 Nevertheless, do not rejoice that the spirits submit to you, but rejoice that your names have been written in the heavens."* What we see here in Luke 10 is Yeshua giving a nod to how the enemy fell from heaven and in particular the narration we read about it in Isaiah.

The reason I go through all that and mention this passage in Isaiah is that in Genesis 3 the enemy is projecting his own thoughts of himself, his own problems with himself upon us. Projection in psychology is the idea that one attributes one's own ideas, feelings, or attitudes of themselves on to others. For example, if someone thinks they have bodyweight issues and then projects their own issues on others, they may continually (whether directly or indirectly) tear down other people's bodies based on their own poor self-body perceptions.

This is exactly what the enemy is doing. We see in Isaiah 14 that HaSatan wanted to be God, his ambitions were to become El Elyon, he wanted to sit on the throne in heaven. Because of this, he was cast out of heaven. But, he sees God creating mankind specifically in His image and likeness and everything going on in creation itself and he says, "If I can't have God no one can, if I can't be like God then no one can…" So he goes to Eve, particularly because he knows Adam is the spiritual authority, and if he goes to Adam he'll likely have a fight. But, Eve isn't the spiritual authority, so he goes to her knowing if he can just get her to cave, then Adam will likely cave with her. So he says to Eve, **"Did God really say, 'You must not eat from all the trees of the garden'?" 2 The woman said to the serpent, "Of the fruit of the trees, we may eat. 3 But of the fruit of the tree which is in the middle of the garden, God said, 'You must not eat of it and you must not touch it, or you will die.'" 4 The serpent said to the woman, "You**

most assuredly won't die! 5 For God knows that when you eat of it, your eyes will be opened and you will be like God, knowing good and evil." (Genesis 3:1b-5)

He already knows what's going to happen because he has experienced it himself. He wanted to become like God and was kicked out of heaven, and in Genesis 3, through his projection, the enemy is trying to get humanity to fall prey to the same issues. And we see that this is the first lie mentioned in Scripture. We go back to Genesis 1:26 and it says: ***26 Then God said, "Let Us make man in Our image, after Our likeness!"*** We're already created in God's image and likeness, and we are already as "like-God" as we were ever meant to be. Adam and Eve were created perfect because they were created in the image and likeness of perfection. You can not become any more like God than being created in the image and likeness of God. The only step from there is to try imperfect perfection, to dethrone God, and take His place.

Then we go on a little further in this passage in Genesis 1:26b-27: ***Let them rule over the fish of the sea, over the flying creatures of the sky, over the livestock, over the whole earth, and over every crawling creature that crawls on the land." 27 God created humankind in His image, in the image of God He created him, male and female He created them.***

So God's already said He's created us in His image and likeness, the second thing He has done is He gave us dominion, power, and authority over the things of this world. So, the enemy is cast out of heaven and he has given up any sort of dominion and power he may have had. But he knew that if he could get us, the ones created in the image and likeness of El Elyon, the ones who were created to be what he wanted to be and could not, what he wanted to forcefully ascend to and could not, he knew if he could make us fall then we'd be in the same boat as him, we'd be cast out of heaven too. The Garden of Eden is like heaven, we'd be cast out of where the Presence of God dwells with us, we'd be cast out of heaven like him. We'd experience the same fate that he experienced. But, he also knows that if mankind falls to his temptation, to his scheme, that we'd be giving him our dominion, power, and authority over things of this world, we'd be giving him power again.

Adam and Eve walked with God likely every day they were in the Garden. I like to picture them walking hand in hand with God in the Garden like a child and his father. We get to experience God, we get to talk to God, we get to know God personally in an intimate relationship. And the enemy is upset because he no longer gets to experience those things. But, the enemy knows he can get his power back if he can weaken us, if he can take it from us. This is exactly what the enemy is trying to do in Genesis chapter three, he's trying to destroy our intimate relationship with the Lord and he's trying to take our power away from us.

Where it becomes even more interesting is we were created in the image and likeness of God. This means not only did we have free will, because it was given to us by God, but we had the power, the authority and the ability to overcome temptation because we were created to be perfect. Not only did we have free will, but we had the ability to overcome temptation because with our free will we should be striving for our will to be in line with God's. So, as we look at the creation-like verses in the Gospels, what we see immediately after the recreation of creation in Matthew 3 and Luke 3 is that Yeshua comes out of the water, crosses the Jordan, and goes into the wilderness where He is tempted/tested by the enemy for 40 days. As He's fasting and being tempted, the enemy is throwing Scripture at Him.

One of the temptations the enemy offers is, "If you just bow before me I will give you power, dominion, and rulership over all the world." First off, this is God in flesh standing before him. Second, power, dominion, and rulership over this world were given to who? God gave it to us, and we handed it over to the enemy… So, though this temptation may sound like a lie, it does have truth in it. God did not give the enemy that power, we did. Yeshua walking on earth and offering His life as a sacrifice for us was to restore creation, it was to restore our power and authority, it was to restore our ability to be in His Presence again.

Notice as Yeshua is tempted by the enemy He overcomes that temptation, He does not succumb to it. He redeems the mistake Adam and Eve made in falling to the enemy's temptation. He redeems their giving into temptation. He redeems the failure of humanity, He redeems our sin. It gets even more interesting, Yeshua came to bring atonement and salvation. Atonement from what? Sin. Sin came into the world because we gave in to the temptation of the enemy and gave our authority to the enemy; because we walked against the ways of God even though the Presence of God was in our lives; because we chose to step out of the will of God and ultimately to be kicked out of the Presence of God. Yeshua came to bring atonement, to bring Salvation, to bring redemption so that with the outpouring of the Ruach HaKodesh in Acts 2 we can be restored in our power, dominion, and authority over things of this world.

See how this all comes back together again? We were given authority over the things of this world. Guess what are things of this world? Death, despair, sickness, depression, etc. These are not things of the Kingdom of Heaven, they are things of this world and they exist because humanity chose sin over the will of God. They exist because of Adam and Eve's failure to live out what they were created to be. So, Yeshua comes—God Himself robed in flesh—to tabernacle among us in order to restore all of this. He redeems our sins, He redeems our mistakes, He redeems our history of failure over and over and over again to show us that walking in our free will to overcome the temptation of the enemy is possible. When the Power and Presence of the Living God is a part of our life, He will restore our power, dominion, and authority over things of this world.

When Yeshua was asked how to pray in Matthew 6:9-13 it is interesting the words that He chose: **9 "Therefore, pray in this way: 'Our Father in heaven, sanctified be Your name. 10 Your kingdom come, Your will be done on earth as it is in heaven. 11 Give us this day our daily bread. 12 And forgive us our debts as we also have forgiven our debtors. 13 And lead us not into temptation, but deliver us from the evil one.'**

So right there in Yeshua's prayer, He sums up not only what He came to do in delivering us from evil, but He sums up in reverse everything we've messed up since creation. Notice He says, "*Your will be done on earth as it is in heaven...*" Who has dominion and authority over heaven? HaShem! HaShem has dominion and authority over heaven. Yeshua is our *Melech Mashiach*, our King Messiah, who sits on the throne for all eternity. He has dominion and authority over heaven and has given us—His creation—dominion and authority over the earth. If we're going to operate properly in and walk out this authority we have over things of this earth effectively, the only way we're going to do so is if we do so aligning what we are trying to do with His will. What is His will? A spotless bride. What is his will? A bride that cares more about being in His Presence than anything else.

If we take all of what has happened since creation and we dumb it down to just a quick concept, we see this: We were created to live eternally in the presence of God. We sinned, God kicked us out of His presence, but He wasn't done with us and He refused to give up on His creation. He places His Presence in our midst with the *Mishkan* (Tabernacle) and *Beit HaMikdash* (Temple), literally His physical presence in our midst as they see the Shechinah of God in the midst of Israel. So, His presence resides within our midst but we cannot be in His presence, only the high priest (which is a foreshadowing of Yeshua making the way for us) can go into the Holy of Holies. The community of Israel cannot enter in, we are separated from the Holy of Holies. Then we go to the Gospels and we see Yeshua, so now the literal Presence robed in flesh. Before we had the Tabernacle and Temple, the temporal residence for the Glory of God, now we have the eternal house, the very image and likeness, the Shechinah of God. Now it's not just His Presence that dwells in our midst in a tent, but instead, it is He Himself robed in flesh dwelling among us. After the death, burial, and resurrection, what does God do…? He pours out His Ruach HaKodesh. His Ruach HaKodesh (His literal presence) now resides, indisputably, within our very hearts and lives. So now it's not a matter of whether or not we can go into the Presence of God, because His presence is now within us. As much as it broke the heart of God when Adam and Eve sinned while they were physically within His presence, how much more does it break the heart of God now that He is physically within us?

So He places His presence in us, restores us, redeems us, and provides atonement and salvation for us so that ultimately we can be restored to be back in His presence again for eternity. Notice with God it is all a cycle, it is all to bring us back to where he originally wanted us to be in the first place.

CHAPTER 3

As we talk about the Ruach HaKodesh, the Holy Spirit, and the way that the Ruach interacts in our lives throughout this book, what I want us to grasp, what I want us to take hold of is that the Ruach HaKodesh isn't something we just haphazardly use and throw away or that we flaunt and make a big scene with. We talked about Luke 10:18 earlier, but if we read that in context and go back simply one verse, we read *(Keep in mind the connection to the seventy elders of Israel, which we will discuss in great detail later on.)*, ***17 Then the seventy returned with joy, saying, "Master, even the demons submit to us in Your name!" 18 And Yeshua said to them, "I was watching satan fall like lightning from heaven. 19 Behold, I have given you authority to trample upon serpents and scorpions, and over all the power of the enemy; nothing will harm you.*** (Luke 10:17-19) Again, He's restoring the image and purpose for which we have been created. He has created us to have victory over the enemy, the only way we can have victory over the enemy is through Yeshua's salvation and ultimately through the power and presence of the Living God in our lives. So He says, ***"Behold, I have given you authority to trample upon serpents and scorpions,"*** this isn't a new authority, this is the authority we've had since the foundations of creation, we just subjected it to the enemy and Yeshua has given it back to us, He's restoring us. ***"20 Nevertheless, do not rejoice that the spirits submit to you, but rejoice that your names have been written in the heavens." 21 In that very hour, He was overjoyed in the Ruach ha-Kodesh and said, "I praise You, Father, Master of the universe, that You have hidden these things from the wise and*** *discerning and revealed them to infants. Yes, Father, for this way was pleasing to You."* (Luke 10:20-21)

We as believers are still infants. The people He is talking to, they were not the most pious and studious of the Jewish community, they were not the ones who were buried nose deep in the Torah, Mishnah, and Gemorah every waking moment of their life. These were the ones who were consumed with life. The ones who were consumed with their faces in the books all the time didn't respond to Him in the same way these guys did, those who were deemed wise were not recognizing what was going on. But, those who were infants, young in the faith, not viewed as "wise" by man were the ones who were fully alert to what God was doing and were open to being used by Him.

22 All things have been handed over to Me by My Father. No one knows who the Son is except the Father, and who the Father is except the Son and anyone to whom the Son chooses to reveal Him." 23 Then turning to the disciples, He said privately, "Blessed are the eyes that see what you see! 24 For I tell you, many prophets and kings desired to see what you are seeing yet did not see, and to hear what you are hearing yet did not hear." (Luke 10:22-24)

Everything God has done from the time that He kicked Adam and Eve out of the Garden has been for the single purpose of us being in His presence again, for the single purpose of restoring our authority over things of this world. Here's where it gets a little tricky, Revelation tells us that heaven and earth will be rolled away and the new heaven and new earth will descend upon the earth. So, in all reality, where will we spend eternity? Here, a better here. A perfect here. A restored and redeemed here. A here that we as humanity have not destroyed. And I don't mean just destroyed it ecologically speaking, but we've destroyed it through allowing sin to reign in our lives.

I long for the day when the feet of my Messiah return to the Mount of Olives and the Mount of Olives is split in two because I'll know the time has come that we will soon spend eternity with our Heavenly Father. In the meantime, while we wait for that very hour, which could be tomorrow for all we know, looking at Scripture Yeshua says no man knows the hour or time but the Father. So, we can look at Scripture and get a pretty good idea of what's going on around us and see that it could be any day now, could still be 10, 15, 50 years or more off, but it could be any day now. So, it's more important now than ever before that we realize the importance of walking in the Ruach HaKodesh and let His Holy Presence operate through us in such a mighty and powerful way that it changes the lives of everyone we come into contact with. Because what we have been given the presence, power, and anointing of the Ruach HaKodesh for is not for yours and my sake, but the sake of those in the world. We have been given the power of the Ruach HaKodesh to restore our dominion over things of this earth, and I don't mean the ability to walk up to a lion and command its mouth to be shut (although that would be a cool party trick), I don't mean to be able to go out and name all the animals as Adam did. But, what I do mean is spiritually and Scripturally speaking the dominion we have been given is over the works of the enemy. We have dominion over hasatan, He likes to make us think we don't, he likes to demean us and destroy us because he wants to constantly bring humanity down to this place where we don't think we are worthy of the Presence of the Lord.

But, the reality is that sickness, death, despair, depression, anxiety, woundedness, pain, brokenness, suffering, etc., all of these sorts of things are things of this world, things of the enemy, they are the consequence of sin and we've been given dominion over sin. It is our duty, our purpose, being bought by the Blood of the Lamb, being covered in the Blood of the Lamb, being anointed in the Ruach HaKodesh, it is our purpose in Messiah to bring that Life to the world around us.

Throughout this book, we are going to look in-depth at what it looks like when the Spirit of God moves among humanity, at what the impartation of the Ruach HaKodesh looks like. The terminology used throughout the *Tanakh* (Old Testament) is called the Mantle of the Spirit of God, we're going to look at what that is and how it is passed from one to another. We're going to look at what authority we actually have in the power of the Holy Spirit. We're going to lay a solid foundation so that as the Body of Messiah we'll have unified Biblical foundation of what a move of the Ruach HaKodesh looks like so that we are able and willing to allow the Ruach to move in our midst in a way that God wants. ***"Your will be done on earth as it is in heaven..."***

God wants to live in our midst, He wants to operate in our lives, He wants to use us to bring freedom to the oppressed. Notice in the passage in Luke 10 the elders come back to Yeshua and say, "We're casting demons out in Your Name..." Notice when Yeshua is praying for healing He says, "Get up and walk." He doesn't beg for it, He demands it, and that same power of the Ruach is in us. It's there. We have to walk in the enacted power of God, we have to walk in the overflow of the power and presence of God in our midst. We have to understand that this power and authority was given to us at the foundations of creation itself and that everything God has done since then has been to restore us in His presence, to restore His presence in our lives and to restore our dominion and authority over things of this world. Not for our sakes, but for HIs Kingdom. Just like Yeshua says in Luke 10, don't rejoice in the fact that the enemy is scared of you, don't rejoice in the fact that you're able to cast demons out, don't rejoice in the fact that the demons quake in fear at the reality of who God is in our lives. But rejoice that our names are written where? In heaven above, in the Lamb's Book of Life. We have to understand and desire that everything we do must be centrally focused on Yeshua. We don't have the power of God in our lives so we can do whatever we want, but instead, so that He can do what He wants in and through us for His Kingdom; so that we can walk in His ways; so that more will be saved; so more will be set free; so that more will find the love of God that He has for His bride.

We've been given the power of the Ruach HaKodesh so that we can affect the world around us for His glory. Far too often, too many within the Body of Messiah have diminished or damaged the image of what the Presence of God in our lives looks like. There are a lot of people afraid of what it looks like when the power of God moves. It can get a little crazy sometimes… When the Spirit of God moves and people start falling it can be unnerving. When people start speaking in tongues it can be unnerving. When people start prophesying it can be unnerving. When someone gets up out a wheelchair and starts running laps it can be unnerving. But, it's what God wants, it's what God wants to do through us.

There are those who have been afraid of what the move of the Ruach looks like or they have realized (and you've got to understand, if the Presence of God in the Ruach HaKodesh isn't working through us it's because we're likely living in that three-letter word… S-I-N) that the sin in their lives is hindering the Presence of God in their lives. So, over the centuries there have been those who, for one reason or another, the Spirit of God wasn't operating through, and they created theologies that destroy the power of the Ruach in the life of a believer today. There are denominations in the Body of Messiah that teach that the power of the Ruach HaKodesh was only for the days of the Apostles and hasn't been active since.

This is just not Scriptural, it's also not the experience I've had as a believer. I am alive today because of the healing and miraculous hand of God. I have had car accidents that should have killed me, yet here I am. I have had illness, severe asthma, a potential hole in my lung, sever bronchitis, the doctors said it would be very dangerous for me to walk outside my house because of the dirt and dust in the air. Believers gathered together in the power of the Ruach HaKodesh, laid hands on me, and prayed in the Name of Yeshua for healing, and miraculously all was gone and I am still standing today. I have seen things happen because of the power of God. I watched my grandmother profess her faith in Messiah Yeshua on her death bed in hospice and watched the way that the Presence of God changed her countenance. She passed away two days later, but the day she professed her faith she was glowing, she looked like she was restored and renewed, she looked like she could get out the bed and live for years to come. And I have countless more testimonies like this, as I am sure many of you reading this book right now do as well.

The Presence of God changes our countenance not because some luminary light comes on, but because the Presence of God overtakes and becomes our countenance. In Numbers 6:24-26, Aaron is instructed to bless *B'nei Yisrael* (Children of Israel) in a very specific fashion—*24 'Adonai bless you and keep you! 25 Adonai make His face to shine on you and be gracious to you! 26 Adonai turn His face toward you and grant you shalom!'* Notice how two of the lines of this blessing have to do with the face of God being upon us. This is not some ethereal concept, it is literal. Moses came down from the mountain and His face was radiating. When people see God in our lives they see light, the radiant Glory of God. However, some denominations teach cessationism, in other words, that the gifts of the Ruach HaKodesh, the activity of the

Ruach HaKodesh has ceased. It is believed that it was active in the first century, during the days of the Apostles, but since then has ceased and no longer operates in followers of Messiah. We have to understand that cessationism is wrong, it is inaccurate. The Spirit of God has not ceased to operate in His people. We may very well be guilty of choosing to cease operating in the Spirit, but it has not ceased to operate through His people.

We also need to understand that there are aspects of the way that we, the Body of Messiah, understand how the Spirit works, or think we understand, that is just flat out wrong too. For example, far too often we see the gift of tongues used in the wrong way or in the wrong scenario, or people trying to prophesy and it not coming true... This does not mean God doesn't operate in these ways, He does. But, as with everything that God does there is order. It is imperative that we understand and grasp the order in which the Ruach HaKodesh operates in our midst, and the reality that He is in fact still operating in the Ruach in our midst. He wants to overfill and overflow our lives with His Spirit, not for our sake, but His. He wants to use His radiant Glory shining off of us, His countenance upon us, to impact others around us.

Bottom line, here's why I believe this is so important for us to get a hold of, we live in a day and age where simply preaching the Gospel is ineffective. It is ineffective for the same reason we trump up cessationism because people see the sin in our lives. In the world we live in today, people look straight through our garbage. We can run our mouths about God all day long, but if our life is a total wreck the world will look straight through it and they'll see the mess that we are. But, when we entirely submit our lives to the Ruach HaKodesh they see the power of God in our lives, and when they see the power of God in our lives, and in turn experience the power of God in their own lives, then they're willing to listen to us preach the Gospel and know that it is real.

When the Ruach HaKodesh is everything in our lives the world will recognize they're not looking at a pile of junk anymore, they're seeing God in us standing before them. When they see signs, miracles, and wonders they see God in their midst and their hearts are open to the truth of the Gospel.

When we lay hands on and pray for someone who has struggled for years with shattered discs in their back and they feel the overwhelming warmth of the Spirit of God and experience complete healing, then they are truly open to the Gospel. When we are praying for someone who has lost their sight and suddenly they can see again, they are open to the Gospel. When we speak Life into someone who has struggled for years with depression and suicidal thoughts and all of the pain and anger melts away and joy takes over, then they are truly open to the Gospel. Yeshua says in John 14:12-14–*12 "Amen, amen I tell you, he who puts his trust in Me, the works that I do he will do; and greater than these he will do, because I am going to the Father. 13 And whatever you ask in My name, that I will do, so that the Father may be glorified in the Son. 14 If you ask Me anything in My name, I will do it.* This is not a maybe, this is a promise. The power of the Holy Spirit is available to us so that we can walk and live in its authority over things of this world. Yeshua says through the authority of the Ruach we can do potentially greater things in His Name than He did, let the weight of that sink in.

As I mentioned previously, the days we live in are a "Post-Truth Era" and it is believed by most that there is no finite truth. What is truth for me may not be truth for the next person, and their truth may be different than the next. But, as believers in Messiah, we know there is only one Truth, Messiah Yeshua, and anything contrary to that is the work of the enemy working against the Kingdom of God. In the "Post-Truth Era," it is more imperative that we operate in the latter rains that are being poured out on us than ever before.

The early rains were in Acts 2, we've been in the rainy season since then, and I believe we are living in the latter rains now. In Israel you have the rainy season from basically November through March, that rainy season is agriculturally vitally important. But, there is potential for way more harvest when you experience the miracle of early rains and latter rains. If there are going to be early rains they fall torrentially in October, and latter rains fall torrentially in April. In years with early and latter rains, there are phenomenal harvests and gains. Acts 2 was the early spiritual rains and there was phenomenal harvest, hundreds and thousands were added that were saved. We have seen a kind of constant and steady but minimal harvest since then. I believe we are in the days of the latter rains now and there will be a phenomenal harvests again, but we need to get on board with what God says about His Ruach HaKodesh so that we can affect the community around us with the Presence and Power of God.

CHAPTER 4

We now transition into the life, journey, and ministry of Moses and how the Ruach HaKodesh moved through him. We see that through Moses there is redemption, deliverance, and freedom that was brought to B'nei Yisrael through him, and then in that deliverance and freedom, he brought them to the Presence of God. Interestingly enough this is a pattern that we see in the Body of Messiah when we allow Adonai to be the ruler in our lives through the Atonement of Messiah—we find redemption, deliverance, and freedom, and through that, we are brought into the Presence of God.

Let's take a look at Exodus 3, we see Moses has spent 40 years in the wilderness and he's come to a point where the Lord begins to deal with him in regards to his calling and purpose.

1 Now Moses was tending the flock of his father-in-law Jethro, the priest of Midian. So he led the flock to the farthest end of the wilderness, coming to the mountain of God, Horeb. 2 Then the angel of Adonai appeared to him in a flame of fire from within a bush. So he looked and saw the bush burning with fire, yet it was not consumed. 3 Moses thought, "I will go now, and see this great sight. Why is the bush not burnt?" 4 When Adonai saw that he turned to look, He called to him out of the midst of the bush and said, "Moses, Moses!" So he answered, "Hineni." 5 Then He said, "Come no closer. Take your sandals off your feet, for the place where you are standing is holy ground." 6 Moreover He said, "I am the God of your father, the God of Abraham, Isaac and Jacob." So Moses hid his face, because he was afraid to look at God. 7 Then Adonai said, "I have surely seen the affliction of My people who are in

Egypt, and have heard their cry because of their slave masters, for I know their pains. 8 So I have come down to deliver them out of the hand of the Egyptians, to bring them up out of that land into a good and large land, a land flowing with milk and honey, into the place of the Canaanites, Hittites, Amorites, Perizzites, Hivites and Jebusites. 9 Now behold, the cry of Bnei-Yisrael has come to Me.

Through the call that God gives to Moses, we will see that the Ruach HaKodesh is a teacher. John 16:13– *13 But when the Spirit of truth comes, He will guide you into all the truth. He will not speak on His own; but whatever He hears, He will tell you. And He will declare to you the things that are to come.* We'll see the evidence in Moses' life of the Ruach HaKodesh (who is the Spirit of Truth John mentions) doing this very thing, leading, guiding, and directing him.

Moses was a type and shadow of the restoration of dominion, the restoration of the Presence of the Lord, the restoration of freedom and deliverance. We also see that there are two types of experiences, in Exodus 3 & 4 and Exodus 19 & 20, in regards to encountering the Presence of God. In Exodus 3 & 4 Moses has an individual experience with the Shechinah and is immediately desperate to draw closer and hear more. Whereas with Exodus 19 & 20 there is a corporate experience with the Shechinah and the nation immediately desperate to move away and hear no more.

So what happens in this individual experience of Moses? We begin to see how Moses is receiving the mantle of the Ruach HaKodesh. What is this mantle? Is it an anointing? Yes. Is it a calling? Yes. Is it a stamp of approval? Yes. If we look at Isaiah 61:1-2 which Yeshua quotes in Luke 4:18, *18 "The Ruach Adonai is on me, because He has anointed me to proclaim Good News to the poor. He has sent me to proclaim release to the captives and recovery of sight to the blind, to set free*

39

the oppressed, 19 and to proclaim the year of Adonai's favor." So the Spirit of the Lord that was on Yeshua and was foretold about in Isaiah can be seen working in the life of Moses as well.

Moses' individual experience, what exactly happened? He was herding sheep on Mount Horeb (Sinai) and saw a bush that appeared to have spontaneously combusted and yet was not being consumed, or burned up completely. He saw this with his eyes physically, which was an experience the Lord used to get his attention to reveal His plan to him. The next thing we see is that Adonai's voice calls forth from the burning bush to Moses, Moses heard the call of Adonai. It is important that when the Ruach HaKodesh is calling that we can understand and perceive who that voice is and listen. Moses' bold response to the call of HaShem's voice was *"Hineini"* (Here am I). Next, the Lord says, "Do not come any closer, take off your shoes, you're on holy ground."

We'll see as we move forward that this is a setup for what is going to happen for the corporate experience for the nation of Israel.

Adonai introduces Himself to Moses and Moses immediately hides his face. That seems to be a typical reaction because of the fall of mankind. Remember when Adam and Eve heard the Lord walking in the Garden in the middle of the day they ran and hid from His Presence. Here Moses recognizes he is standing before the Presence of the Lord and he hides himself, or his sinfulness in the Presence of God. As a side note, later when Moses' encounters the Presence his face becomes radiant from the encounter and glows, Israel becomes fearful of his glowing face and he has to cover his face then too. Except in this situation, it is to protect the Countenance of the Lord from Israel's sinfulness.

God reveals to Moses (which is a greater spiritual revelation as well) that He has seen the affliction of His children, B'nei Yisrael, and that He has heard their cries. Because of His love for them, He is going to use Moses to bring redemption and freedom to them for them to inherit the promises of God and to place His Presence in their midst.

We can take a deeper spiritual dive in the text and recognize that what God is doing ultimately in the Exodus of Israel is removing them from under a worldly system, one that is representative of the greater worldly system the enemy has instituted around us. He is removing them from a system and governance established by man, from religious rites established by man, from rulership established by man. He is redeeming them into a system, not of this world, He is beginning a work of drawing His people, and through them all of His creation, back unto Himself from under the grip of the enemy.

So God tells Moses He is sending him right back from where he came, right back from where he fled for his life, right back into Egypt, and He is sending Moses there to set the people of Israel free. Moses asks Adonai point blank, "When Israel asks who sent me, what do I say?" And the Lord very simply says, "Say *I Am* sent you!" *I Am* answers a lot. When we come to an understanding that the Lord is what we need, what we should desire, what we long for, *I Am* is all we need, then we are in a good place.

Moses isn't quite there yet. He's still got a few objections he wants to try to run by God (probably in hopes of getting out of this gig he never asked for...). He says, "But God, I don't speak so well..." And the Lord responds and negates the complaint. Moses tries to argue with HaShem a total of five times about why he doesn't think he's the right man for the job, and all five times the Lord shuts down Moses' arguments. And if we're honest, we probably find ourselves in this exact same position all the time... One of my favorite examples of this is when we are in the checkout line at the grocery store and feel the Lord's leading to talk to the person behind us, and we go through the, "I'm too busy; this isn't the right time or place; why me?; I'm in a hurry; etc" rather than simply heeding His leading.

I have experienced very similar conversations/ arguments with the Lord in my own life. About three years after my wife and I got married we felt the Lord begin to call us to New York. I am a Jewish believer, I have grown up in a Messianic Jewish home and synagogue, my father and father-in-law are both Messianic Jewish rabbis, I was training to be a Messianic Jewish rabbi, and my first response to God's call was, "I'm not ready for New York, Jews in New York will eat me alive..." We ended up moving to New York anyways, we ended up involved in leadership in a fantastic Messianic synagogue in Long Island, we found ourselves living in a village in a county that was predominately Jewish and I ended up working for a while in a village that was predominately Chasidic. We were being used in amazing ways to impact the lives of Jewish and non-Jewish people with the Good News, and as much as I'd like to say I learned my lesson once and for all on arguing with God, I can't say that I'm perfect at immediate submission yet, but I am working really hard at it...

Adonai tells Moses that He is going to send his brother Aaron with him to Pharaoh to speak for him. What we end up seeing in this type and shadow account of the beginning of Israel's Exodus is that Moses is set up to act as God and Aaron will act as his prophet (this in no way implies that Moses thought he was God). This becomes a physical foreshadowing and lesson of how God would speak through His prophets throughout Israel's history. A prophet is ultimately a mouthpiece that proclaims the truth of the Lord, the Word of the Lord to His people.

God encourages Moses, and not only does He encourage him by saying, "You can do this, and you will do this, and you will be successful." God graciously lays out an entire plan for Moses, and God says, "Oh, by the way, as a sign that this is My will and My desire, as a sign that it is truly the God of your forefathers, the God of Abraham, Isaac, and Jacob leading you on this adventure, you and the people you are going to free will come back to this very mountain to encounter and worship me in the same way."

Oddly, the Lord allowed for Moses to find himself uniquely qualified for the task at hand. Not only was he a shepherd and prepared for the job of shepherd a spiritual flock, but he also has been in this same wilderness for 40 years. He knows the land, he knows the terrain since he helped his father-in-law Jethro as a shepherd. He has been to this mountain before and here he is receiving prophetic insight from HaShem that these things were going to happen. His unique qualifications go even farther than that though. He was a Hebrew himself. He grew up in Pharaoh's home, raised as the grandson of Pharaoh, and for all intents and purpose was raised to potentially sit on the throne himself one day. He knew the ins and the outs of Egypt, he knew how things operated. He recognized the plight of the people of Israel long before he fled Egypt himself, as a matter of fact, it was his recognition of their plight that caused his fleeing.

In Exodus 4 we see Moses return to Egypt and the beginning of what would ultimately lead to the freedom and redemption of Israel from their grip.

18 So Moses went, returned to his father-in-law Jethro and said to him, "Please let me go, so I may return to my kinsmen who are in Egypt and see whether they are still alive." Jethro said to Moses, "Go in peace." 19 Then Adonai said to Moses in Midian, "Go, return to Egypt, for all the men that sought your life are dead." 20 So Moses took his wife and his sons, set them on a donkey and returned to the land of Egypt. Moses took the staff of God in his hand. 21 Adonai said to Moses, "When you go back to Egypt, see that you do all the wonders before Pharaoh that I have put in your hand. Still, I will harden his heart, and he will not let the people go. 22 You are to say to Pharaoh, "This is what Adonai says: 'Israel is My son, My firstborn. 23 So I have said to you, Let My son go, that he may serve Me, but you have refused to let him go. Behold, I will slay your son, your firstborn.'"

27 Now Adonai said to Aaron, "Go into the wilderness to meet Moses." So he went and met him at the mountain of God, and kissed him. 28 Then Moses told Aaron all the words of Adonai with which He had been sent, along with all the signs that He had commanded him to do. 29 Then Moses and Aaron went and assembled all the elders of Bnei-Yisrael. 30 Aaron spoke all the words that Adonai had spoken to Moses and did the signs in the sight of the people. 31 So the people believed. When they heard that Adonai had remembered Bnei-Yisrael and had seen their affliction, they bowed their heads and worshipped.

Adonai prepares Moses with exactly what he is to say to Pharaoh when he arrives in Egypt. Along the route, Adonai reunites Moses with Aaron (who Adonai had already called to meet Moses along the way) and Moses told him of everything that had happened, of all the signs and wonders and of what he had been commanded by the Lord to do. Then they both rushed to the elders of Israel and shared everything with them and immediately their hearts were lifted and they fell down in worship before the Lord. I would imagine that this immediate response was likely a very encouraging sign in and over itself to Moses and Aaron of the will of God.

CHAPTER 5

After all the ups and downs, all of the joy and heartache, all of the signs and wonders Israel is finally cast out of Egypt and they begin their journey into the fulfillment of the promises of God. Along the way to Sinai Israel experiences a number of signs and wonders, often predicated by their grumbling against the Lord—signs and wonders that should enhance their faith, yet they never really seem to do so. This is where we find ourselves in Exodus 19, as Moses and Israel see the fulfillment of the sign Hashem said He would give Moses of the nation returning to the very same mountain and encountering Adonai in a similar fashion on a grander scale and worshipping Him there.

In Exodus 19 beginning with verse 3, we read—*3 Moses went up to God, and Adonai called to him from the mountain saying, "Say this to the house of Jacob, and tell Bnei-Yisrael, 4 'You have seen what I did to the Egyptians, and how I carried you on eagle's wings and brought you to Myself. 5 Now then, if you listen closely to My voice, and keep My covenant, then you will be My own treasure from among all people, for all the earth is Mine. 6 So as for you, you will be to Me a kingdom of kohanim and a holy nation.' These are the words which you are to speak to Bnei-Yisrael." 7 So Moses went, called for the elders of the people, and put before them all these words that Adonai had commanded him. 8 All the people answered together and said, "Everything that Adonai has spoken, we will do."*

We are beginning to see a pattern here. Moses saw the burning bush which was not consumed, from the burning bush the voice of Adonai called Moses to draw near and listen. In Exodus 19 we're going to see the entire mountain ablaze and smoke rising yet the mountain is not consumed, and the voice of Adonai will call the people of Israel to draw near and listen.

Then Moses reported the words of the people to Adonai. 9 Adonai said to Moses, "I am about to come to you in a thick cloud, so that the people will hear when I speak with you, and believe you forever." Then Moses told the words of the people to Adonai. 10 Adonai said to Moses, "Go to the people, and sanctify them today and tomorrow. Let them wash their clothing. 11 Be ready for the third day. For on the third day Adonai will come down upon Mount Sinai in the sight of all the people. 12 You are to set boundaries for the people all around, saying, 'Be very careful not to go up onto the mountain, or touch the border of it. Whoever touches the mountain will surely be put to death. 13 Not a hand is to touch it, but he will surely be stoned or shot through. Whether it is an animal or a man, it will not live.'

Again we see the continuation of the pattern. When Moses saw the burning bush he wanted to rush to it to check it out. Adonai cried out from the fire telling him to not come any closer for he is on holy ground. Here Adonai tells Moses to not let the people come too close, to not let them touch the base of the mountain. This is because they too were on holy ground. We're beginning to see that the mantle that was placed on Moses is also being placed as the calling of the nation of Israel. That's very important because as we continue through this study we're going to begin to see how this mantle of the Spirit is passed on all the way up to when we see the fulfillment of the calling for the mantle to be placed on Israel in Acts 2. Remember, we are tracing the mantle of the Holy Spirit from the foundations of creation through today so that we can have a solid understanding of how we are to operate in the Spirit within a biblical context today. So these patterns are extremely important to pick up on.

When the shofar sounds, they may come up to the mountain." 14 Then Moses went down from the mountain to the people, consecrated them, and then, they washed their clothing. 15 He said to the people, "Be ready for the third day. Do not draw near your wives." 16 In the morning of the third day, there was thundering and lightning, a thick cloud on the mountain, and the blast of an exceedingly loud shofar. All the people in the camp trembled. 17 Then Moses brought the people out of the camp to meet God, and they stood at the lowest part of the mountain. 18 Now the entire Mount Sinai was in smoke, because Adonai had descended upon it in fire. The smoke ascended like the smoke of a furnace. The whole mountain quaked greatly. 19 When the sound of the shofar grew louder and louder, Moses spoke, and God answered him with a thunderous sound. 20 Then Adonai came down onto Mount Sinai, to the top of the mountain. Adonai called Moses to the top of the mountain, so Moses went up. 21 Then Adonai said to Moses, "Go down and warn the people, lest they break through to see Adonai, and many of them die. 22 Even the kohanim who come near to Adonai must consecrate themselves, so that Adonai does not break out against them." 23 Moses said to Adonai, "The people cannot come up to Mount Sinai, for You are the One who warned us, saying, 'Set boundaries around the mountain, and consecrate it.'" 24 Then Adonai said to him, "Go down. You are to come back up, you and Aaron with you. But do not let the kohanim and the people break through to come up to Adonai, or He will break out against them." 25 So Moses went down to the people and told them.

We continue with the development of this pattern that the Lord established. Moses saw the burning bush and it was not consumed. Now the nation is seeing the mountain ablaze and it is not being consumed. Remember we're looking at there being an individual call on Moses which was a type and shadow of a corporate call on Israel. Now we're talking about B'nei Yisrael's call and how prophetically the Lord showed and did to Moses what is now being shown and done to Israel. Adonai's voice calls out to Moses on Mount Sinai; Adonai's voice calls out to Israel from Mount Sinai. Moses responded Hineini; Israel responds in a similar fashion as they say "*Kol d'ber Adonai na'aseh*—Everything that Adonai has spoken we will do." The Lord tells Moses not to come any closer and to take off his shoes because he's on holy ground; to Israel, Adonai says don't come any closer, wash and cleanse yourself for you're on holy ground (my paraphrase). Moses hears the voice of the Lord and he hides his face; Israel hears the Lord's voice and they say, "His voice is too much, we can't hear it again or we'll die!" This is the same response, they are hiding from the Lord as well.

If we're ever in a place in our lives where we don't want to hear God's voice, that's a pretty good indication that there's something in our lives that is not right, that is outside of the will of God, that is not walking in righteousness. Rather than hiding our faces from the Lord in those situations we should probably fall on our faces before the Lord and say, "Hineini" and return in T'shuvah. This should be one extremely valuable lesson we learn from Adam and Eve, from Moses, from B'nei Israel, etc. Because, if we are honest with ourselves, there isn't anything we can hide from an all-knowing God. He is already well aware of our failure and He is already ready for our return. That feeling of shame and regret is not of God, it is a ploy and tactic of the enemy to keep us from seeking the Face of God and hearing His voice.

What is happening here is that we are seeing this process that the Lord began of deliverance and freedom. Israel's journey of freedom from slavery in Egypt in which they had no control, no dominion, no authority over anything and moving into the promises of God is a foreshadowing of what God has provided for us in the Sacrifice of Yeshua. Much like the blood upon the doorpost brought freedom to Israel, Messiah's blood upon our hearts brings us freedom from the reign of the enemy. It restores to us the dominion, power, and authority of the Ruach HaKodesh. And it allows us to encounter the tangible and literal Presence of God again.

Ephesians 4 talks about what has often been called the "Five Fold Ministry" and presents what is actually four roles not five (shepherd and teacher are meant to be one role). If we look at the life and ministry of Moses we realize that he, in essence, actually filled at one point or another, and at times all at once, with each and every one of these roles mentioned in Ephesians 4. Not only that, but each of these roles is Ruach inspired and Moses didn't operate in any of them at all until after he received the Mantle of the Holy Spirit upon him. None of these things would have been possible at all without the Holy Spirit overcoming him and leading him in HaShem's purpose and plan for him.

We'll begin to see the continuation of a pattern moving forward in this book that there are certain emphases that are brought upon salvation, deliverance, freedom, and dominion that comes with the Presence of God. His desire for us is to, in the power of the Ruach HaKodesh, take dominion over things of this world, to be free of sickness, disease, disorder, confusion, anxiety, etc. If you've lived for any length of time in this world you'll know that the system of the world around us is a system of confusion, disillusionment, and disorder, it is a system established specifically for the purpose of keeping a separation between Creator and creation. But when we're willing to submit to God and allow His Ruach HaKodesh to empower us in His calling for our lives then we will begin to be lead into all truth just as Moses was and we will begin to find ourselves coming free from slavery to the world around us.

This is exactly what we see in Moses' life. At first, he wanted to rebel against the call of God, but eventually, he gave in and he received the power of the Holy Spirit. Through the power of the Holy Spirit, he was empowered to walk in his calling and he leads the entire nation of Israel to freedom. You and I are called into the same great calling, we are called to lead those trapped in slavery to sin and those in darkness to freedom in the marvelous Light of Messiah. You and I are empowered by the same Ruach to walk out our calling as disciples making disciples. We have much to learn about the mantle of the Ruach HaKodesh as we continue through this study, much to see about what the Bible actually says about operating and living in it, and much to see about just how powerful His Spirit really is and how much He can do through us in His Spirit if we simply submit to Him.

Understand that as a follower of Messiah Yeshua the Ruach HaKodesh has in fact called you by fire (just as Moses saw on the bush, just as Israel saw on the mountain, just as was seen on the heads of the disciples in Acts 2). He has put an anointing on your life and He has given you freedom. Just as Moses was called by Adonai and empowered by the Ruach to lead Israel into freedom, you and I have been called by Adonai and empowered by the Ruach to lead a dark and lost world into freedom in Messiah. If you don't believe me, take a look at the Great Commission in Matthew 28–**18 And Yeshua came up to them and spoke to them, saying, "All authority in heaven and on earth has been given to Me. 19 Go therefore and make disciples of all nations, immersing them in the name of the Father and the Son and the Ruach ha-Kodesh, 20 teaching** *them to observe all I have commanded you. And remember! I am with you always, even to the end of the age."* Ultimately, this is the same call and the same promise given to Moses, just on a much larger scale.

The Lord is telling us the same message today that He was speaking through Moses in days of old: He is our freedom, He is our deliverance, He is our Presence, He is our peace, He is the Living God who is inside of us and has made us a holy Tabernacle. I encourage you to walk in the calling, gifting, and anointing that the Ruach HaKodesh has empowered you for, just as we see Moses doing. If we do, we will see signs, wonders, miracles, revelation, we can receive words of knowledge and wisdom and all of these things the same as Moses did. When we do, we will begin to understand that the truth of the Great Commission is that it is our duty to pick up the call and mission of Yeshua that we spoke of earlier from Luke 4:18 (Isaiah 61:1-2)—*18 "The Ruach Adonai is on me, because He has anointed me to proclaim Good News to the poor. He has sent me to proclaim release to the captives and recovery of sight to the blind, to set free the oppressed, 19 and to proclaim the year of Adonai's favor."*

See, the calling that was upon the Patriarchs, that was upon Moses, Joshua, Elijah, and Elisha; the calling that was upon Yeshua and the disciple is the same calling that is upon us today as followers of Messiah. From the beginning of time, in Genesis when the Spirit was hovering over the face of the seas, that same Spirit is residing within us. He has been showing us through types and shadows in the Tanakh that He has always been with us and has always wanted to lead us. It is the same Spirit that empowered Yeshua as He began His ministry and the same Spirit that raised Him from the dead. If we have the same Spirit and Power of God then why don't we live like it today? I believe we are in a day and age where we need to wake up to our burning bush encounter, to our Sinai on fire encounter, we need to cry out to Hashem, "Hineini! Kol d'ber Adonai na'aseh!!!" (Here am I! Everything Adonai has spoken we will do!)

CHAPTER 6

Now we are going to look at a very specific kind of change of direction in our discussion on the Ruach HaKodesh, and the way that the Spirit operates or interacts with us and through us. We've set up now a foundation where we've discussed that the Ruach has been active in the world since creation. We see Scripturally that it's not like all of a sudden God decided in Acts 2 that He needed one more part of Himself, but that God has always existed as God and that all of the aspects of God, or the way He reveals Himself to us, have always been a part of who He is. He has not changed and He will not change, as Hebrews 13 says, ***"[He] is the same yesterday, today and forever."*** We are the ones that seem to always be changing, more often than not, uselessly.

But when God gets a hold of us things go in a different direction. So in this chapter, we are looking now in a different light as we look at the Ruach HaKodesh and the way it moves from an individual to a multiplicity. Earlier we looked at the Ruach HaKodesh upon Moses, or, perhaps a better way to word it, the mantle of the Holy Spirit—the anointing of God—that Moses, operated in and how God spoke to the nation of Israel through Moses. So, in this chapter, we will be following this same concept of the mantle of the Ruach HaKodesh as we look at the 70 elders. If you are unfamiliar with the 70 elders from the Torah you can open up to Numbers 11 and read all about them.

But we're going to be looking at what the narrative of the 70 elders in Torah tells us about how a portion of the mantle of the Ruach HaKodesh that was upon Moses was taken and placed upon each of the 70 elders. And this is the beginning of what we see scripturally of the

Ruach HaKodesh upon the masses, upon those who follow the Lord and a transition that is a foreshadowing of what was to come that we now know as the outpouring of the Holy Spirit in Acts Chapter 2. This also foreshadows the outpouring of the Ruach HaKodesh going from a single individual, or specific individuals, at specific times (as seen throughout the Tanakh) to the entirety of the body of Messiah and the availability of the power of the Spirit to those that believe in Messiah.

So, Numbers Chapter 11 we see right out the gate that Israel appears to be following the same theme as tends to be the case with a large majority of the Torah...

1 The people were murmuring in the ears of ADONAI about hardship,...

In other words, the people were grumbling and complaining, they were griping, they were less than satisfied with the scenario in life that they currently found themselves in.

...and when Adonai heard, His anger burned. The fire of Adonai blazed among them, ravaging the outskirts of the camp. 2 The people cried out to Moses, so Moses prayed to Adonai and the fire died out. 3 The name of that place was thus called Taberah because fire from Adonai had burned among them. 4 The grumblers among them began to have cravings, so Bnei-Yisrael began to wail repeatedly, saying, "If we could just eat some meat!

Notice how Israel doesn't skip a beat, right? Israel complains and grumbles against God and instantly God becomes angry and the fire of the Lord begins to rage and it ravages, it burns the outskirts of the camp. In other words, God is saying, "Look, I'm not trying to kill you all but I am trying to wake you up to the direction that you're going, that you're walking in the wrong way." And Israel's response is along the lines of, "Oh we're sorry, we're sorry. God forgive us." And as quickly as Israel repents of their actions, God brings an end to the judgment that is occurring. Then Israel, immediately afterward, starts grumbling and complaining again and they say, "If we could only have meat. Oh, remember the fish and the meats and all the grand food we had to eat in Egypt?" How quickly we forget just how rough things were in Egypt…

Then we pick up again with verse 10…

10 Moses heard the people wailing by their families, each man at the door to his tent. Adonai's anger became very hot, and Moses was troubled.

11 So Moses asked Adonai, "Why have You brought trouble on Your servant? Haven't I found favor in Your eyes—that You laid the burden of all these people on me? 12 Did I conceive all these people, or did I give birth to them, that You should say to me, 'Carry them in your bosom just as the nurse carries an infant'—to the land You promised to their fathers? 13 Where can I get meat for all these people? For they wail to me saying, 'Give us meat to eat!' 14 I am not able to carry all these people by myself! The load is too heavy for me! 15 If this is how You are treating me, kill me now! If I have found favor in Your eyes, kill me please—don't let me see my own misery!"

So Moses is fed up, he's done, he's over it all. Have you ever felt like this before? He is over everything, he could care less about Israel at this point. He wants to be free and clear of them, and so much so that he says "Lord if I've found favor in your eyes just kill me. Get it over with, don't put me through this stress anymore, I can't handle it and these people are too much for me to deal with. Just rid me of their misery."

Then we move down to verse 16 which picks up with,

16 Adonai said to Moses, "Bring me 70 of the elders of Israel whom you know to be elders of the people and their leaders. Take them to the Tent of

Meeting, so they may stand with you there. 17 Then I will come down and speak with you there, and, I will take some of the Ruach that is on you and will place it on them. They will carry with you the burden of the people, so you will not be carrying it alone."

Up to this point, only a few people were allowed to go to the Tent of Meeting, to the Tabernacle. Only a few could actually physically encounter the presence of the Lord there. The first was Moses. The second was Aaron the high priest. More specifically the high priest, whether that be Aaron or his sons who would follow in his calling.

That was it. Nobody else was allowed to go into the presence of the Lord—only Moses and Aaron. So here the Lord agrees with Moses, the stress of the people is way too much for one man to carry. Remember, Exodus tells us there were six hundred thousand men of fighting age of Israel. That means that there was an excess of as many as a million and a half people when you add women and children. And that is just considering those that are blood descendants of Abraham, not to mention that Exodus tells us that there was a mixed multitude that left with them. So you're talking about this vast amount of people, likely as many as three to five million people total, that are standing here grumbling and complaining. So one man is looking at this angry mob of upwards of five million people. No wonder he's crying, "Just kill me now. Get it over with because they're going to kill me either way. Just kill me now."

So God says, "You're right... It's too much. Bring 70 elders, 70 recognized leaders of Israel." And notice the way Adonai words it, He says, "Bring me 70 of the Elders of Israel *whom you know to be elders of the people and their leaders.*" So very specifically the Lord is telling Moses to call forth people whom he knows the calling of leadership is upon.

We can read in 1 Timothy 3 Paul's description of the calling of a leader and what a leader looks like and how they should live their lives and carry themselves. So obviously there is this recognizable characteristic to a leader. And in this particular case, we're dealing specifically with leaders, we're not dealing with the ultimate masses as we do in Acts 2. But the scenario serves as a type and shadow of what would happen in Acts 2 as the Ruach moves from individuals to masses.

So the Lord is saying that you will clearly see who these leaders are, who these elders of Israel are. Bring these 70 elders with you to the Tent of Meeting and I will meet with you there and a portion of the Ruach I placed upon you, I will take and I will place upon them.

We continue with Verse 18,

18 "Now to the people say: Sanctify yourselves for tomorrow, because you will eat meat, for you wailed in Adonai's ears saying, 'If only we could eat meat! It was better for us in Egypt!' Now Adonai will give you meat and you will eat!

The end of this chapter is where we read about the second account of the quail being brought in. Remember, in the first account they cried about meat and God brought in quail to appease their grumbling and nothing negative happened. The second time they cried about meat (which we see here), God brings in quail and a whole bunch of people die. But we go down to verse 21 and it says, *21 Moses then said, "600,000 foot soldiers—the people I am in the middle of---yet You say, 'I am going to give them meat to eat for an entire month?' 22 If flocks and herds were slaughtered, would they have enough? Or if all the fish in the sea were caught, would they have enough?"*

In other words, Moses is saying, "Would they ever be satisfied?" He's not saying, "You know there are six hundred thousand men, if we got every ounce of meat that currently exist on the face of the planet, would they finally be satisfied?" He's saying they will never be satisfied, they will never be happy, no matter what Moses or Aaron or even the Lord ever does for them, they will never be satisfied.

And verse 23, **23 Adonai said to Moses, "Is Adonai's arm too short? Now you will see whether My word will come true for you or not."**

CHAPTER 7

Now we'll skip down to the actual occurrence of the Mantle of the Ruach being placed upon the 70 elders. We've set up why this discussion of the 70 Elders is here, now we're looking at the actual account of the Ruach upon them.

We continue in the text with verse 24, *24 So Moses went out and told the people Adonai's words. He gathered 70 of the elders of the people and had them stand around the Tent. 25 Adonai descended in the cloud and spoke with him. He took some of the Ruach that was on him and placed it on each of the 70 elders. It so happened that when the Ruach first rested on them, they prophesied—but never again.*

The Hebrew in this passage can actually be interpreted in two different ways, one way is what we see here in the Tree Of Life Version (TLV) *"but never again."* However, another way that this is translated and interpreted is *"and it never ceased."* So, one of the ways the Hebrew can be understood contextually here is that when the spirit was placed upon them they began to prophesy and never ceased. Now, why is it important that we notate the idea that it never ceased, not whether or not it ever ceased with them? I think it's got more to do with the connection of when the Spirit moves there is often prophecy that occurs. Now we have in the Body of Messiah, especially today and looking at the world around us and the way things are when we talk about a prophet in the body of Messiah, far too often we're speaking of a prophet with a misunderstanding of what a prophet is. See, we often look at the concept of a prophet as though they're a soothsayer or a seer of the future. But that's not scripturally what a prophet actually did. Now there were (and still are) times when God shares a vision of the future in prophecy, and we see that in numerous of the prophets in the Tanakh, such as the destruction of the Temple. But more often than not, when those "here's what's going to happen in the future" discussions come up, it's often followed by, "and if you just returned to the Lord that will all settle and it won't happen." When we look scripturally at Isaiah, Jeremiah, Ezekiel, Samuel, or at any number of the other prophets that exists in the Bible the one thing that a scriptural view of a prophet all has in common is this a prophet says, "Thus says the Lord" and "Repent now and return to the Lord."

The prophet speaks the Word of the Lord, speaks forth the truth. And I don't mean just like, "oh the Lord put this message on my heart, you need to cut me a check for a hundred dollars. Thus says the Lord." No that's not what we're talking about. We're saying he speaks the word of the Lord, which could be a direct message from the Lord, or it could be The Word, the Scriptures, the Bible, he speaks the Word of the Lord. And in doing so, the purpose is to call people to repent, to return to God in faithfulness, to make t'shuvah, which is the Hebrew concept of repentance. The concept of t'shuvah is that you're walking in the wrong direction, you realize you're walking in the wrong direction, you stop dead in your tracks, and you turn around 180 degrees and you walk back to the arms of the Lord. That is what true repentance is. Many times as believers today our idea of repentance is, "Oh, God I messed up I'm sorry, forgive me. Ok cool." We go on about our way doing the same thing over and over again. But that is not true repentance. True repentance is you stop what you're doing hard and fast and you return to the Lord. And so a prophet biblically, when we look at the overarching narrative of the scriptures and we look at the context of the Bible of what a prophet is, a prophet is one who speaks the word of the Lord for the purpose of drawing people back to the Lord, of calling people to faithful repentance to the Lord. And it's important that we grasp that idea, that we understand that a prophet is not somebody that merely tells of what's going to happen in the future, but specifically calls people to the Lord. And with that, we set up our discussion as we move forward in this passage.

Continuing with Numbers chapter 11 verse 26, *26 Two men, however, had remained in the camp.* So keep in mind everything that just happened occurred at the Tabernacle, at the Tent of Meetings. This all occurred at the presence of the Lord where nobody else could be but the 70 elders, Moses, and Aaron. *The name of one was Eldad and the name of the other was Medad. The Ruach rested on them. They were among those listed, but they had not gone out to the Tent.* So for whatever reason they didn't quite make it to the Tent Meeting, to where the Presence of the Lord was. But God is faithful. God said give me 70 elders, Moses brought the name of seventy elders and these two were on that list. They didn't quite make it there, 68 were there, two were in the camps, and he still put the portion of the mantle of the Ruach HaKodesh upon them. They were among those listed but they had not gone out to the tent. *So they prophesied in the camp.* They began to do exactly what the others did, but they did it in the camp in the middle of the people, while all the others did so in the Presence the Lord where none of the camps could see it.

No wonder the people in the camp weren't scared of what happened at the Tent of Meeting and it didn't surprise them or shocked them at all. But then all of a sudden Eldad and Medad started speaking and prophesying, which again if we're talking about a call to repentance, these are people who are grumbling against the Lord. These are people that are continually remembering back to the "grand old days" in Egypt, with a slight misremembrance of what actually occurred in

Egypt and that it wasn't quite so grand. But they're grumbling against the Lord. So here they begin to prophesy and if we look at the scripturally contextual definition of a prophet, they are calling people to repent. No wonder they were getting scared...

Verse 27 continues, **27 A young man ran and told Moses and said, "Eldad and Medad are prophesying in the camp!" 28 Joshua son of Nun, the assistant of Moses since his youth, cried out and said, "Moses, my lord, stop them!"**

Now, real quick let's think back to our previous discussions. We talked about how when the presence of the Lord was revealed what is it that Moses did when in early parts of Exodus he saw the Shechinah upon the burning bush? Moses covered his face, he hid from the Presence of the Lord. As we've said previously, we know that there is a connection to Adam and Eve whenever we sin and we recognize the Presence of the Lord with us we try to hide ourselves right. It's like we think we can cloak who we are as though God can't see what we're doing and what and who we really are. When in reality what God wants us to do is be open and be honest with Him because He already knows the truth and He just wants to gently bring us back to Himself. So here the camps of Israel begin to hear these two men prophesy when the Spirit falls on them they become scared to death. Joshua comes running and says, "Hey Moses you got to tell these dudes to stop, stop this now." In a sense, this is similar on a national scale to Moses covering himself in the Presence of the Lord. They are afraid of the presence of the Lord just like they were in Exodus 19 and 20 when the voice of the Lord spoke from Mount Sinai. And just like at Mount Sinai when the nation cries out in fear for the voice of the Lord to stop lest they die, Joshua cries out to Moses to make this revelation of the Spirit of God stop because the nation is yet again afraid of the revelation of God among them.

And what was Moses' response? **29 "But Moses said to him, "Are you jealous on my behalf? If only ADONAI would make all the people prophets! If only ADONAI would put the Spirit on all of them!""**

And this is the catch if only Adonai would put the spirit on all of them. If only Adonai would make them all prophets. If only Adonai would put His Ruach on all of His people...

Next Moses and the elders of Israel returned to the camp. As we look at this we understand what we're seeing Moses saying: "Look, Joshua, don't get upset. Don't get jealous. Don't worry about me." First and foremost we know this is Joshua's future because the Mantel of the Ruach is taken off Moses and put on Joshua when Joshua becomes the leader of Israel and takes over for Moses and walks in Moses' footsteps leading Israel into the Promised Land. But in the meantime, Moses says look I wish this happened to everybody and it's a foreshadowing, this whole event is a foreshadowing.

This whole narrative is foreshadowing of what's to come. We know that when Yeshua walked on earth he operated in the Ruach HaKodesh, He operated in the power of the Spirit of God, the Spirit of God is His authority. He spoke life into the dead. He spoke to those that were unable to walk, he spoke reinvigoration of their legs so they could get up to walk. When there were those that were stricken with demonic oppression and so on, He proclaimed deliverance for them, He cast that out of them through the Ruach HaKodesh, the presence of the authority of the Lord that was upon Him. And ultimately in Acts 2, after His death, burial, resurrection, and ascension, the Ruach HaKodesh was poured out on a mass level for all believers. Just like we saw here with the mantle of the Ruach HaKodesh that was upon Moses, a portion of the mantle of the anointing of the Spirit that was upon him is placed on a mass level upon the 70 elders. This was a foreshadowing of what would happen in Acts 2. It is a foreshadowing of Yeshua, operating in the Spirit and then all of a sudden the Spirit was available for all. Ultimately Moses, who likely didn't truly understand that it was prophetic, this prophetic statement that he longed that Adonai would put his Spirit upon all and that all would experience the presence of the Ruach HaKodesh becomes reality in Acts Chapter 2.

Not only in Acts Chapter 2 where Jews and converts to Judaism experienced the outpouring of the Ruach HaKodesh because of their faith in Messiah but just a few chapters later we see, in Acts 10, at Cornelius' house the exact same experience on those of the nations. Moses says in Exodus 11:29, he says if only Adonai would put the Spirit on all of them. He isn't just speaking of the people of Israel. I think he's speaking prophetically of all. He may specifically be considering Israel because that's his immediate reality, but prophetically, God is speaking of everyone. He desires to put His Spirit upon all. But the qualifier for that to occur, the precursor for that to occur is faith in Messiah, faith in the atoning Blood of the Lamb that we can be washed clean of our sins so that His Ruach HaKodesh can reside within us because then we are a clean vessel, a clean Tabernacle for His Presence.

Now what's interesting with this is there's a correlating story in the Brit Chadashah, in the New Covenant writings, of this particular account. I mean literally the exact same numbers and everything. Luke Chapter 10 beginning verse 1, *1 Now after these things, the Lord assigned seventy others and sent them out by twos before Him into every town and place where He Himself was about to go. 2 And He was telling them, "The harvest is plentiful, but the workers are few. Therefore, beg the Lord of the harvest to send out workers into His harvest."* Then he goes on with instructions on how they were to operate as they were ministering and so on.

But then we go down to verse 17, the 70 *Sh'lichim* (emissaries, sent out ones) these are disciples of Yeshua who were sent out. Now we know by what happens next beginning in verse 17 that the Ruach HaKodesh was upon them, the mantle of the anointing of the Holy Spirit was upon them. We know this because of what happens in verse 17, **17 Then the seventy returned with joy, saying, "Master, even the demons submit to us in Your name!"** Now it's one thing to speak the name of the Lord, the name of Yeshua, and say, "In the name of Yeshua I command *blah blah blah blah blah*." It's another thing when the authority of the Ruach HaKodesh is behind those words.

The mantle of the Ruach HaKodesh, the mantle the anointing, I believe, just like with Moses and the 70 elders, and the correlating image here, the mantle of the anointing in the Ruach HaKodesh that was upon Yeshua a portion was placed upon the 70 Sh'lichim, the 70 sent out ones, the 70 emissaries here in Luke 10. They went out and they began to speak life into people's lives, they began to cast demons out, and they began to prepare the way for the coming Messiah who was about to enter into the cities, which is what Messiah sent them there for in the first place.

Verse 18, **18 And Yeshua said to them, "I was watching satan fall like lightning from heaven. 19 Behold, I have given you authority to trample upon serpents and scorpions, and over all the power of the enemy; nothing will harm you. 20 Nevertheless, do not rejoice that the spirits submit to you, but rejoice that your names have been written in the heavens."** In other words, your names are written in the Lamb's Book of Life. Why? Because of the blood atonement of Messiah, because of faith in Messiah.

We briefly discussed this passage in Luke 10 earlier in this study when we looked at Yeshua discussing the enemy's, hasatan's, fall from heaven and we equated that to the prophets where it talks about him falling from heaven. What we see as we said before is the Ruach HaKodesh interacting in our lives, the anointing of the Ruach HaKodesh, the mantle of the anointing is in our lives to restore to in us the authority and the dominion that we have over things of this world right—death, sickness, despair, depression, demonic activity, etc., in the lives of those that we interact with and in the world around us. We have the authority in the Ruach HaKodesh, we have the power in the Ruach HaKodesh to have dominion over things of this world which is what we were given in the first place in Genesis. That's what, as we said before, God spoke to Adam, "I've given you dominion and authority over things of this world." We sinned and handed that dominion and authority to the enemy and with the outpouring of the Spirit of God in Acts 2 what we end up having is a restoration of that dominion and authority being given back to us.

As we've already discussed, when Yeshua was tempted by hasatan, hasatan said I have the authority to give all of this over to you. Sadly, he did, in fact, have this authority, but it wasn't authority given to him by God, it was authority given over to him by us. We were given that authority by God. We allowed him to have it when we sinned, when we allowed him to tarnish the work of God in our lives, the perfection of God's creation, we gave him that power, dominion, and authority over things of this world and he took full access of it and had fun with it and ruined the world around us. And so with the blood atonement of Messiah, the cleansing blood of Yeshua, the whole purpose was that we could be washed clean that we could be restored by the power the Ruach HaKodesh, the anointing of the Ruach HaKodesh to be able to have dominion, power, and authority over things of this world. And so what we see here, and I think that as believers today we miss out on this idea, we miss out on the fact that this is actually a part of what being empowered by the Ruach HaKodesh is. It tells us here in Verse 17 that these 70 Sh'lichim came back as it says in Luke 10:17, *"Then the seventy returned with joy…"*

See, they were excited. They were ecstatic because they just saw the Lord work through them. They just saw these great things and they were excited. *"Master even the demons submitted to us in your name."* As believers today in the 21st century we find ourselves so far removed from the first-century body of Messiah and we are so separated from the realities of what is possible in the power of the Ruach HaKodesh. We are so inundated with two thousand years of man-made, baseless theology trying to water down, undo, explain away or just outright eliminate the power the Ruach HaKodesh among the body of Messiah that we don't actually have a way to conceptualize what is truly available to us in the authority that is restored to us in the Ruach HaKodesh.

The Holy Spirit has not ceased working… We have ceased trusting in Him. We have ceased allowing Him to operate in and through us. We have ceased believing in Him, at least in terms of the way that the word of God tells us to believe in Him.

We have told God, just like Israel of old, "Oh, things were better in Egypt. We had it so much easier in Egypt. Sure there were chains but at least we were fed." We have told God, "Oh yeah, I mean You are literally living in us now. You've washed me clean. That's awesome and you've done all of this that I can shine Your Light into the world around me. I get it and that's cool, I'm with that. Oh but you want me to do something… I don't want to do that. I'm not on board with that… Oh, you want to empower me to do it, I don't think so…

"It's scary. You know healing people, that's scary, I don't want to do that. It's weird when somebody starts walking and they haven't been able to walk in years. That's weird. I don't want a part of that. Oh, you mean when their arm that's been bound up for four decades all of a sudden stretches back out and has full mobility again. No, I don't want to see that, that's creepy, God, that's some horror movie stuff, I don't want that. How about we just have this nice, quaint, superficial loving relationship? I don't really want to get into all of that."

But the reality is *"all of that,"* and so much more, is exactly what God wants to do through us. It is exactly how God wants to use us.

And on the other side of the pendulum, there are those who do not believe in cessationism, they do not believe that the gifts and the power of the Ruach HaKodesh ceased after the first century. But instead, they believe it is in hyperdrive. With these, you've got people that are jumping pews and holy rolling, or screaming that they feel their flesh is on fire because the Spirit the Lord is on them, or they're "drunk in the spirit." And all of this really weird sort of behavior.

But that's not at all what we see biblically either, anywhere. As a matter of fact, it was a trumped-up accusation in Acts 2 when the non-believers saw what was happening among the believers. It was a baseless accusation because the non-believers didn't understand what was happening before their eyes. It was just an accusation birthed from their lack of understanding. *"Oh this is crazy, they must be drunk. What other explanation could there possibly be…?"* So this whole "drunk in this spirit thing" is garbage. It wasn't them saying, "Oh, it's as if they must literally be drunk, they must have had too much to drink before they came to the Temple for Shavuot." No, it was just a trumped-up accusation.

But then Peter began to explain what happened to the folks that were there, thousands from every tribe and tongue that were there at Shavuot. (Which by the way is going to happen again, just read Zachariah… We will gather for the Moedim again at the temple in the millennial reign.) As we see here, the Bible is very careful to express that there are men from every tribe and tongue, both Jew and proselyte (those that converted to Judaism) that are at the Temple—not some arbitrary upper room, a theory that doesn't work because you can't get thousands of men there. But they were at the Temple in Acts chapter 2 and they hear and see what they don't understand and all of these things that are happening are foreign to them. But, I believe what they heard was these men who were believers and who spoke Hebrew as their native tongue and who were impacted by the Ruach HaKodesh begin to preach the Gospel of Yeshua in their own languages, from these Israeli men that did not speak these many languages.

I do not believe that they heard these men from the Galilee speaking in some weird "random noises" that no one has ever heard before, they heard the men speaking in their own languages that the believers did not normally speak. And they knew every word and understood and they thought the only way that this can happen is if the believers were drunk. It was a spiritual accusation against the Lord. But the reality is they were instilled with the authority that was given to them from the foundations of creation. They were re-instilled with the authority of the Ruach Kodesh and that's why at the end of this account after Peter shares the message with those that were there it says, *"and thousands were added that day that were saved."*

Thousands were saved because the Power of God moved upon and through the early believers and they weren't afraid. When the Ruach HaKodesh fell, the Talmidim weren't afraid like the camps of Israel were when they saw these two guys, Eldad and Medad, out speaking and prophecy as the anointing of the Ruach fell on the 70 elders in the Torah. They weren't afraid of the presence of the Lord, they weren't afraid of the activity of the Ruach Kodesh among them. Instead, they were energized and excited by it. They were ecstatic because the Lord was now in their midst again. The Lord had a place to dwell among His people.

They knew Messiah came, the Talmidim understood Scripture… they understood Scriptural prophecy… they understood that Daniel 9 says the Messiah has to come before the destruction of the Temple. So, if Messiah came it won't be long before the temple would be destroyed. As a matter of fact, Daniel gives an exact reference to how many years before the Temple's destruction the Messiah would come. The disciples did the math, they knew it wasn't long for this world that the temple would exist. It wasn't long before the physical and permanent-intended dwelling place that the Lord resided in among His people was going to be destroyed. They recognized that there was now a temporal dwelling place for the Presence of the Lord again among His people. And a temporal dwelling place is as it was intended to be with the Tabernacle in the wilderness, as it was intended to be for almost 400 years that the Tabernacle rested in Shiloh in the north of Israel.

It was recognized that the Lord was now dwelling among His people—literally in His people. It wasn't something foreign because it was something they were prepared for after reading the Torah parasha every single week. You've got to understand that the Torah cycle was established roughly five hundred years before Messiah walked on Earth. So for five hundred years leading up to Peter and the disciples being empowered by the Ruach HaKodesh the Jewish people had been reading about the 70 elders in numbers chapter 11 and understood that when the Spirit of God moves, things start to happen. There was a great expectation that when the Lord becomes a part of our lives in a very real and active way things start happening.

They expected and they were prepared, they understood what was going on. They were not shocked or surprised, it was not some shock-and-awe event. The fact is that now they understood what was always God's intentions. And then as though reading about it in number Chapter 11 wasn't enough, in Luke 10 we get a refresher course with the 70 emissaries that Messiah single-handedly chose and sent out with an anointing of His Ruach HaKodesh. I don't think He sent them out unarmed and unprepared. He sent him out with a portion of His Ruach upon them, the same Ruach that He operated in. Now We begin to see how all of this comes together.

See, a lot of times in the body of Messiah we've had these ideas, especially with some of the modern revivals that have occurred, there's this notion that we can just breathe on people and they will fall right out. Maybe if they do it's because we had a little too much garlic or something at lunch… I don't know. But this isn't how it works in the Scriptures. In the Bible, the Ruach is placed upon somebody as an impartation. It's not something that just brushes over us. It's an impartation, as a matter of fact, quite often in the Scripture when we talk about the mantle being transferred the idea is in a laying on of hands for the impartation. That is not to say that it's specifically and only this way, but biblically there is a direct impartation, it is a transference if you would. The Ruach HaKodesh doesn't suddenly become less in me because God used me for an impartation of his Ruach on somebody else. On the contrary, we both are impacted by His Ruach HaKodesh. As it is increased among creation, the power of His Ruach is increased among God's people.

So in Numbers 11, we see this impartation of the mantle, the authority of the Ruach HaKodesh from Moses to the 70 elders. Then we see the same exact thing in correlation occurs in Luke 10 with the impartation of the mantle of the anointing of the Ruach HaKodesh upon Yeshua's 70 emissaries. And in Acts 2 we see a grander scale of the same events, a holy impartation.

See, when the wind blows it just keeps on going, right? But when there's an impartation it becomes a part of who you are. It becomes a part of our DNA, it becomes a part of our very reality, an extension of our very body.

And so what we see that numbers 11 and Luke Chapter 10 is a direct correlation, we see an exact replica. Numbers 11 was a foreshadowing of what happened in Luke 10 and of what would happen. In turn, they both were a foreshadowing of Acts 2 when the impartation of the Holy Spirit went from being on a micro-scale to a macro scale. When it went from a couple of people to a grand mass of believers and thousands were added that day that came to faith. And at the end of Acts 2, there were those being added daily that were coming to faith, they were receiving impartation of the Holy Spirit, they were being overcome with the anointing of the Presence of the Lord. Later in Acts when Cornelius' household, who were all gentiles, gathered together and Peter preached to them the exact same thing occurred there. There was an impartation of the mantle and authority of the Ruach. The Ruach was on Peter and was then imparted upon the gentiles gathered at Cornelius' house. And things continued to replicate from then on over and over and over again for the last 2000 or so years. This is the way it has always worked, with exception to the fact that within the body of Messiah we have decided to redefine the way the Spirit of God moves and operates primarily because we still operate in the same fear as the camps of Israel when Eldad and Medad began to prophesy in their midst.

CHAPTER 8

Now let's go to 1 Corinthians 14 and look at something really unique and interesting. Here Paul recounts—or in a grander scale sort of quotes directly from Moses. 1 Corinthians 14:1 says, *"1 Pursue love and eagerly desire spiritual gifts, but especially that you may prophesy."* Why is it so important to prophesy? What exactly is a prophecy? Simply put, a prophecy is a word of the Lord calling us to repent. It is not just a foretelling, it is not telling somebody's future or rubbing some crystal ball or whatever else. It is the word of the Lord calling for repentance. Can there be a foretelling of what will happen? Absolutely… But very often when we see that in Scripture it is a condemning foretelling. In Isaiah when it says that the walls of Jerusalem will be destroyed, that Jerusalem will be ripped down, that it will be run over by the Babylonians, will be destroyed by the men that would come from nations, and Israel will be scattered among them. These are all condemnation prophecies, HaShem speaks to the consequences of Israel's choice to sin. However, in each and every one of these situations the next thing that follows in Isaiah and Jeremiah (and all the other biblical prophets speaking similarly), *"But if you just return back to the Lord, if you just make T'Shuvah, if you just repent, then these things will not happen." [My paraphrase]* Prophecy is always and solely intended to be the word of the Lord for repentance.

Paul's heart here is the cry of the Great Commission from Yeshua's words in Matthew 28, *"All authority in heaven and on earth has been given to Me. Go therefore and make disciples of all nations…"* Therefore going to all nations and lead men to salvation. What is the foundational responsibility for one to receive Salvation? It is repentance. Why should we prophesy?

Because the word of the Lord goes forth to call men to repentance.

Paul continues with 1 Corinthians 14:2, *"2 For one who speaks in a tongue speaks not to people but to God—for no one understands, but in the Ruach he speaks mysteries. 3 But one who prophesies speaks to people for building up, urging on, and uplifting. 4 One who speaks in a tongue builds up himself, but one who prophesies builds up the community. 5 Now I want you all to speak in tongues, but even more that you would prophesy. One who prophesies is greater than one who speaks in tongues—unless he interprets, so that the community may be built up."*

Paul says he wished that all would speak in tongues, but even more so he wished all would prophesy. What does Moses say? He wished that all would prophesy, he wished that all would experience the Spirit of the Lord as the 70 elders did. See, these biblical examples of a Ruach-led faith and life wished that the Ruach would be upon all and that all would prophesy. Why do both Moses and Paul proclaim the same vision for the children of God? Because they knew that if we are impacted and led by the Ruach HaKodesh then we will be used by God to lead people in repentance back to the Lord. It's not about a show, it's not about any sort of theological, denominational, or ideological agenda, it's not about profiting from the gifts of the Ruach... The impartation of the Ruach upon the Body of Messiah is for the distinct purpose of drawing people back to God because His Presence is now in the midst of man.

Let's look at one more important comparison here, and this is where things get complicated, this is where we decide that we're either getting on board or just getting out of the way. This is a pivotal point in the discussion as we look at the Ruach HaKodesh, where either we are willing to let the Lord do what He wants to do and use us for His purposes or we just walk away and wash our hands of it and let God do something with someone else. We've got to understand the gravity of what it means to be imparted with the Ruach HaKodesh, to be empowered in the authority of the Holy Spirit. We have to understand the weight and the magnitude of what this means. So the next thing we read in Numbers immediately after the 70 elders and the quell is what happens in Chapter 12.

Number chapter 12 verse 1, *1 Then Miriam and Aaron spoke against Moses on account of the Cushite woman he married, because he had married a Cushite woman. 2 They asked, "Has Adonai spoken only through Moses? Hasn't He also spoken through us?" Adonai heard it."* Miriam and Aaron get a little jealous and they get presumptuous and speak against Moses, the Lord's anointed. Notice how they word this, they don't say, "Hasn't the Lord also spoken to us…?" Instead, they very specifically say, "Hasn't He also spoken THROUGH us?" In other words, there was an impartation of the Ruach HaKodesh—the anointing and the authority of the Holy Spirit—that was upon Miriam and Aaron. There was an impartation, a portion of the mantle of the Ruach that was upon Moses, Aaron, and Miriam, not just Moses. And we know this because they say hasn't He spoken through us, haven't we prophesied because of the spirit of the Lord? Again prophecy, not fortune telling, but prophecy and calling people to repentance, calling people back to the Lord.

"*3 Now the man Moses was very humble, more so than anyone on the face of the earth."* (This is my favorite example of humility… Who wrote the Torah? Moses did and Moses says Moses was the most humble man that ever lived. That's my kind of humility…) Although I joke about Moses writing about his humility, the reality is we can see the truth of Moses' humility by his immediate reaction every time Israel messes up and the Lord threatens to wipe them out. The very first thing Moses does is fall on his face and beseeching the Lord on behalf of the people immediately. There's no doubt, there's no thought, there's no missing a beat, he falls on his face before the Lord crying out for mercy, every single time and that takes a true depth of humility.

"4 Immediately, Adonai said to Moses, Aaron and Miriam, "The three of you, come out to the Tent of Meeting." So the three came out. 5 Adonai descended in a column of cloud, stood at the entrance of the Tent of Meeting, and called to Aaron and Miriam. The two of them stepped forward. 6 "Hear now My words!" He said. "When there is a prophet of Adonai, I reveal Myself in a vision, I speak to him in a dream. 7 Not so with My servant Moses. In all My house, he is faithful. 8 I speak with him face to face, plainly and not in riddles. He even looks at the form of Adonai! Why then were you not afraid to speak against My servant Moses?" 9 Adonai's anger burned against them, and He left them."

Then we see that the cloud lifts and that Miriam is covered in tza'arat, or what is often translated as leprosy, but it's worse than that. This is actually where we get the Jewish tradition that tza'arat, leprosy, is a punishment for *lashan harah*, literally evil tongue or speaking badly about other people. Adonai says to Miriam and Aaron, no doubt you are a prophet and I've spoken through you, but when I speak through you and other prophets, it is through dreams and visions. But with Moses, I speak face to face as a man speaks to a man. I speak to and through him differently. He has even seen the form of the Lord, the Shechinah—the Divine Glory—as we read about with Moses hidden in the cleft of the rock and Adonai allows him to see His backside as He passes.

Miriam and Aaron messed up greatly, and not just because they spoke about Moses behind his back, not just because they were speaking lashan harah. But they grossly messed up because they misunderstood the weight, the power, the grand responsibility that goes along with being empowered by the Ruach HaKodesh. the responsibility. When you have authority in the Spirit of God you are held to a different standard. You are held to a higher standard when it comes to sinning when the Presence of God resides within you. That doesn't mean that the Lord is no longer merciful and gracious, He absolutely is, but there's a different type of consequence that goes along with it.

Think about, the number of pastors who have fallen to sexual immorality in recent decades, there's a grander scale of consequence that goes along with that. Think about the number of lives that were negatively impacted because of those scandals. People that put too much faith in a man, to begin with, but then the negative impact on hundreds of thousands of people. Because when we are empowered with the Ruach HaKodesh, when we are imparted with the authority of the Holy Spirit, we're held to a different standard by God.

The Hebrew National brand hot dog tagline is probably one of my favorite marketing tag-lines ever. As believers, their tag-line is even more true to our lives than it is even to the company that developed it. They say, "We answer to a higher calling." As followers of Messiah who are filled with the Holy Spirit our lives should be lived for the sole purpose of emulating Yeshua HaMashiach, and as such, how much more fitting is the tagline for our own lives than simply a marketing ploy for hot dog company?

The world around us sins all day long and they've got a punishment that's coming if they're not washed by the Blood of the Lamb. And there is an eternal consequence… Those of us who have found Messiah, those of us who are empowered by the indwelling of the Presence of the Lord have the authority to speak over the things of this world. But guess what sin is…? It is a thing of this world, it's not a heavenly thing and we have the authority to speak over it, we have the authority to avoid it, we have the authority to avoid temptation. As a matter of fact, we are called to emulate Messiah and what is it Messiah did…? He avoided the temptation of sin His entire life. We have the authority. On our own, we don't have the ability, but with the power of the Ruach HaKodesh, we have the authority.

When we sin we answer to a higher calling. We answer to a higher authority. We answer to a higher consequence because it's not just our lives. If non-believing Joe Schmoe down the road sins it doesn't change anybody's life, everybody expects him to sin anyways. That's what sinners do—they sin. But if we, as believers, sin it affects a lot more people. Especially in this day and age that we live in, people see right through us. They see right through the show we want to put on. That's why it is that much harder for the message of the Gospel to be shared because we can preach it all day long but the people that we preach to, that we minister to, they see right through us. They see that what we say and what we do, how we believe and how we live, they don't always match up… We have been imparted with the authority of the Ruach HaKodesh and we don't even relish it in our own lives much less impart it and share it with others. We don't walk in it in the way that we're supposed to in our own lives, our own ministries, our own families, our own households, our own congregations, or our own jobs.

When people see us what they should see is the Shechinah of the Living God. When people see us they should be impacted by the Presence of the Lord. When people see us their lives should be changed just because the Presence of the Lord was in their midst. They shouldn't have to wait till at some point in their lives they finally decide that maybe they should read the New Testament. They should see the work of the New Testament, the work of grace, mercy, love, and forgiveness in our lives. They should see the work of the

Ruach HaKodesh, they should come to us and want what we have.

I will wholeheartedly and unhappily concede that cessationism exists, but it's not that God has ceased to operate. It's not that the Ruach has ceased to operate in our midst. It is that we have ceased to believe in the operation of the Ruach HaKodesh. We have ceased to allow the Ruach to lead our lives. We have ceased to allow the Ruach to guide our steps. We have ceased to allow the Ruach to move through us to impact lives. We have ceased to allow the Ruach to empower us to speak healing and life into people's lives. We have ceased to allow the Ruach HaKodesh to direct us to people that need to hear the Good News. We have ceased to allow the Ruach HaKodesh to map out every one of our footsteps day by day.

Proverbs says that a man plans his steps, but the Lord will guide our feet. We seem to have gotten hung up on the first part of that. We plan our own plans but we forget that the Lord is supposed to guide our feet. How does He guide our feet? By the Holy Spirit! The way he maps things out for us and sometimes those footsteps the Lord is directing us on is directly into the lives of somebody that needs to see the work of the Lord in our lives. But we have ceased to allow the Lord to direct our footsteps.

It's not just whether or not this job or that house or this trip is something that we should or shouldn't do. It's not just giving the Lord control and guidance in our lives in the sense of making decisions. But more specifically allowing Him to direct our footsteps for the purpose of His Kingdom, for His ways, that we may be used by Him. As we are empowered by the Ruach HaKodesh we do have one unifying gift and that is prophecy. I mean a biblical understanding of prophecy, that is to speak the Word of the Lord into people's lives for them to repent. This requires that we must do it with the compassion, grace, and mercy that we saw from Yeshua.

Notice Yeshua sits with the Samaritan woman at the well, Yeshua didn't beat her down because she sinned. Yeshua didn't act like He was holier than thou — and He actually was. He very graciously said Your sins have been forgiven, go and sin no more. He very graciously called her into the Kingdom. He very graciously led her to repentance. God did not call us through the power of His Ruach HaKodesh to bash people because they don't believe the same way we do. He called us to let His Light shine in a way that other people want to know what we believe, that other people want to know what we have, that other people want to experience the love and the forgiveness that we have experienced.

The question I have for you right now, the thing I want us to start to wrap our heads around as this study continues to develop from here is, are we willing to wholeheartedly relegate our lives to the leading the Ruach HaKodesh? Are we willing to recalibrate and really align our ideology, our interpretation of scripture, our theology to understand what the Holy Spirit wants to do among us?

The children of Israel were scared when they saw the elders prophesy in their midst, but they were scared for the same reason they were scared at Mount Sinai. They weren't scared because it was something freaky, they were scared because they heard the voice of the Lord. They were trembling at the core because they heard the voice of the Lord. How often do people recognize the voice of the Lord speaking through us? Or are we simply regurgitating what we've always been told or what we think instead of allowing the Lord to speak through us?

The reality is the Ruach HaKodesh is upon us but because of that, we are held to a higher standard. It is more important as believers empowered by the Ruach HaKodesh that we truly walk not just in repentance once, but for the remainder of our lives. That we walk in the power of the Ruach in a way that changes and impacts other people's lives. This is why we are spending the time digging through this study on the Ruach HaKodesh so that we understand that there is way more to this than the way we have watered down and damaged the message of the Presence of the Lord in our lives over the last 2000 years. We're living in the days of the latter rain and it is time that we grasp how the Lord really wants to operate through his Ruach in our lives.

CHAPTER 9

Now we are going to take a look at Joshua. The Book of Joshua has been taught, primarily in the perspective of leadership. But, in the following pages, we are going to take a much deeper look at Joshua's life, his service *under* Moses, and his role *after* Moses, especially as it pertains to a discussion of the Ruach HaKodesh *l'dor v'dor* (generation to generation).

As we're going to be focusing in this section on the Holy Spirit's impartation from anointed to anointed and from generation to generation, let's begin with looking at Joshua 24 beginning with verse 1.

1 Then Joshua assembled all the tribes of Israel to Shechem, and summoned Israel's elders, heads, judges and officials. So they presented themselves before God. 2 Then Joshua said to all the people: "Thus says Adonai, God of Israel: 'From ancient times your fathers—Terah, the father of Abraham and the father of Nahor—lived beyond the River and worshipped other gods. 3 Then I took your father Abraham from beyond the River and led him through the entire land of Canaan and multiplied his offspring. I gave him Isaac, 4 then to Isaac I gave Jacob and Esau. To Esau I gave Mount Seir to possess it as his own, but Jacob and his children went down to Egypt. 5 "So I sent Moses and Aaron, and I plagued Egypt with what I did in its midst, and afterward I brought you out. 6 I brought your fathers out of Egypt. When you came to the sea, the Egyptians pursued your fathers to the Sea of Reeds with chariots and horsemen. 7 But when they cried out to Adonai, He put darkness between you and the Egyptians, then He brought the sea upon them, and it covered them; and your eyes saw what I did to the

Egyptians. Then you stayed in the wilderness for a long time. 8 "Then I brought you to the land of the Amorites who were living beyond the Jordan. Though they fought against you, I gave them into your hand, and you possessed their land when I destroyed them from before you. 9 Then Balak son of Zippor, king of Moab, rose and fought against Israel. He even sent and called for Balaam son of Beor to curse you. 10 But I refused to listen to Balaam; instead, he had to keep blessing you. Thus I delivered you from his hand. 11 "Then you crossed over the Jordan and came to Jericho, but the men of Jericho fought against you—the Amorites, the Perizzites, the Canaanites, the Hittites, the Girgashites, the Hivites and the Jebusites—but I delivered them into your hand. 12 Then I sent the hornet before you and it drove them out from before you—the two kings of the Amorites—not by your sword or your bow. 13 I gave you a land on which you had not labored, and cities that you had not built and you have settled in them, vineyards and olive groves that you had not planted, that you are eating. 14 "Now therefore, fear Adonai and worship Him in sincerity and in truth. Get rid of the gods that your fathers had worshipped beyond the River and in Egypt, and worship Adonai. 15 If it seems bad to you to worship Adonai, then choose for yourselves today whom you will serve—whether the gods that your fathers worshipped that were beyond the River or the gods of the Amorites in whose land you are living. But as for me and my household, we will worship Adonai!"

Here we're seeing a picture where Adonai is speaking through Joshua at the end of the book proclaiming to the Children of Israel, "Look at all that Adonai has done for you…" Joshua is laying out and making his case plain before Israel that everything that has happened up to this point was not because of him but because of Adonai. Often people will look at Israel at this point and be totally amazed at the leadership of Joshua… But, if we look at it from this perspective then we are approaching this whole thing wrong. Really, it has been the Ruach HaKodesh through Moses, through Joshua, through the 70 elders that continued to lead Israel even to this point.

If we go back to Numbers 11, it's interesting that when the impartation of the Ruach HaKodesh was given to the 70 elders, who was the one saying to Moses, "Make them stop, the people are scared!"? It was Joshua.

Numbers 11:24-29—*24 So Moses went out and told the people Adonai's words. He gathered 70 of the elders of the people and had them stand around the Tent. 25 Adonai descended in the cloud and spoke with him. He took some of the Ruach that was on him and placed it on each of the 70 elders. It so happened that when the Ruach first rested on them, they prophesied—but never again. 26 Two men, however, had remained in the camp. The name of one was Eldad and the name of the other was Medad. The Ruach rested on them. They were among those listed, but they had not gone out to the Tent. So they prophesied in the camp. 27 A young man ran and told Moses and said, "Eldad and Medad are prophesying in the camp!" 28 Joshua son of Nun, the assistant of Moses since his youth, cried out and said, "Moses, my lord, stop them!" 29 But Moses said to him, "Are you jealous on my behalf? If only Adonai would make all the people prophets! If only Adonai would put the Spirit on all of them!"*

So, it's really interesting, we see the end cap of Joshua standing before the Children of Israel and saying, "Choose this day whom you will serve…" And then we see Joshua toward the beginning of his experience with the Ruach HaKodesh, as he sees the elders receiving the impartation and he's crying out, "Hey, we've gotta stop this craziness!!!" And Moses, as level-headed and Ruach-led as possible, corrects Joshua and awakens him to the reality of what HaShem is doing among His people.

Joshua was Moses' primary protege and was a young leader of Israel being raised up when the account of the 70 elders occurs. By the time he gets to what we read earlier from Joshua 24, we see that Joshua has given full surrender to the Ruach HaKodesh. So, what exactly happens in between...? What happens from his doubt and fear in Numbers 11 to his standing before Israel boldly encouraging them to choose Adonai in Joshua 24? This "in-between" is what we are going to focus primarily on in this section.

An impartation from the Ruach HaKodesh is not just a one and done deal. The reality is, in order to be a leader within the Household of God one must not only experience an impartation at the beginning of their ministry. They must continue to walk in that impartation, to experience the impartation, to operate in the impartation, and to receive fresh impartation of the Ruach. Just because we may see a young person who appears to have the characteristics and ability for leadership, who appears to have a calling toward leadership, does that mean that that young person will be a perfect leader? No... Leaders need to be groomed, they have to be trained and taught. What we see here is a type and shadow from Moses to Joshua, we see discipleship in the life of Joshua. A good leader may have charisma and ability to be able to speak and teach, but if they are terrible as a leader, or even as a person, such as being manipulative, controlling and harsh, they are not ready to be a leader. They will tear people down, rather than build people up, and the role of a leader in the Body of Messiah is to build up the Body.

That's what we begin to see here with Joshua and Moses. We see it very similarly here in the Torah as we do with Yeshua and his talmidim. What we see of discipleship and training with Yeshua isn't the first time we see this played out. Where the Lord begins to reveal to us the reality of the impartation of the Ruach HaKodesh from generation to generation is right here with Moses and Joshua. By the time we get to Joshua 24 and Joshua's grand speech encouraging Israel to dedicate themselves entirely to the Lord, we see the fruition of that mentorship, impartation relationship that Joshua was nurtured in under Moses.

Here we are with a man who goes from crying out in fear, "We've got to stop this!" to a man standing in the *dunamis* (power), standing in boldness saying "be strong and courageous!" So, how do we get there? How exactly does the journey from fear and trepidation at the presence of the Ruach to full submission to the impartation of the Ruach, as we see in Joshua's life, occur?

We see that as a young man Joshua was raised up at the side of Moses to learn from and be mentored by him. If you take the time to read from Numbers 11 through the end of the book of Joshua, there are some extremely valuable lessons to learn here. So, let's now focus on a few of those lessons that the Ruach HaKodesh was revealing to him through the life and ministry of Moses that he needed to become the leader Israel needed next.

Joshua spent 40 years serving under Moses' leadership. That's a pretty long time, especially by today's standards. Today, for whatever reason, things are just done differently, mentorship just doesn't happen like it did in Moses' day… You have people who come up and go to grade school, then middle school, then high school —and we know how high school kids are, they're ready to take over the world, you can't tell them anything because they think they already know everything (and we've all been those teens too...). Then you see folks in their late teens and early 20s as they decided to go to college or to pick up a trade and they work in those areas for a few years, and they think they are suddenly ready for management or leadership of some sort. Then you've got folks in their late 20s telling people in their 40s and 50s how to do their job, and everything seems flipped upside down…

But here we see that Joshua is 40 years old and he's learning, he's come out of Egypt and is now beginning to learn under Moses. It says a lot for someone to be able to be content where you are right now, no matter where you are in life until God promotes you (in this case, in the Ruach HaKodesh) to wherever you're going next. Contentment is a very difficult thing, it goes against our fallen human nature. But in today's society where everything is so readily accessible we rarely even wait on God for an answer anymore. Rather than turning to God, we turn to Google. And this removes the working of patience (which is a fruit of the Ruach—Galatians 5:13-26) in contentment.

One of the most important things Joshua had to learn was contentment. Moses modeled and displayed the idea of contentment in God's calling, in God's direction, and in the assignment God had given him. And Joshua needed to learn the value of contentment and trusting the Ruach's leading in that place of contentment, which is something he witnessed in his mentor. Moses got frustrated with the situation some times, he wanted to move forward, to move out of the wilderness, he wanted to see Israel walk in the fulness of God's promises. But, there's a difference between having the drive to continue to pursue the things God has in store and being content with where you are. Contentment doesn't mean you're simply kicked back and relaxing in the recliner and not doing anything… Contentment is recognizing God has you in point "A" and He wants to take you to point "B," and trusting in God for guidance and direction on what to do and how to be the most effective for the Kingdom in the meantime.

When the Ruach HaKodesh had been imparted in Numbers 11, Joshua did recognize something different was happening and that others were able to be led by the Ruach and prophesy. But, with that, just because other people can have the ability to prophesy, to heal, to teach, or whatever Spiritual gift it may be, it does not take from who God has appointed/anointed for leadership. Moses was still the leader. This is still true today, especially within the Body of Messiah. In our congregations, the rabbi or pastor is the spiritual authority and leader, even if there is someone who may be more gifted in certain areas, the person God has established as the appointed authority is the leader. And it is our responsibility as part of the community to recognize that God-given authority and faithful submit to it, just as we witness in the life of Joshua and Moses. This is a lesson Joshua learned with regards to contentment.

Joshua was able to see contentment modeled before him. One of the great events Joshua was able to witness was the rebellion of Korach (Numbers 16). Korach challenged Aaron's authority as the high priest and Moses' authority as the leader of Israel. Korach wasn't satisfied or content with the calling he had as part of the Levitical order responsible for caring for the *Mishkan* (Tabernacle), he wanted to run the Mishkan and to be the leader of Israel. So, the ground swallows him up and he and his buddies vanished that day before everyone's eyes. Joshua learned to be content with where he was because he also saw how (not just once either…) people rose up against Moses and Aaron, and he saw the consequences of what happened when this occurred.

Another thing that Joshua learned that he was able to witness as he was mentored under Moses, was humility and intercession. What happened every time Moses was challenged and every time B'nei Yisrael rebelled against God? Moses fell on his face before the Lord in intercession. What a fantastic, right-before-your-eyes kind of example for Joshua to witness. We're talking about lessons that are not just learned from someone laying on hands and sending someone out immediately. The Brit Chadashah makes it clear that we are not to be quick to lay hands on anyone. There is a necessity for training, for mentorship, for development, to learn faithfully under the tutelage of the Lord's anointed before we step out to fulfill our calling. As with everything in the Kingdom of the Lord, there is order and structure, and being raised up in the anointing of the Ruach HaKodesh is no different. The discipleship/mentorship part is also seeing these things in the leader that you're following, the mentor exuding those characteristics, those traits, the fruit that comes from the Ruach HaKodesh, and us taking those in.

Moses was always humble, he interceded on behalf of his brothers and sisters who were in sin. Moses on many occasions fell on his face before the Lord on behalf of those he led. How important a lesson do you think that was for Joshua to witness as a mentee under Moses? How important of a lesson is that for us today? Imagine how much different life could be if when things went wrong at work, rather than blowing up about the situation we fell on our faces before the Lord and sought His face on the matter. What about our friends and family who have not yet come to know Yeshua as Messiah? What if we continually fell on our faces in intercession for them? Want to see your career take off? Want to see your family become restored? Want to see your calling take form? Want to see your city changed? Racial reconciliation? Revival break out? We need to return to

the examples we see in the Bible, examples like Moses—
and later Joshua—who fell on their faces in intercession
on behalf of those they served in both the good times and
the bad. Moses is the prime example of what God
desires from us in these difficult situations. Adonai wants
us to bring things to Him first, and ask Him what He
wants us to do.

Joshua saw contentment—Moses was content
where he was as a leader. Joshua saw what happened
when others stepped out of contentment and attempted
to rise up against God's anointed. Joshua saw a leader
who was humble and willing to set aside his own
thoughts and feelings and intercede on behalf of others.

What else did he learn from the example of
Moses? He learned to obey God's commands. Wasn't
that one of the things God continue to encourage Israel
to do throughout the Torah? "If you'll obey my Word, I will
provide and care for you, I will protect you, etc." Israel is
in a covenant relationship with the Lord, which expected
both parties to uphold their end equally in partnership. If
we obey God's commands the "blessings and curses" of
Deuteronomy talk about how God says, "If you honor
God's Word you'll be blessed in the city and in the fields,
etc." A lot of people like to just focus on the blessings, but
they don't like to talk about or deal with consequences on
the other side. But in the same section of Deuteronomy,
the Lord also says, "If you do not honor God's Word then
you will be cursed in the city and in the fields, etc." As a
matter of fact, in Deuteronomy—as Israel is receiving
their final instructions from Moses as their leader—God
spends a greater amount of time focusing on the
consequences of breaking covenant than on upholding
covenant. Isn't it better just to obey God?

It's not always easy upholding covenant,
especially because the flesh is weak. Joshua watched as
Moses navigated this all the time, imagine how many
times Moses' flesh wanted to take control and solve a few

problems the bare-knuckle way. But, he was faithful, and on the rare occasions when his flesh got the better of him Moses was immediately repentant. And this is who Joshua got to mentor under, the example he would later strive to emulate as Israel's next leader.

So, we see throughout this that Joshua, who is being groomed, is learning all these priceless lessons. Remember, we're talking about impartation and full-submission to the Ruach, not a one-and-done experience, but a life-time impartation.

CHAPTER 10

The next lesson Joshua learns we see in Deuteronomy 6:4-9: *4 "Hear O Israel, the Lord our God, the Lord is one . 5 Love Adonai your God with all your heart and with all your soul and with all your strength. 6 These words, which I am commanding you today, are to be on your heart. 7 You are to teach them diligently to your children, and speak of them when you sit in your house, when you walk by the way, when you lie down and when you rise up. 8 Bind them as a sign on your hand, they are to be as frontlets between your eyes, 9 and write them on the doorposts of your house and on your gates.*

    If the Lord were speaking these words for the first time to us today it would probably sound more like: Do these things when you get up in the morning, at the gas station, when you're on social media, when you take the kids to school, when you're at work, when you're at the store, when you're driving your car and someone cuts you off, etc... The core of what HaShem is saying here is that we are to display our love for Adonai at all times and in all situations, ancient or modern. The Ruach HaKodesh is our strength to allow us to continue to carry on as witnesses and disciples of Yeshua before all and no matter where. This is no more important than in our own homes, before our spouses and our children.

    Moses lived out a depth of love and obedience to the Lord that we must learn from and model in our own lives. Joshua got to witness it first hand and it was the foundation of what he would ultimately model his leadership and personal spiritual life after. Now, as we mentioned before, this most certainly doesn't mean Moses never messed up... He was just as proficient at jacking everything up as you or me. The difference is that

Moses was swift in repentance, his heart sought constantly after reconciliation with the Lord when he fell short of the glory. Joshua may not have been Moses' physical son, but he was most certainly Moses' spiritual son, and he modeled Deuteronomy 6:4-9 out faithfully before him, and before all Israel.

Another lesson that Joshua experienced serving under Moses is confidence in battle. And it is vitally important for us as believers in the 21st-century world to grasp this reality, as there is a constant spiritual battle going on all around us. The closer we draw to the Lord the harder the enemy attacks in our lives. We've got to remember that in battle, the enemy uses all his resources available to try to bring down their greatest threats. And the enemy isn't an idiot, he isn't going to waste his time on anyone that isn't a threat, so if you are experiencing the enemy's attack it is because he sees you as a threat for the Kingdom of God.

Joshua 1:6 says, *6 Chazak! Be strong! For you will lead these people to inherit the land I swore to their fathers to give them.* And this is a message which was similarly relayed by the Lord to both Joshua and Israel several times in the book of Joshua.

Deuteronomy 20:1-4 says, *1 "When you go out to battle against your enemies and see horse and chariot—a people more numerous than you—do not be afraid of them. For Adonai your God, the One who brought you up from the land of Egypt, is with you. 2 When you draw near to the battle, the kohen will come forward and speak to the people. 3 He will say to them, 'Hear, O Israel, you are drawing near today to the battle against your enemies. Don't be fainthearted! Don't fear or panic or tremble because of them. 4 For Adonai your God is the One who goes with you, to fight for you against your enemies to save you.'*

That's a powerful lesson that Joshua had to learn and a powerful lesson for us to take to heart today. But, it also goes much deeper than that. The less sin we allow into our lives the more confidence we have in the Lord. What happens when we allow sin to control our lives? Remember when Yeshua was on the stake He looked up to heaven and cried out, "Father, why have you forsaken me?" We have to understand that that was the first time Yeshua felt the presence of sin in His life because the sin of the world was transferred to Him. So, perhaps the way we should better understand His heart's cry is more akin to, "Father, what is this forsakenness that I feel?" He had never felt forsaken before, so what was the difference from everything He had experienced up to that point and the moment Yeshua cried out to His Father? The difference was the presence of sin. When we live a life that is enveloped in sin we will feel forsaken, we will not feel like we are children of God, we will not feel like our identity is in the One who has conquered the world, who has overcome the flesh. When we understand our identity is in Him because He has created us in His image and likeness then what happens in that mindset is we can stand up boldly and proclaim, "the Lord has given me this battle!" And we can march forward with full confidence in victory because He has given us this battle and He'll fight for me.

To reiterate what we've covered thus far, Joshua learned some very key characteristics of operating in the Ruach HaKodesh while serving as a mentee under Moses. He witnessed these very important traits of spiritual leadership firsthand. Under Moses, he learned how to be humble, how to be teachable, how to be content, how to be obedient, and how to be confident in the Lord. These are some of the most important lessons of leadership that Joshua learned, but for us today gleaning from their life in the impartation of the Ruach

HaKodesh, these are even more important for us to understand as a foundation to faithfulness to the Lord.

Another lesson Joshua learned was not to complain. When we complain, aren't we really accusing God of not doing His job? Isn't that why Moses was really mad? When accusations were tossed out complaining against Moses, against Aaron, or even against HaShem weren't acting like the accuser of the brethren. They were accusing Moses and Aaron of not being in the image of God. They were accusing God of not upholding His end of the covenant, of not knowing what's best for them. When, in reality, it was B'nei Yisrael not upholding their end. And if we're honest with ourselves, we act the same way… How often have we made poor choices and when the proverbial poop hits the fan we cry out, "God, how could You have let this happen…?" We begin to blame God for our stepping outside of His Will. Isn't that exactly what we saw in the Garden of Eden? When the enemy comes to Eve, he accuses her of not being made in the true image of God.

We have to be able to see that when we gripe, grumble, moan and complain about our circumstances (which there is always a lesson to learn out of these circumstances) then we are negating what God is trying to get through to us. We're trying to derail the lesson the Ruach HaKodesh wants to teach us. When we complain we are accusing God of not being who He says He is. When we complain about our leaders we are accusing them of not being God's anointed. But isn't our calling to praise, exalt, and glorify Him? Aren't we to understand that He's the Lord of the battle, that He's going to protect us through it, that He is the victorious One? Joshua learned that when you continue to rebel against God you'll be in the wilderness for decades rather than weeks…

Perhaps one of the most important and powerful lessons Joshua learned while serving under Moses was the lesson of intimacy. God wants us to be intimate with Him, and He with us. It goes back to that idea of a covenant relationship, that we become one with Him. Have you ever had a time of intimacy with the Lord that was so powerful that you were overwhelmed with so much love that all you could do was cry? A time where words are not enough and anything you might say would ruin the whole thing.

The world today has it all wrong, the world's view of intimacy is not true intimacy. It is not a picture of what a marriage relationship with the Lord looks like. See, that's what a godly marriage between a husband and wife is supposed to look like, it is supposed to be a mirror image of the intimacy between the bride of Messiah and her Groom. What is better, immature love or mature love? Immature love is powerful, it is a raging fire, it burns unbridled, but it is also way too easy for immature love to simply be a lustful counterfeit. Mature love is going to have that power, that electricity, but it is also going to have that glue that holds it all together. This is the discipleship process, the process the Lord is carrying us through if we will continue to live our lives for Him, in the Ruach.

When you're a young/new believer you are on fire for God, you are completely consumed in the emotional side of the intimacy with your Bride Groom, but if this immature love doesn't continue to blossom into a mature intimacy with the Lord then it is far too easy for the flame to be snuffed out. There is nothing wrong with having that fire, with a true zeal for the Lord, but it is in the small things, the daily walk, the daily communion, in the daily relationship with the Bride Groom that that intimacy matures and grows into something lasting, something that cannot be crushed no matter what attacks arise. It is in this mature intimacy that a relationship with the Lord becomes the priority, not just an emotional rollercoaster. As a matter of fact, one of the most important keys to mature intimacy in a relationship is devotion and devotion requires faithfulness.

These are the things that Joshua continued to see in Moses. He watched as Moses went up the mountain and spent 40 days completely encompassed in the Shechinah of Adonai. He watched as Moses returned, not once, but twice (albeit because of Israel's mistakes) with the Word of God. He watched as Moses went up the mountain into the Presence of God and would descend again with His face aglow with the Shechinah. He witnessed Moses receive the divine download to be relayed to B'nei Yisrael. He watched as Moses' intimacy with HaShem was operated on some other plane, some other wavelength. This is how a deeply matured intimacy between a husband and wife operates, they can finish each other's sentences, they can sense how the other is feeling, they can read the micro-expressions on their partners face and know every thought rolling through their head. Joshua watched as Moses' intimacy with the Lord continued to develop over the years, and Joshua consumed the example and emulated all he could from what had been lived out before him.

There's something to be said of people who have walked with the Lord for a long time. They may not be jumping pews and swinging from chandeliers, but there is a wisdom, a knowledge, an understanding that comes from deep within those people. And there is something so valuable to be gleaned from their example of deep intimacy with the Lord.

So we see how in Joshua's development as a leader empowered with the Ruach HaKodesh there are these two bookends. The first is in Numbers 11 where Joshua is freaked out by the impartation of the Ruach HaKodesh on the elders and cries out to Moses saying, "You've gotta stop this now!" The second is in Joshua 24, wherein his maturity of intimacy in the Ruach Joshua boldly urges Israel, "Choose you this day whom you will serve!" The story in between is not one where Moses empowers and then walks away. But rather it is one of great discipleship, of mentorship, it is one of an example in the true character of a Spirit-led leader. It is the very embodiment of Deuteronomy 6:4-9's command to teach the children and to walk by the way.

We have to continue to be diligent. We have to keep in mind that the things that God has shown us, He wants us to continue to pass on to future generations. We see how Moses discipled Joshua, we see how Yeshua discipled, we see how those disciples made other disciples. This discipleship shouldn't just be an impartation of head knowledge either, it MUST BE an impartation of the Holy Spirit, it MUST BE a building up into mature intimacy. As believers, we must take this to heart, we must recognize that it is our duty and responsibility to continue this pattern laid out in Scripture. Who are you mentoring in the Ruach? Who are you taking time to disciple to further maturity in intimacy with the Lord? Who are you investing in?

CHAPTER 11

Up to this point, we've taken a deeper look at the Ruach HaKodesh as the mantle was placed upon Moses. We've spent some time looking at Moses, Aaron, and Miriam and how the Ruach moved through each of them. We've looked into the impartation of a portion of the Mantle of the Ruach being placed upon the 70 elders in Numbers. In the last section, we looked specifically at the impartation of the Ruach being transferred from the first generation of the leadership of Israel (Moses) to the second generation (Joshua). Now we look at similar circumstances, but specifically from a little bit of a different perspective. Here we're going to be looking at Samuel, Saul, David and Solomon, and the way we see the Holy Spirit upon each of these individual's lives.

Let's begin this discussion in 1 Samuel chapter 1, here we see an all-too-familiar story in the Scriptures about a woman, in this case, named Hannah, who is barren. She is married and her husband also has another wife and she has no problem having children. Her husband, Elkanah, goes every year to the Mishkan, he brings his entire family to worship HaShem, he brings offerings for the Lord and he prays for his barren wife, Hannah, to become pregnant. Peninnah, the wife who has children, gets a larger portion of the offerings that they eat in the Presence of the Lord because of her children and she often rubs it in the face of Hannah. The narrative, ultimately, alludes back to the story of Jacob, Rachel, and Leah.

Here in 1 Samuel 1, we see the heart of Hannah as she is praying at the Mishkan and pouring her heart out before the Lord. She says beginning in verse 10, *10 While her soul was bitter, she prayed to Adonai and wept. 11 So she made a vow and said, "Adonai-*

Tzva'ot, if You will indeed look upon the affliction of Your handmaid, remember me and not forget Your handmaid, but grant Your handmaid a son, then I will give him to Adonai all the days of his life and no razor will ever touch his head."

Do you recognize what this promise Hannah is referencing to is? It is the Nazarite vow of Numbers 6. There is more to the Nazarite vow, he also will not be able to eat or drink anything of the vine and so on. But she's saying to the Lord, "If you give me a child he will be especially dedicated to you his entire life." She prays and she prays, pouring her heart out before the Lord, and she's praying silently, and I imagine she looked kind of like someone who is unable to read silently without their lips moving. But, either way, she was praying silently, but her lips were moving. The High Priest, Eli, comes by and sees her and asks her (this is my paraphrase), "Why are you drunk already? You need to get your life together..." She responds that she's not drunk she is simply praying to the Lord. Eli says to her, "Whatever you're praying for, may the Lord bless you and give you your request," because he can see the passion with which she is beseeching the Lord.

Hannah goes home and, to her great surprise, she gets pregnant. The next year as Elkanah is getting ready to go to the Mishkan to worship the Lord and present the offerings Hannah tells him, "I'm going to stay behind this year, I told the Lord that as soon as our son is weaned that I would be dedicating him to the Lord and he would remain in service at the Tabernacle. So, I'm going to stay here and take care of him until that point." She names him Shmuel in Hebrew, which is Samuel in English, and it means "God hears." The root word of Shmuel is "shema," the same word used in the Jewish liturgical prayer known as the Shema from Deuteronomy 6:4—*Shema Yisrael Adonai Eloheinu, Adonai Echad/Hear oh Israel the Lord your God, the Lord is On*—and she called him

Shmuel because, as she says in 1 Samuel 1:20b, *She called his name Samuel, "because I have asked Adonai for him."* She recognized that Adonai heard her cry and answered her prayers.

She names him Shmuel and dedicates him to the Lord. She goes with Elkanah the next year and hands Samuel off to the service of the Lord at the Tabernacle as she promised. From then on she doesn't see Samuel again except for the one pilgrimage a year when Elkanah would take his family to the Mishkan to worship. On these trips, she would bring him clothing and provisions, but when they returned from the Tabernacle Samuel remained behind to continue to serve HaShem.

Picking up again in 1 Samuel 1:25, *25 After they slaughtered the bull, they brought the boy to Eli. 26 "It's me, my lord!" she said. "As your soul lives, my lord, I am the woman that stood by you here, praying to Adonai. 27 For this boy I prayed, and Adonai has granted me my petition that I asked of Him. 28 So I in turn dedicate him to Adonai—as long as he lives he is dedicated to Adonai." Then he bowed in worship there before Adonai.*

We skip forward and we see Hannah's prayer, we see the sons of Eli and how they are evil and the way they treat the people of Israel. Then in 1 Samuel chapter 3, we begin to see the call of Adonai upon Shmuel's life. Shmuel becomes a prophet, a "seer" as it is related in the narrative as Saul comes to him looking for his father's donkeys a few chapters forward. Shmuel becomes a judge of Israel, an overseer of God's people. He is what we can consider the final judge of Israel before the kings of Israel take over with Saul, and then the Davidic line after him.

1 Samuel 3:1 picks up, *1 Now the boy Samuel was in the service of Adonai under Eli. In those days the word of Adonai was rare—there were no visions breaking through.* In other words, in those days people

were not receiving the Word of the Lord to relay to Israel, they were not prophesying; in those days the Word of Adonai coming forth from the mouth of a messenger was rare. Which, as we've well established at this point, means that there was no one operating in the mantle of the Ruach HaKodesh

2 One day, Eli was lying down in his place— now his eyes had grown dim so that he could not see, 3 and the lamp of God had not yet gone out. This isn't speaking of the lamp as in the soul within him, it is speaking of the Ner Tamid, the Menorah in the Tabernacle. Remember, it wasn't long after this that the Philistines waged war against Israel and Eli's two sons took the Aron HaBrit (Ark of the Covenant) out to battle thinking that the God of Israel would fight for them. They were still outside the Will of God, but they take the Ark to battle and the Philistines take off with the Ark.

1 Samuel 3 continues, *Samuel was lying down in Adonai's Temple, where the ark of God was. 4 Then Adonai called, "Samuel!" So he answered, "Here I am." 5 Then he ran to Eli and said, "Here I am, for you called me." But he replied, "I didn't call—go back to sleep." So he went back and lay down.*

It happens two more times, Samuel hears the Lord call forth his name and he responds then runs to Eli the High Priest to see why he called. To which Eli continues to respond that he hadn't called him and, more or less, "I am trying to sleep, leave me alone with all this meshugash, and go back to sleep…" However, the third time Eli starts to recognize what may be going on and he says, "Hey listen, Samuel, this is the Lord speaking to you. Don't miss out on it because it doesn't happen much anymore…" And we pick up in verse 9, *9 So Eli said to Samuel, "Go back to sleep, and if He calls you, say: 'Speak, Adonai, for Your servant is listening.'" So Samuel went back and lay down in his place. 10 Then Adonai came and stood and called as at the other* times, *"Samuel! Samuel!" Then Samuel said, "Speak, for Your servant is listening." 11 Then Adonai said to Samuel, "Behold, I am about to do something in Israel at which both ears of everyone that hears it will tingle...* Then the Lord goes on to talk about removing Eli and his household from the priesthood and the Land and holding to these promises He made to Eli.

So, at this point, we begin to see the exact moment in which Shmuel begins to have this interaction with the Ruach HaKodesh and the anointing of the mantle of the Ruach that is upon him. You may find yourself asking, "What in that passage makes us think that there is any sort of anointing of the Holy Spirit upon Samuel as there was on Moses or Joshua?" The simple answer is that he hears the voice of the Lord, in particular in a very literal audible sense. But we also know from Moses to the 70 elders and from Moses to Joshua there was a transference of the mantle of the Ruach HaKodesh that was made from one to another. When we go forward to Saul and later David being anointed as king we see the same kind of transference of the mantle of the Holy Spirit. Samuel anoints both of these future kings of Israel and he lays hands on them and there was an impartation of a portion of the mantle that he carried that was placed upon Saul and David as the leaders of the nation of Israel.

It can only work that way, especially before the outpouring of the Ruach upon the Body of Messiah in Acts 2 in which it is available for everyone. In the Tanakh what we're seeing is that the mantle of the Ruach is accessible for anyone the Lord chooses. In Acts 2 what we see shifts is that the mantle of the Ruach is accessible for anyone that God chooses, the difference is He's chosen everyone and now we have the opportunity to choose to come into this covenant relationship with Him. In this, now, the Ruach is available for all who believe in Messiah Yeshua's sacrifice, and not just for a select few that HaShem hand selects over the generations.

We see that throughout the Tanakh there are instances and situations in which the Lord calls forth specific individuals for the sake of placing the Ruach HaKodesh upon them for His purposes. It is their job, just as Shmuel does here, to say, "Here I am Adonai, your servant is listening." And from this moment forth he takes on the role and calling for which the mantle of the Holy Spirit was placed upon him, to be a prophet and in essence a judge of Israel. He becomes the one to whom Israel looks to hear from the Lord for guidance and leadership.

Then we go to verse 19 and we read, *19 So Samuel grew up and Adonai was with him, and let none of his words fall to the ground.* In other words, anything the Lord said to him he spoke forth to Israel. He never ignored the word of the Lord or allowed it to come back void. *20 Then all Israel from Dan to Beersheba knew that Samuel was entrusted as a prophet of Adonai. 21 Adonai started to appear once more in Shiloh, for Adonai revealed Himself to Samuel in Shiloh by the word of Adonai.*

Now early on in 1 Samuel chapter 3, we read that there is no longer any appearance of the Lord, or at least that such an event is few and far between. Up to this point, no one in Israel heard the voice of the Lord anymore, there were no longer dreams and visions among His people because Israel had already started to separate themselves from the God of Abraham, Isaac, and Jacob. So Samuel is one of the first people in which we see this continuum, and revival of sorts, of the word, the voice, and the Presence of the Lord coming forth and the outpouring of the Ruach HaKodesh upon an individual with Israel again. And so we read, *21 Adonai started to appear once more in Shiloh...* Shiloh is where the Tabernacle stood, it is where the Glory of the

Lord rested upon the Ark of the Covenant. So, all of the sudden now, because of Samuel's faithfulness and willingness to serve the Lord and the anointing upon him the Lord began to show His Glory to Israel again.

What did we say previously about a prophet's job? It is to speak the Word of the Lord. And the Word of the Lord is always what? "Return to Me!" It is always a call to T'shuvah, to true repentance. So Samuel's job as a prophet of Adonai, as is the case of Isaiah, Jeremiah, Ezekiel, and others, is to speak forth the Word of the Lord to usher His people back to Him. Their job is not specifically to speak forth future visions and fortune-telling. Although telling the future can be a part of prophecy, the point of prophecy is always to speak the Word of the Lord and to call people to T'shuvah. If we look at Isaiah and Jeremiah as examples, that is exactly what we see over and over again. They continually relayed a message from the Lord that more or less said, "Here's what God says is going to happen, at some point in the future there will be destruction. But, God just wants you to return to Him in faithfulness, and if you simply make T'shuvah all of that will be forgotten or pushed off."

CHAPTER 12

So, all of a sudden as Samuel is serving under the mantle of the anointing of the Ruach HaKodesh as a prophet and judge over Israel, we begin to see something that God had previously prophesied over Israel. Let's look back at Deuteronomy 17 beginning with verse 14, *14 "When you come to the land that Adonai your God is giving you, possess it and dwell in it, and you say, 'I will set a king over me, like all the nations around me,' 15 you will indeed set over yourselves a king, whom Adonai your God chooses.* In other words, once the Lord has done everything He said He is going to do for you, you're going to become arrogant, you're going to become conceited, you're going to become too comfortable in the land that you're in and where you're at. The Lord says Israel will do the exact opposite of everything the Lord said to do. God said to be different from the nations around us, He called Israel out to be set apart righteous and holy, to be an example of holiness for the nations. But, God warns there will come a day when Israel will cry out that they will give themselves a king *to be like all the nations around them.*

So the Lord says, *5 you will indeed set over yourselves a king, whom Adonai your God chooses.* In other words, as we read in other places in the Bible, God places people in positions of power and authority for His purpose. We may not always understand it, and we certainly may not always like it. Hitler was a very evil guy, he did a lot of very evil things… But, the Lord used what Hitler did and the destruction that he caused to ultimately bring about revelation of the reality and prophecy of the reestablishment of the nation of Israel as a Jewish homeland. Ultimately this began what we recognize as the fulfillment of end-time prophecy, and the ushering in of the Return of Mashiach. We see that Hitler was way outside the will of God, but God used the authority He gave him to bring about His purposes. We don't have to understand it, we just have to trust that God knows what He is doing and He will be faithful to fulfill His promises.

We continue to examine this passage from Deuteronomy 17, *15 you will indeed set over yourselves a king, whom Adonai your God chooses. One from among your brothers will be appointed as king over you—you may not put a foreigner over you, who is not your brother. 16 Only he should not multiply horses for himself or make the people return to Egypt to multiply horses, because Adonai has said to you, "You must never go back that way again." 17 Nor should he multiply wives for himself, so that his heart does not turn aside, nor multiply much silver and gold for himself.*

If we look at Solomon, he is considered the wisest man that ever lived. The one thing he asked of God was to be given the wisdom to lead God's people. Solomon is still considered one of the wisest and most righteous men that ever lived, yet, do you realize that in the first few years of his reign as king of Israel appointed by HaShem that he broke every single one of those commands we just read in Deuteronomy 17? He broke every single one right out of the gate and is still considered the wisest.

The Lord says there will come a day in which you will desire to be like the nations around you. When that day comes you will ask for a king, you will ask to have a king like all the nations around you. The reality is, Israel wasn't supposed to do this, having an earthly king was never God's intention for Israel. Who is supposed to be the King of Israel? Adonai. The Lord is our king, we should not have a king over us on earth. He is the Lord of heaven and earth and we should submit to His will and authority. But alas, Samuel was approached with the inclination of Israel to step outside the will of God and ultimately bring about this exact warning we just read about in Deuteronomy 17.

In 1 Samuel 8 we read, *1 Now when Samuel grew old, he appointed his sons as judges over Israel. 2 The name of his firstborn was Joel and the name of his second Abijah—they were judges in Beersheba. 3 His sons, however, did not walk in his ways, but turned aside after dishonest gain—they took bribes and perverted justice.* As an interesting rabbit trail, there is almost an exact mirror of what Samuel's sons did here and what Eli's (the high priest Samuel served under) did. Both men's sons are serving under righteous men and their hearts turned astray.

We pick up again in 1 Samuel 8:4, *4 Then all the elders of Israel gathered together and came to Samuel at Ramah, 5 and said to him, "Behold, you have grown old and your sons do not walk in your ways. Now appoint for us a king to judge us—like all the nations."* To paraphrase Deuteronomy 17, the Lord says there will come a day when you've come into the Land, you've taken it, and settled it and you will approach and say, we want a king over us like all the nations around us. Here in 1 Samuel 8, that day of which Moses prophesied has finally arrived. *6 But the matter was displeasing in Samuel's eyes when they said, "Give us a king to judge us." So Samuel prayed to Adonai.* Samuel gets upset, a righteous zeal rises within him at B'nei Yisrael. He recognizes that Israel's King should ONLY be HaShem, they shouldn't have an earthly man sitting on a throne in Jerusalem (or anywhere else for that matter) acting as king over them, because the King of Israel sits on the Throne in the Holy of Holies of the Heavenly Mishkan.

We are to live and operate in His Presence, but we cannot live in His Presence if our allegiance is divided. Yeshua says in the Besorah (Good News) that a kingdom divided shall fall. So, we can't have an earthly king and a

Heavenly King and give our full allegiance to both. Especially when we're looking at Israel which is a nation God has ordained specifically for His purposes. How can we walk fully submitted to His purposes if we're also walking submitted the purposes of man as well…?

So, Samuel gets upset, and in this righteous anger he does a really wise thing, he consults the Lord as opposed to just spewing out rage-filled vitriol. (Imagine how much better our witness would be if we acted like Samuel… Imagine if when we get upset about things in our lives rather than just acting out we turned to the Lord in prayer…) Samuel takes the time to pause and to seek the voice and will of the Lord.

So, although Samuel recognizes Israel is stepping outside the will of God, he seeks the Lord's guidance. And what is it the Lord does as Israel has now fulfilled the prophecy of Deuteronomy 17:14-20…? The Lord doesn't just give them a king, He gives them the exact kind of king they are looking for, one exactly like all the nations around them. Because when we, as humans, are looking for a king, we aren't looking for some wimpy little guy to be king… We want the guy that's going to lead us into valiant battle on a stallion, we want the guy who's bigger than everyone else, this big, burly, strong-man who stands head and shoulders above everyone else. This isn't always God's pick though, is it? But here, God gives Israel exactly what they were looking for, because He knew they needed it to understand exactly how wrong they were in asking for a king.

We now move forward to chapter 9 of 1 Samuel, in which Samuel meets Saul for the first time. It's an odd encounter, it was a Book-of-Acts-like vision (think Peter's vision in Acts 10) that brings about the encounter. The donkeys of Saul's father run off and Saul is sent out to find them. He searches high and low but is unable to locate them, so he ends up deciding to go to the man being called "the seer," which of course is Samuel. The

Lord knew Samuel wasn't ready for this meeting yet, so the Lord speaks to Samuel and says (paraphrasing), "Hey, Shmuely, this time tomorrow this young guy is going to come to you, and by the way... He's going to become king..." The Scriptures tell us that Saul was a big dude, that he stood head and shoulders above everyone else. Saul was big, bulky, strong, valiant, and brave, in other words, he was everything a human would expect in a king. So the Lord tells Samuel that this guy Saul is going to be the first king of Israel.

In chapter 10 of 1 Samuel we read, *1 Then Samuel took the vial of oil and poured it on his head. Then he kissed him and said, "Has Adonai not anointed you ruler over His inheritance? 2 When you leave me today, you will find two men near the tomb of Rachel in the territory of Benjamin at Zelzah, and they will say to you: 'The donkeys you set out to look for have been found—behold, your father has dropped the matter about the donkeys and is worried about you saying, "What should I do about my son?"'* And it goes on to talk about how Saul was to come back to Samuel at a specific time and how everything would work out from there. But, as all of this is going on we see that Saul has been anointed as king over Israel and Israel gets exactly what they asked for. However, Samuel's heart is zealously broken for Adonai. The narrative of Saul's beginning continues on and in chapter 11 we see Saul's first victory in battle.

In chapter 12 we see the prophet Samuel begin to pour his heart out and rebuke Israel. This is where we see that righteous anger, that righteous zeal, I believe empowered by the Ruach HaKodesh, begins to speak forth. Beginning in verse 1 we read, *1 Then Samuel said to all Israel, "Behold, I have listened to your voice in all you said to me, and have set a king over you. 2 Now here is the king who will go before you, while I am old and gray. Also here are my sons with you. I have gone before you from my youth to this day. 3 Here I am. Witness against me before Adonai and before His anointed. Whose ox have I taken or whose donkey have I taken? Whom have I defrauded or whom have I oppressed? From whose hand have I taken a bribe to look the other way? I will restore it to you." 4 They replied, "You haven't defrauded us or oppressed us or taken anything from anyone's hand." 5 Then he said to them, "Adonai is then a witness against you, and His anointed is a witness this day that you have not found anything in my hand." "He is a witness," they replied. 6 Then Samuel said to the people, "It is Adonai who appointed Moses and Aaron and who brought your fathers up from the land of Egypt. 7 So now, stand still, so that I may plead with you before Adonai concerning all the righteous acts of Adonai, which He did for you and your fathers.* And then Samuel goes on to begin to declare all HaShem has done for Israel to this point.

.   Then in verse 11, we continue, *11 Then Adonai sent Jerubbaal, Bedan, Jephthah and Samuel, and delivered you from the hand of your enemies on every side, so that you might live securely. 12 But when you saw Nahash king of the Ammonites marching against you, you said to me, 'No! But a king must reign over us!'—even though Adonai your God is your king. 13 "Now therefore, here is the king whom you have chosen and whom you have asked for, and behold, Adonai has set him as king over you. 14 If you fear Adonai and worship Him, and listen to His voice and do not rebel against the command of Adonai, then both you as well as the king who reigns over you will be following Adonai your God. 15 But if you do not listen to the voice of Adonai and rebel against the command of Adonai, then the hand of Adonai will be against you and against your fathers.*

16 Now stand by and see this great thing that Adonai will do before your eyes.

What we see is that in this righteous anger and zeal of Samuel (which, by the way, Saul never lives by) he begins to tell Israel exactly where and how they messed up and he begins to speak the Word of the Lord. As a matter of fact, most of what we read about in the latter half of 1 Samuel 12 is a near-exact replica of what we read about in the Torah. "If you and your children just honor God's words and obey His commands you will live long in the Land and prosper…" It is all repeated here, and it is repeated over and over again throughout the Tanakh as a whole as a call to God's people to stand upright (the very definition of righteousness) before HaShem. What we see is this prophet of the Lord who is empowered by the Ruach HaElohim boldly speak the Word of the Lord.

Now I want to transition to look at Saul because we've seen the way Samuel interacts with the Ruach HaKodesh and how he prophesies and speaks forth. But, now the Ruach, at least with these next several individuals we will be looking at (starting with Saul), is upon a different type of individual. We're not just looking at the Spirit upon a prophet like Moses, Joshua, and Samuel, now we'll be looking at the impartation of the mantle of the Ruach upon the earthly king of Israel.

So, we're going to turn back a little bit to verse 9 of 1 Samuel chapter 10, ***9 Then it happened, as Saul turned his back to leave Samuel, that God transformed his heart, and all those signs came to pass that day. 10 When they arrived there, at the hill, behold, a band of prophets did meet him, and suddenly, the Ruach of God overtook him, and subsequently, he prophesied among them.***

So, first off, Saul leaves Samuel from this initial encounter, and the first thing that happens is God transforms his heart. This almost sounds like Salvation, right…? At Salvation God begins to transform our hearts so we can walk in His ways (and sometimes we need to allow Him to do a lot more transformative work in our hearts for sure). Here He transforms Saul's heart and then, he is empowered with the Ruach HaKodesh. The passage says, "**the Ruach of God overtook him.**" The Ruach didn't just sit on his shoulder like the little conscience angels we see on tv saying, "Do this and do that…" The Ruach didn't just haphazardly come into his life and then leave him. No, the Bible says the Ruach OVERTOOK him. The Spirit of God overtook Saul and he began to prophesy.

The passage continues from verse 11, **11 So when all who knew him formerly saw him prophesying with the prophets, they said one to another, "What has happened to the son of Kish? Is Saul also among the prophets?" 12 (Someone there asked, "Who is their father?") Therefore it became a proverb, "Is Saul also among the prophets?" 13 When he finished prophesying, he came to the high place.**

Immediately upon Saul receiving the anointing as king from Samuel, he is told, "a series of things will happen before he is standing before Israel as their king, but God is going to bring it all to pass, You are God's anointed." Notice how that is worded, "You are God's ANOINTED…" That doesn't mean he is going to always do what is right, but he is God's anointed. Moses was God's anointed and he messed up, Joshua was God's anointed and he messed up. As humans, we mess up, even being the anointed of God, we are going to mess up, that's just how it is in the fallen world. The key is T'shuvah, to return, to HaShem's grace and mercy. The difference is that Saul doesn't come back around, he doesn't make T'shuvah. Why is that? It's because Saul is who B'nei Yisrael thought they needed as king, he isn't God's idea of what a king should be. But when we get to

113

Melech David (King David) things change in this way. David is called "a man after God's own heart." David is a type and shadow, a foreshadowing of Mashiach Yeshua.

So, what we see with Saul is that Saul isn't a man after God's own heart. Saul is exactly what Israel wanted, and Israel got exactly what they asked for. Israel wanted this big, beefy, brave man as king that would lead them into battle and they could be proud to follow behind. They got exactly that, he stood head and shoulders above everyone, he was a perfect specimen of machismo. Samuel says, "Here, God is giving you the king that YOU want." But, in Deuteronomy 17 the Lord says He will give us the king that He chooses. So, He has chosen and anointed Saul, but He hasn't chosen him for the same purposes that He chose David. But He has chosen Saul for His purposes, as a wake-up call to Israel. With Saul, HaShem is saying to Israel, "If you want to be like the nations around you, then this is what you get. You get a train wreck, because all the nations around you are train wrecks, and all their leaders are train wrecks. But, this isn't ultimately what I have in store for you."

CHAPTER 13

The Ruach HaKodesh is upon Saul, and I think a lot of times we lose sight of that. We lose focus on the reality that even though Saul was clearly, over and over again, outside the will of God, the Ruach HaKodesh was upon him. Then we move to David who later receives the anointing. Notice David is anointed as king, but it is years before he ever sits on the throne of Israel. What does he do? He humbly awaits his turn, because he recognizes that Saul is still the anointed. David has several opportunities to kill Saul, to get rid of him, and to make his own life easier and to make things potentially better for the nation of Israel. But he recognizes the anointing that is still on Saul and he's not going to touch that. But Saul, on the other hand, even though he has the Holy Spirit upon him, isn't going to walk faithfully with the Lord.

The very next thing we see is that Saul makes a misguided sacrifice. Let's take a look at just some of the section headings through the next couple of chapters in the Tree of Life Version. In 1 Samuel 13, we see "Saul's Misguided Sacrifice." 1 Samuel 14 we see "Saul's Rash Vow" which ends up causing him all sorts of problems and consequences. We go forward to 1 Samuel 15 and we see "Saul spares Agag of Amalek." God told Israel in the Torah to wipe out Amalek completely because of the way they treated Israel coming from Egypt to the Promised Land, and Saul makes a treaty with them instead. Over and over again Saul does these things that go completely against the will of God.

Then appears this young man named David. So Samuel, who was already an old man when Saul came on the scene, and the Lord says to him, "Alright, so Israel got what they wanted and they're going to deal with the consequences for a while. But, now I want to show you the king that I desire and I want you to go search him out." So, in chapter 16 of 1 Samuel we see where Samuel anoints David as king.

We read, beginning with verse 1, *1 Now Adonai said to Samuel, "How long will you grieve over Saul, since I have rejected him as king over Israel? Fill your horn with oil and go. I am sending you to Jesse the Beth-lehemite, for I have selected for Myself a king among his sons."* And it's really interesting, considering that Melech David was a shadow of Mashiach Yeshua, to think about where Yeshua was born, in Bethlehem, and where David was from.

We continue, *2 But Samuel replied, "How can I go? If Saul hears of it, he will kill me." Adonai said, "Take a heifer with you and say: 'I have come to sacrifice to Adonai.' 3 Then invite Jesse to the sacrifice, and I will let you know what you are to do. You will anoint for Me whom I tell you." 4 So Samuel did what Adonai said and went to Beth-lehem. The elders of the town came out to meet him trembling, and asked, "Do you come in shalom?" 5 "In shalom," he said. "I have come to sacrifice to Adonai. Consecrate yourselves and come with me to the sacrifice." He also consecrated Jesse and his sons and invited them to the sacrifice. 6 Upon their arrival, he saw Eliab and thought, "Surely, Adonai's anointed one is before Him."* Samuel gets ahead of himself and is thinking here, "Hey, this dude is big and bad like Saul maybe this is who God has chosen to anoint as the next King of Israel, Eliab strikes me as kingly…"

Continuing in verse 7, *7 But Adonai said to Samuel, "Do not look at his appearance or his stature, because I have already refused him. For He does not see a man as man sees, for man looks at the outward appearance, but Adonai looks into the heart."* So, Israel got the king they wanted in Saul because they were only considering the outward appearance. Eliab had a kingly-like outward appearance. But, that wasn't what God was trying to show Samuel, He wanted Samuel to understand God is not concerned with the outward appearance, He is concerned with the heart, with the inward appearance.

We pick up again with verse 8, *8 Then Jesse called Abinadab and made him pass before Samuel. But he said, "Neither has Adonai chosen this one." 9 Then Jesse made Shammah pass by and again he said, "Neither has Adonai chosen this one." 10 Thus Jesse made seven of his sons pass before Samuel. But Samuel said to Jesse, "Adonai has not chosen any of these." 11 Then Samuel asked Jesse, "Are these all the boys you have?" "There's still the youngest," he replied. But right now, he's tending the sheep."* I want to take a moment to pause and let this sink in real quick… Saul was exactly what humanity thinks should be king, he was the prime idea of a king, he was big, he carried himself with a sense of authority, he was bold, he was fearless. But, then God chooses David as the next king, and it is through David's lineage that we get the kingship lineage of Israel, and ultimately we get Messiah.

Yet, as we watch all of this play out, we realize that there is a drastic difference between Saul and David. When Samuel goes to Jesse's house and is looking for who God chooses as the next king of Israel, he says, "Hey, bring all your sons out to me." Jesse lines up the first seven of his sons, Jesse doesn't even think to go get David from the fields. David is not only the least likely to be thought of as king over the nation of Israel, but his own father couldn't even see the potential. His own father who loved him couldn't see the potential in him. Notice, God says I don't look at the outside, I only look at the inside. For us, as believers, it is as equally painful a statement as it was encouraging for David because as believers we like to live on the outside like everything is ok, like we're honoring God as we're supposed to. We're keeping this, we're doing that, we're worshipping the right way, we're doing missions, we're giving financially, we're praying and in the Word, but in reality, a lot of the time everything is jacked up on the inside. We think no one sees what's going on on the inside because on the outside we're putting on a good show, and we're right, the folks around us in the world don't know any difference (and are equally messed up). But the Lord knows, because the Lord doesn't care about the outside, He is concerned with the inside. To the Lord, the outside doesn't matter at all until the inside is right.

Continuing with the latter part of verse 11, *"Send and bring him," Samuel said to Jesse, "for we will not sit down until he comes here." 12 So he sent word and had him come. Now he was ruddy-cheeked, with beautiful eyes and a handsome appearance. Then Adonai said, "Arise, anoint him, for this is the one." 13 So Samuel took the horn of oil and anointed him in the midst of his brothers. From that day on Ruach Adonai came mightily upon David.*

It overtook Saul, it came mightily upon David. Notice a theme in the way the Bible words this, a portion of the Mantle was taken from Moses and placed upon the 70 elders, a portion of the Mantle was taken from Moses and placed upon Joshua. Even down to the account of Samuel anointing Saul we see the imagery of the oil being poured on Saul and the Ruach overtaking him, and now here it says, *From that day on Ruach Adonai came mightily upon David.*

Interestingly enough, the next verse in this chapter says, *14 Now the Ruach Adonai had departed from Saul, and an evil spirit from Adonai terrified him.*

And from this moment forward David begins to serve in Saul's household and under Saul. Saul doesn't realize that this is a divinely orchestrated apprenticeship. When Saul does realize what is going on and there is this spiritually oppressive battle that is now going on within Saul, as he catches on to the anointing now upon David he starts to try to kill him. From this moment through the end of 1 Samuel, David is patiently awaiting whatever the Lord is going to do with and/or to Saul. He runs for his life, he teams up with Philistines, he does whatever he needs to stay alive, and while this is all happening he is patiently awaiting God's timing because he is fully aware that Saul is still God's anointed. He may recognize Saul is not in God's will, he may recognize that the Ruach is no longer upon Saul, he may recognize the spiritual battle, bordering on psychosis, raging with Saul, but no matter what Saul is still God's anointed until God decides otherwise.

As believers, we need to recognize and understand the value of this lesson because a lot of times we get upset about something happening and we handle it all wrong. In Matthew 18 Yeshua teaches a fantastic lesson about dealing with conflict in your congregation: *15 "Now if your brother sins against you, go and show him his fault while you're with him alone. If he listens to you, you have won your brother. 16 But if he does not listen, take with you one or two more, so that 'by the mouth of two or three witnesses every word may stand.' 17 But if he refuses to listen to them, tell it to Messiah's community. And if he refuses to listen even to Messiah's community, let him be to you as a pagan and a tax collector.*

There's proper order in Scripture to everything, and David realizes that is the case even in this scenario. David is the anointed next king of Israel, he has the "right" to go and wipe Saul out if he wanted to... but, that isn't God's way of handling these situations. It would definitely have been Saul's way, it is exactly what Saul is trying to do to David. So, recognizing God's timing is in control, David patiently waits.

How many of us in our lives realize that when the Ruach HaKodesh is leading us to do something, we often have this idea that it must be happening right now? The Lord said this is going to happen and we want it to happen NOW. It is exciting and invigorating. However, sometimes the Lord's plan is for it to happen a little further down the road, and He is simply giving us a heads up so we can get prepared for what He wants to do. When David was a young boy and was fighting Goliath, he wasn't ready to sit on the throne, not even a little bit. He had no clue what that responsibility would entail, he had no training or development regarding leadership and kingship. He had the chutzpah for sure, but he wasn't ready to sit on the throne. Even though David had the anointing already, he had to sit under Saul for a while to learn how a king operates, to learn both the good and the bad.

As a rabbi coming up, I trained under different rabbis in various congregations. I needed this so I could learn what works and what doesn't work, what's good and what's not. I needed this to learn how to develop into the leader that our congregation needed. That doesn't mean that these lessons were necessarily easy, that doesn't mean there wasn't some degree of "growing pains" in the process, but it was needed. And in the end, it was vastly more valuable than I could have ever imagined, and I don't think I could ever thank the rabbis I worked under enough for the time, energy, and care that they put into the rabbi and man of God I am today. The way we do things in our synagogue is made up of a combination of things that I've experienced and learned in other synagogues that work, and there are things we don't do based off the fact that I was able to witness first hand that they didn't work well or wouldn't work well in our context. So, we need to realize that we have to see what is happening around us and watch what the Lord is doing in His anointed who goes before us. If we are anointed by God we must be willing to wait our turn and watch what He is revealing to us in that time of growth and development. God is never going to move faster than His timing, and just because we feel His anointing, just because we've received His vision, that doesn't mean that it is an immediate move. More often than not, as we see in Scripture, there is a time where the current anointed and the coming anointed are running the relay race hand-in-hand before the transition: Moses and Joshua, Saul and David, Elijah and Elisha, Yeshua and His Talmidim, Paul and Timothy, just a few examples to hit the point home.

For David, what God was revealing to him was a lot of how not to be a king… In 2 Samuel chapter 1, we see David mourn for Saul and Jonathan. Notice, Saul was the king of Israel, David was the successor of the throne of Israel by divine decree, and Saul had attempted to kill David over this very issue numerous times. Yet David mourned with great sorrow at the death of Saul, he didn't rejoice at the death of Saul, he didn't rejoice now that Saul was officially out of the way. How often as believers do we have David's attitude as seen here? Or better yet, in contrast, how often as believers do we see something happen to the anointed of the Lord and they fall from where the Lord has raised them and instead of us mourning with them and sharing in that sorrow and helping to restore them, we poke fingers, make snide remarks, spread gossip and slander, laugh at them, etc…? We've got great lessons to learn in operating in the power of the Ruach from the interactions of David and Saul.

Now David has every right to climb the throne of Israel and take his (literally) God-given place as King. But instead, he takes time to mourn the death of the king who went before him. He takes time to mourn the death of the anointed. He begins to operate from that moment forward in his anointing from God. The reality is the anointing of the Holy Spirit was upon both Saul and David, the Bible says the Ruach overtook Saul and it came mightily upon David. The mantle of the Ruach was upon both of them and there are lessons to be learned by us today from both of them.

We see the mantle was upon Saul and he squandered it away, the anointing of the Holy Spirit was upon him, he had the opportunity to lead Israel in righteousness before the Lord. But, instead, he began to make rash decisions, he harms Israel, he causes the nations around them to attack Israel. He causes unholy desecration before Israel, he began to break down Israel's faith in the Lord, and he hurt the image of the Lord that is supposed to come forth from the Lord's anointed.

Then we have David, and although he definitely made some mistakes (that whole Bathsheba thing was pretty messed up, to say the least…), yet the Bible says that HaShem called David "a man after God's own heart." Although he made mistakes, he made it a point to make T'shuva, to repent and faithfully return to the Lord. He didn't squander the gift of the Ruach HaKodesh as Saul did, instead David developed in the gift of the Ruach. Every decision he made he tried to bring before the Lord to make sure he strove to walk within the will of God for the nation of Israel. When he failed to bring a decision before the Lord and things blew up in his face he went out of his way to fall on his face before HaShem in repentance. That is the example to set for how to walk in the Lord's anointing.

When we think of leaders today, we think of what the world around us tells us a leader should be. But, God's idea of a leader is something completely contrary to the world's opinion. When God says He can use someone, it is usually someone no one else would consider. Typically, it is the exact opposite of what the majority would look for in a leader. Remember, David's own father didn't think God could do anything with this kid and left him out in the field. No one thought much of Yeshua, He would speak and great wisdom would come forth and people would say, "Wait, aren't you from the Galilee? What could you possibly know…?" Paul begins to preach and every one second-guesses him because they immediately thought, "Wait, aren't you the guy who was killing believers just the other day…?" Peter hates Gentiles, and who is the first person God calls to lead Gentiles to Salvation? Peter. And he witnesses the Ruach fall upon a house full of Gentiles just as he experienced at the Temple on Shavuot in Acts 2. God generally chooses the least obvious, mainly because what is obvious to God is not going to be obvious to sinful man. What God looks at is the heart and what we typically look at is simply the exterior.

We see in both scenarios that Saul and David are both empowered by the Ruach HaKodesh. Both are overcome by the Ruach HaKodesh. Both have the anointing of the mantle of the Ruach HaKodesh upon them. Both have the ability to prophesy as we often see happen when the Ruach is upon someone. One squanders it and wastes it away, while the other walks boldly in righteousness. Righteousness doesn't mean we will always make the right choices and never mess up, Paul says we've all fallen short of the Glory of God. I believe righteousness has as much, if not more, to do with if and how we return than it does with how we walk it out.

Then we see Solomon, Shlomo in Hebrew, in 1 Kings 3. David dies and there is this crazy jockeying for the throne of Israel and Solomon is the one who is already anointed as the successor to the throne. (By the way, as an aside, notice how often in the Bible we see generation after generation of fathers and sons battling the same battles as we see with David and Solomon ascending to the throne.) Notice again, as we said before, God seems to always choose the least obvious. Solomon is the son of a messed relationship, of a tremendous mistake that David makes with Bathsheba.

As a matter of fact, look at the account of Yeshua's lineage in the Gospels, you'll notice there are four women mentioned. Each of these women is in one way or another considered by society to be women of ill-repute due to perceived or literal sexual promiscuity. First, there is Tamar, who tricked her father-in-law Judah into thinking she was a prostitute and sleeping with her. Then there is Ruth, when the book of Ruth says she "laid at Boaz's feet" this is likely a Hebrew idiom meaning she slept with him, or consummated their relationship. Then there's Bathsheba (Solomon's mom) that David saw bathing from his window and pursued her romantically even though she was married and he got her pregnant, then ultimately had her husband killed to try to cover up his mistake. And then there's Miriam (Mary) who, although she didn't actually do anything wrong, to the world around her, she was an unmarried woman who was pregnant, which means by the unknowing gossiper she was perceived as a whore.

So, as we see looking at the lineage of Yeshua (which includes David and Solomon) it is filled with people who made, or were perceived to have made, tremendous mistakes. And although many of these people would not be our first choices as fantastic leaders of God's people, they were God's choice, He anointed them for His purpose because He sees the inside (the heart) while we can only see the outside (the failures of flesh). Solomon was a bastard in the eyes of society, yet God chose him to be the anointed king of Israel, and God chose to put the mantle of His Holy Spirit upon him to lead Israel.

In 1 Kings chapter 3, after Solomon has officially secured his throne and his reign in Israel, beginning with verse 5 we read: **5 At Gibeon Adonai appeared to**

Solomon in a dream by night, and God said: "Ask for what should I give you?" 6 Solomon said: "You have shown my father Your servant David great lovingkindness, as he walked before You in truth, righteousness and uprightness of heart toward You. Indeed, You have kept this great lovingkindness for him by giving him a son to sit on his throne, as it is today. 7 So now, Adonai my God, You have made Your servant king in my father David's place. I am but a youth. I don't know how to go out or come in. 8 Your servant is amid Your people, whom You have chosen—a great people, too numerous to be numbered or counted. 9 So give Your servant a mind of understanding to judge Your people, to discern between good and evil—for who is able to judge this great people of Yours?" 10 Now it was pleasing in the eyes of Adonai that Solomon requested this thing. 11 So God said to him: "Because you asked for this thing—and have not asked for yourself long life, nor asked for yourself riches, nor asked for the life of your enemies, but asked for yourself understanding to discern justice—12 behold, I have done according to your words. I have given you a wise and discerning mind, so that there has been none like you before you, nor shall anyone like you arise after you. 13 Moreover I have also given you what you did not request—both riches and honor—so that no one among the kings will be like you all your days. 14 Furthermore, if you walk in My ways, keeping My statutes and My commandments, as your father David walked, then I will lengthen your days." 15 Then Solomon awoke and took note of the dream. So he went to Jerusalem, stood before the ark of the covenant of the Lord, and offered up burnt offerings and fellowship offerings. Then he made a feast for all his courtiers.

Paraphrasing this account, Solomon hears the voice of the Lord asking, "What would you like Me to do for you?" And Solomon's response is, "Who am I to be able to lead Your people? These are Your people, You have chosen them, called them forth for Your purposes. There are way too many to be numbered, who am I and what would I know about leading them? The thing I ask is that You give me Your wisdom to lead Your people as You would have them be led, as You would have them judged, as You would have them kept unto Yourself." He has the chance to ask God for literally anything, and God has said He would give him whatever he asks for, and all he asks for is the wisdom to lead God's people as God would see fit, in other words, God's wisdom. From where do we get God's wisdom? The Ruach HaKodesh, the Presence of the Lord within us, His indwelling. As Solomon is asking for God to give him His wisdom, I truly believe what he is asking for is an indwelling of the Holy Spirit.

Solomon is the anointed one, the chosen one. The Ruach is upon him as it was on his father David before him, as it was Saul, as it was Samuel, as it was Joshua and Moses and so on. Solomon's desire is not for riches and wealth, it is not for long life, it is not for peace, but his desire is for the wisdom of the Lord to lead the people of Israel. The way I would interpret that, not that his heart proved to always be in that direction, is that he asked for the wisdom to lead Israel in HaShem's ways so that Israel may remain righteous and holy before Him, so that Israel will always walk faithfully before the Lord.

When the Ruach HaKodesh is placed upon us as believers, when we are washed by the Blood of the Lamb and filled with the Holy Spirit, it is not for our benefit, it is not so we can go out and do magic shows with all the wonderful signs, wonders and miracles He can do through us. He gives us His Spirit that we can lead people in righteousness to Him. Saul received the anointing of the Holy Spirit and he wasted it. Samuel received the mantle of the Ruach HaKodesh and he faithfully walked hand in hand with the Father for his entire life, serving the Lord with all he had, and fearlessly standing before Israel and proclaiming the Word of the Lord with all his might. David was filled with the Holy Spirit and he waited patiently for the Lord's timing. (How many of us can honestly say we do that in our own lives...?) He waited patiently for years for the Lord's timing, he risked his life, he risked his future, laying his life aside so he could follow the will of the Lord. When the Lord's timing came about, David served the Lord as a man after God's own heart. His son, Solomon, arises and honoring the example his father set before him, as a man after God's own heart, his reply to God's request was simply for the wisdom to lead God's people in God's ways.

As believers, these are examples we are supposed to live by. Often, unfortunately, we tend to be more like Saul and squander the gift of the Holy Spirit. As a blanket statement, the Body of Messiah as a whole is guilty of being too much like Saul in that regard. Think about it, how many denominations exist that believe in cessationism, that the Spirit of God no longer operates among His people today. But this just isn't biblical... However, on the other side of things, there are plenty of denominations and believers that make a fool of God before the world around us by making the empowering of the Holy Spirit look like something it simply is not. How many leaders are there that act like they're operating in the Spirit of the Lord solely for the sake of their own benefit, gain, and profit?

We have to learn to be more like David, we have to be men and women after God's own heart. None of us, if we're honest with ourselves, would look at ourselves and think we'd be God's choice... I can promise you there are way more people in this world that would look at me and think, "Who is this guy? Why would God have chosen him? I would have never picked him… There's no way I would have ever thought this hot mess would be a leader of God's people." Most of us probably assume the world around us would think the same of us. We all know our pasts, we all know our failures, and we all know there are plenty of nay-sayers who also know the same things about us and would quickly leave us in the field like Jesse did David.

Thankfully, God is more concerned with the inside than the outside, because He sees His potential on the inside and knows if we simply allow Him to reign in our hearts, then our outside will fall in line with what He's doing on the inside. The Lord has chosen each one of us, He has called and anointed each one of us for His purposes. He has given us the wisdom of His Ruach HaKodesh to lead people to righteousness in His ways and in the Blood of the Lamb. It is important that we as believers grasp this, that we understand it, and that we walk in this power faithfully and fervently. We mustn't make a fool of the Holy Spirit, that we don't make a mockery of it. There are way too many people in the world today that look at the Body of Messiah and say, "I want nothing to do with their god because if that's what their god looks like, then he's not a god for me." If this is the case, if this is what people think when they see us, if this is the image and likeness of God that people see in our lives, then we are not acting like men and women after the heart of God.

CHAPTER 14

Next, we're going to take an in-depth look at Elijah and Elisha. There are several key things we can see as we look at these two men in relation to how the impartation of the Ruach HaKodesh can be passed on from person to person, from generation to generation, city to city, country to country, etc.

To give a little background on what is happening biblically as we approach Elijah and Elisha—B'nei Israel has been divided into two kingdoms, the Northern Kingdom is known as the Kingdom of Israel, and the Southern Kingdom is known as the Kingdom of Judah. The Kingdom of Judah was pretty intentional on trying to walk with the Lord and serve Him, whereas the Kingdom of Israel had turned entirely from HaShem as a whole. As the kingship lineage continued to develop, we see a long line (ultimately on both sides) of kings who would lead the people of God astray. This was even taken to the extent of moving the way the descendants of Abraham would worship Adonai, ultimately making their worship look less and less like how we were taught biblically, and more and more like how the nations around us worshipped. So we see these wicked kings have replaced true worship with false worship. (Notice how the enemy will always attempt to produce a counterfeit imitation of faith and how he will always try to get the followers of the God of Abraham, Isaac, and Jacob to go astray in these imitations.)

Honestly, (and chasing a rabbit trail here for a moment) we can even see some of this today in the Body of Messiah. We can see how our whole system of worship as set up by God has somehow migrated from being what we see the Word of God defines as worship, to being a system in which we look at things and decide how we can figure out how to do it better or "improve" things. We can see, as the Body of Messiah continues to splinter with division upon division, denomination upon denomination, that all we've really done is to breed greater disunity in the Bride of Messiah, which as we see in Yeshua's prayer in John 17:20-23 is the opposite of what He wants for His bride.

We first see Elijah pop up on the scene in 1 Kings chapter 17 we immediately find him confronting King Ahab (of the Northern Kingdom). *1 Now Elijah the Tishbite, one of the settlers of Gilead, said to Ahab: "As Adonai God of Israel lives, before whom I stand, there shall be no dew or rain these years, except at my word." 2 Then the word of Adonai came to him saying: 3 "Leave this place, turn eastward, and hide yourself by the Wadi Cherith, east of the Jordan. 4 It will come about that you will drink from the wadi. I have also commanded the ravens to feed you there."*

Oddly, we don't see any background information on Elijah, aside from a description in verse one of what family he is from. The first thing we see from Elijah is, with great chutzpah, he confronts Ahab and declares that there will be no rain, no dew, no precipitation in the Kingdom of Israel. Here is this prophet who doesn't seem to come from anywhere, he just suddenly and boldly appears, and proclaims a judgment (if you will) on the Land.

As we continue on the journey of Elijah's life from here, interestingly, the Bible begins to follow the many miracles that were performed through him. We read beginning with verse 10: *10 So he arose and went to Zarephath. Now when he came to the town gate, to his surprise, a widow was there gathering sticks. So he called her and said, "Please bring a little water in a jar that I may drink." 11 As she was going to fetch it, he called her and said, "Please bring me a morsel of bread in your hand." 12 So she said, "As Adonai your God lives, I have nothing baked, only a handful of flour in the jar, and a little oil in the jug. Now look, I am gathering a couple of sticks, so that I may go in and prepare it for me and my son, that we may eat it and die." 13 Elijah said to her, "Fear not! Go and do as you said, but first make me a little cake from what you have there. Bring it out to me and afterwards, make some for you and for your son. 14 For thus says Adonai God of Israel, 'The jar of flour shall not be exhausted nor shall the jug of oil be empty until the day Adonai sends rain on the land.'" 15 So she went and did according to the word of Elijah—and she and he, and her household ate for many days. 16 The jar of flour was not exhausted, nor did the jug of oil become empty, according to the word of Adonai which He spoke through Elijah.*

I find it very interesting to look at some of the characteristics of Elijah that we can draw upon from just this one passage (not to mention many others that we'll discuss). First, we notice that Elijah is a man of faith, bold, and intentional faith. Second, he spoke with great conviction the words that Adonai gave him. We must realize that speaking by faith is not just speaking whatever you think you should say and expect it to come to pass, but rather to rely on the word of God spoken through the Ruach HaKodesh in us. Faith begins when we read the Word of God, learn the voice of God, and begin to speak what we have learned from the two. Elijah heard God, he spoke only what Adonai had given to him. There was also this unbridled fear of the Lord combined with a lack of fear of man that we see in Elijah.

These are some characteristics that we see displayed even in Moses. Recall how we talked about Moses and Joshua, how there was a mentoring relationship between the two. Joshua then, through this mentorship emulated the same type of characteristics. These were lived out and passed down from Moses to

Joshua, and it was through this hands-on method of teaching by Moses that Joshua was enabled to take on the same walk. Truthfully, the only way Joshua could fully learn to live and act as Moses did was to walk, serve, and minister side-by-side with him, to have a personal relationship with him.

Another miracle we see performed through Elijah was the resurrection of a young boy. This was something that took great faith and boldness, and (as we mentioned earlier) we see an authentic, divinely inspired boldness in him. These characteristics we see exemplified through Elijah as he ministers, as he prophesies, as he performs miracles, and so on are only able to be experienced through the mantle of the Ruach HaKodesh. We can speak out of our own "boldness," what would often be better described by others as arrogance, pride, or crassness, but there's a tremendous difference between those things and the boldness of the Holy Spirit inside of us. The true boldness of the Holy Spirit causes us to speak in faith, to walk in His presence, align our lives with His will, among other things we see exemplified in Elijah throughout this narrative.

Continuing in 1 Kings 17, we'll read briefly about the resurrection of the boy mentioned a moment ago. Keep in mind also, contextually we notice that this is not a new household, this is the same woman and child that Elijah was within the section we read earlier. Beginning with verse 17: *17 After these things, it came to pass that the son of the woman, the mistress of the house fell sick, and his sickness was getting much worse until he had no breath left in him. 18 So she said to Elijah, "What do I have to do with you, man of God? Have you come to me to remind me of my sin and kill my son?"* Isn't it interesting how often people in the Bible who stand firm with God find themselves falsely accused?

Continuing, we read *19 He said to her, "Give me your son." Then he took him from her arms, carried him up to the upper room where he was staying and laid him on his own bed. 20 He cried out to Adonai and said, "Adonai my God, have You brought such evil even on the widow with whom I am staying, by causing her son to die?" 21 Then he stretched himself upon the child three times. He cried out to Adonai and said, "Adonai my God, please let this child's soul come back into his body!" 22 Adonai listened to the cry of Elijah, so the soul of the child came back into his body and he was revived.*

We see yet another powerful characteristic of Elijah in this passage—he was a man of prayer. He didn't wallow in self-pity. He didn't see the boy lying dead and begin to sob incessantly and uncontrollably. He didn't allow this potentially traumatic event to cause his faith to waver at all. Nor did he allow the shock of the condition he found the boy in or the blame the woman was emotionally placing upon him, to cause him to respond merely out of his human nature. Instead, much in the same way as we see with Moses and others, Elijah fell on his face in prayer, he cried out to God knowing that only God had control over this situation and he believed wholeheartedly that God would move.

What we see happen here with Elijah raising this boy from the grip of death itself takes faith, it takes confidence in the Lord. That kind of confidence comes only from the Holy Spirit, the Presence of the Lord dwelling within us, and understanding our place in Messiah. It also comes from a place where we do not allow sin to rule and reign in our lives. Remember, when we are in sin, that makes us feel like we are not children of God. When Yeshua was on the cross, He cried out, "My God, My God, why have You forsaken Me?" What was the difference between this moment and all of His life leading up to this point? The difference was this was the moment Yeshua received the sin of the world upon His shoulders and took the consequence of our sin upon Himself. He experienced the weight and reality of sin for the first time, which made Him feel as though He was forsaken. We have a greater boldness in the Holy Spirit when we are not in sin.

As we continue on our journey of lessons learned in the Ruach through Elijah we come to 1 Kings chapter 18 and what could perhaps be one of the best stories in the entire Bible. Again Elijah is confronting King Ahab, in particular about the people's service of Baal, and we read beginning in verse 20: **20 So Ahab sent word to all the children of Israel and gathered the prophets together at Mount Carmel. 21 Then Elijah approached all the people and said, "How long will you waver between two opinions? If Adonai is God, follow Him; but if Baal is, follow him." But the people did not answer him, not even a word. 22 Then Elijah said to the people, "I am the only prophet of Adonai left, but Baal's prophets are 450 men. 23 Now let them give us two young bulls. Let them choose one bull for themselves, cut it into pieces, lay it on the wood, and put no fire underneath, while I prepare the other bull, lay it on the wood, and put no fire underneath. 24 Then you will call on the name of your god, and then, I will call on the Name of Adonai. The God who answers with fire, He is God."**

Think about the intensity of this scene as it plays out… He puts the challenge out, and not just to Ahab, but at least 450 people total. That takes chutzpah, a definite boldness, an understanding of who God is and what He will and will not do.

Continuing with the rest of verse 24: **All the people responded and said, "It's a good thing." 25 Then Elijah said to the prophets of Baal, "Choose one bull for yourselves and prepare it first—since you are so many. Then call on the name of your god,** *but put no fire underneath." 26 So they took the bull that he gave them, prepared it, and called on the name of Baal from morning till noon, crying, "O Baal, answer us!" But there was no voice—no one was answering. They also danced leaping around the altar that was made. 27 Now when it was about noon, Elijah mocked them and said, "Shout louder! After all, he is a god! Maybe he's deep in thought, or he's relieving himself, or he's off on a journey, or perhaps he's asleep and must wake up!" 28 So they shouted even louder and cut themselves with swords and spears, as was their custom, until the blood gushed over them. 29 When midday was past, they kept prophesying ecstatically until the time of offering up the evening sacrifice. But there was no voice, no one answering, no one paying attention. 30 Then Elijah said to all the people, "Come near to me." So all the people came closer to him. Then he repaired the damaged altar of Adonai.*

This is another really important point to grasp here. As people of God, we are called to repair the breaches that other people have set up in their lives with false gods. That's ministry, that's being a witness in the marketplace, wherever we are. Hasn't the world set up false gods? Haven't they chased after all the "best" this world has to offer: riches, biggest houses, cars, accolades, social media friends and followers, etc. These things can become idols to people. Whatever these idols may be, we're called to be a part of the restoration process in which these idols, these high places, these things that take the place of HaShem in our lives, can be taken down. It is through tearing down these high places that others may see the One True God in our lives and they may overcome them.

Continuing: *30 Then Elijah said to all the people, "Come near to me." So all the people came closer to him. Then he repaired the damaged altar of*

Adonai. 31 Elijah took twelve stones—like the number of the tribes of the sons of Jacob, to whom the word of Adonai had come saying, "Israel shall be your name"—32 and with the stones he built an altar in the Name of Adonai. Then he made a trench around the altar, large enough to contain two measures of seed. 33 Then he put the wood in order, cut the bull in pieces and laid it on the wood. 34 Then he said, "Fill four jars with water and pour it on the burnt offering and on the wood." Then he said, "A second time!" and they did it a second time. Then he said, "A third time!" and they did it a third time. 35 So the water ran around the altar and he also filled the trench with water. 36 Now it was at the time of offering up the evening sacrifice that Elijah the prophet came near and said, "Adonai, God of Abraham, Isaac and Israel, let it be known today that You are God in Israel, that I am Your servant, and that I have done all these things at Your word. 37 Answer me, Adonai, answer me, so that these people may know that You, Adonai, are God, and that You have turned their heart back again." 38 Then the fire of Adonai fell and consumed the burnt offering—and the wood, the stones and the dust—and licked up the water that was in the trench. 39 When all the people saw it, they fell on their faces, and they said, "Adonai, He is God! Adonai, He is God!"

Elijah was a man who stood in front of these 450 false prophets and the king of the Northern Kingdom with boldness and conviction, and this characteristic of Elijah has continued to be a witness for thousands of years. And if you get nothing else out of this discussion of Elijah, I want to make sure you get this man of God's heart! Elijah was not simply bucking the system. He was not trying to stir up a rebellion. He was not trying to win a popularity contest. He was not trying to gain anything for himself. Rather, and most importantly, his only interest was the image of God and the return of the people to Him. Let verses 36 and 37 sink in for a moment, *"Adonai, God of Abraham, Isaac and Israel, let it be known today that You are God in Israel, that I am Your servant, and that I have done all these things at Your word. 37 Answer me, Adonai, answer me, so that these people may know that You, Adonai, are God, and that You have turned their heart back again."*

Elijah sat here and watched as all these fools who are direct descendants of Abraham, Isaac, and Jacob, who are all part of the twelve tribes of Israel, dance around like idiots crying out for a false god to answer them. (Now, granted, we get one of the funniest lines in all the Bible right here from Elijah as he says—and I paraphrase—"What, is your god on the toilet…?") He, much like Moses descending Sinai to find the Golden Calf, sees his brethren worship Baal, a god of Canaan, and even in his greatest zealous anger Elijah's only desire is to see these people make T'shuvah, to see them return to Adonai, the God of their forefathers. His heart is bent on restoration, he isn't trying to make a fool of Baal or the prophets he is facing or even the Israelites who are worshipping Baal. His single aim is to lead these people back to HaShem in faithfulness. He is interceding on behalf of Israel, interceding on behalf of the very same people who have turned their backs on HaShem (over and over and over again), and who likely wanted to kill Elijah themselves. That is humility, that is a heart after God, that is a true ministry, that is the power of the mantle of the Holy Spirit! That is the example we should most importantly be seeking to exemplify as we study about Elijah.

CHAPTER 15

So we see these miracles, and we also see later on that there were others that Elijah performed. But the anointing has to be passed down, the anointing needs to be passed down. So, what happens? We move from Elijah to Elisha. And this isn't some spontaneous transition, Elijah didn't just throw Elisha to the wolves. No, much like Moses and Joshua, Elijah mentored Elisha.

We begin reading again in 1 Kings 19:19— *19 So he departed from there and found Elisha son of Shaphat while he was plowing with twelve pairs of oxen before him, and he with the twelfth. Then Elijah crossed over to him and threw his mantle on him. 20 So he left the oxen and ran after Elijah saying, "Let me please kiss my father and my mother, and then I will follow you." "Come back," he said to him. "For what have I done to you?" 21 So he returned from following him, and took the pair of oxen and sacrificed them and boiled their flesh with the oxen's yoke gear, and gave it to the people, and they ate. Then he arose, went after Elijah and became his attendant.*

The phrase we read here, "became his attendant," sounds very similar to what we read in the Torah about Joshua serving under Moses. Joshua continued to follow and serve with Moses similarly for approximately 40 years. In the narrative of Moses and Joshua, we see the anointing of the mantle of the Holy Spirit passed from one generation of leadership to another. Now we see a prophet with this great power and anointing in the Ruach and we see that he now has an attendant, a mentee if you will, serving with him, and in the same way, the mantle will pass from one to the other.

And what did this attendant do beforehand? He served in the family business, he looked after his family's affairs, he worked on his family's property taking care of the herds and such. But, when he is called but Elijah what does he do? He immediately slaughters the oxen he was in charge of, eats it with all the people, and (for lack of a better way of wording it) he burns the bridge behind him.

Interestingly, that in and of itself is a powerful lesson for believers to learn about the call of God. Often, we feel the call of God and as humans, we try to hold on to a "Plan B" of some sort, a fallback plan—as though God needs us to have a fallback plan. But notice here that Elisha literally burns up the fallback plan, he doesn't have anything left to run back to. He is completely sold out for whatever God has in store in this journey with Elijah. Elisha knew the call from God on his life and he burned all other bridges and figuratively said, "There is no way I will ever turn back."

As we said before, Elijah exemplified these characteristics that we must learn to walk in as men and women empowered with the mantle of the Holy Spirit. These same characteristics were modeled for and emulated by Elisha. He extracted faith, boldness, and prayer (especially intercession); he extracted the ability to listen to the heart of Adonai; he learned how to hear God and how to follow His voice; he learned how to fear Adonai and to walk in His ways. These are some of the most important things that Elisha picked up along the way and characteristics he learned to mold his life around because of the example of his mentor.

Elisha continued to watch Elijah. Interestingly enough, there are no recorded miracles performed by Elisha until after the taking up of Elijah. With Joshua, we see a man who is clearly anointed yet, in great wisdom, faithfully awaits the Lord's timing. With David, we see a boy who is anointed to become king, who receives the mantle of the Ruach and patiently and faithfully awaits the Lord's timing as he willingly serves, and later strives to survive under, the hand of a king who is trying to kill him, but David waits on God no matter what. And alas, we see the same thing with Elisha. He serves under Elijah, he studies intently every word that Elijah says, every prophecy he speaks, every miracle he performs. He consumes as many lessons as he possibly can from the way Elijah walks in the power of the Ruach HaKodesh. But, he never tries to jump ahead of God's timing, he, like those before him, wait patiently and faithfully for the Lord's timing.

Elisha was still learning, he was still training, he was still in need of mentorship. We as believers are learning and being mentored and discipled and we can't be released into ministry yet either. There is a necessity for faithful training and discipleship in ministry in order to be set up for success for the Kingdom, rather than being set up for failure. Sadly, too many are put into ministry roles before they have been properly invested in, often while they are still hurting spiritually and emotionally themselves, and as the old adage goes, "Hurt people hurt people."

Paul says in 1 Timothy 3:6 not to put a new believer into the role of leadership in ministry lest he is susceptible to pride and fall. Why is this? Just because we possess leadership qualities and abilities or an anointing does not mean we are supposed to run headfirst into the ministry. We must be seasoned and tested first, we must be built up and mentored, we must be equipped, we must learn the ins and outs of ministry. This isn't unlike the idea of a driver's license, just because one is 16 years of age and can obtain a license doesn't mean magically they are going to have knowledge and understanding of how to respond to every possible situation on the road. One day you'll get in the car and it will be raining extremely hard and water will be over the roadway, there is dense fog, or traffic is delayed because of a dramatic wreck ahead. How will you have any clue about how to respond to the situations if you are not first taught how to drive safely? The same is true in ministry, just because one has an anointing and has the ability doesn't mean one is magically prepared and ready to jump into leadership.

Someone may be called to preach, or to be in the mission field, or to lead worship, but that doesn't mean calling instantly equals preparedness. There must be discipleship and mentorship. Life and ministry experience is a must. Serving under someone and gleaning from them as the Ruach leads is how this occurs. We see so many examples throughout the Bible of this exact sort of relationship that we must wake up to what the Lord is trying to say to us. This is extremely important in the continuation of the passing down of the mantle and anointing of the Holy Spirit from generation to generation, from ministry to ministry, from prophet to prophet, from pastor/rabbi to pastor/rabbi, from missionary to missionary, etc.

The mantle is passed from Elijah to Elisha, and it is passed in a double portion, and how many miracles does he do? He does double what Elijah did in his ministry. 2 Kings 2: *1 Now it came to pass, when Adonai was about to take up Elijah by a whirlwind into heaven, that Elijah went with Elisha from Gilgal. 2 Elijah said to Elisha, "Stay here please, for Adonai has sent me on to Bethel." But Elisha said, "As Adonai lives, and as you live, I will not leave you." So they went down to Bethel. 3 Then the sons of the prophets at Bethel came out to Elisha and said to him, "Do you know that Adonai is going to take your master away from over you today?" He said, "Yes, I know. Be silent." 4 Then Elijah said to him, "Elisha, stay here please, for Adonai has sent me on to Jericho." But he said, "As Adonai lives and as you live, I will not leave you." So they came to Jericho. 5 Then the sons of the prophets at Jericho approached Elisha and said to him, "Do you know that Adonai is going to take away your master from over you today?" He replied, "Yes, I know. Be silent." 6 Then Elijah said to him, "Stay here please, for Adonai has sent me to the Jordan." But he said, "As Adonai lives and as you live, I will not leave you." So both of them went on.* There was a relentless, unwavering, and devout willingness of Elisha to continue to follow Elijah.

We've talked about the narrative of Elijah's life, and have begun to breach Elisha's, and we've talked about the value of mentorship and discipleship. The whole point to all of this is that the lives and ministries of Elijah and Elisha are a shadow of the ministry of Yeshua and the Talmidim (disciples). If you look at the devotion of Elisha to Elijah, our devotion should be the same (if not greater) toward Yeshua. We should continue to be people who learn from Yeshua, who walk with Him. We should continue to take on His characteristics and emulate them throughout our lives. We should continue to live, move, and have our being in Him. As we read these stories of Moses, Joshua, David, Elijah, Elisha, and others we continue to revisit some of the same themes over and over again. But the greatest of these themes is the necessity to continue to learn from those who have gone before us, those who have paved the way, and we must continue to walk in those ways.

In John 14 we see Yeshua say: *1 "Do not let your heart be troubled. Trust in God; trust also in Me. 2 In My Father's house there are many dwelling places. If it were not so, would I have told you that I am going to prepare a place for you? 3 If I go and prepare a place for you, I will come again and take you to Myself, so that where I am you may also be. 4 And you know the way to where I am going." 5 Thomas said to Him, "Master, we don't know where You are going. How can we know the way?" 6 Yeshua said to him, "I am the way, the truth, and the life! No one comes to the Father except through Me. 7 If you have come to know Me, you will know My Father also. From now on, you do know Him and have seen Him." 8 Philip said to Him, "Master, show us the Father, and it is enough for us." 9 Yeshua said to him, "Have I been with you for so long a time, and you haven't come to know Me, Philip? He who has seen Me has seen the Father. How can you say, 'Show us the Father'? 10 Don't you believe that I am in the Father and the Father is in Me?*

Let's pause there for just a moment. We've now seen how the anointing is passed down, how the impartation has continued to be passed down, how the characteristics of the anointing of the Ruach HaKodesh are passed down. Where does this come from? It comes from the mentors, those who are living godly and righteous lives. As the mentee or disciple moves on he continues to model those characteristics shown by the mentor. What did we just see Yeshua say in John 14? He said, "If you've seen Me you've seen the Father..." He's saying, "The same characteristics that I possess came from Him. If you've seen me, you've seen Him." The reason it is so important for us to grasp this idea from Elijah and Elisha, and so many others, is because this discipleship model is exactly how we are to learn from Yeshua, and from those who He places in our paths to train and develop us in our ministry.

9 Yeshua said to him, "Have I been with you for so long a time, and you haven't come to know Me, Philip? He who has seen Me has seen the Father. How can you say, 'Show us the Father'? 10 Don't you believe that I am in the Father and the Father is in Me? The words I say to you, I do not speak on My own; but the Father dwelling in Me does His works. 11 Believe Me that I am in the Father and the Father is

143

in Me—or at least believe because of the works themselves. 12 "Amen, amen I tell you, he who puts his trust in Me, the works that I do he will do; and greater than these he will do, because I am going to the Father. 13 And whatever you ask in My name, that I will do, so that the Father may be glorified in the Son. 14 If you ask Me anything in My name, I will do it."

We must recognize Elijah and Elisha as a type and shadow. Elisha was given a double portion of the mantle of the Ruach HaKodesh and he did double the spiritual and physical work of God than Elijah did. In John 14 we see Yeshua say, "If you've seen Me you've seen the Father…" and He continues to say, "…he who puts his trust in Me, the works that I do he will do; and greater than these he will do…" That's a powerful statement! He says, "Anything that you ask in My Name, I will do it." Is He speaking of when we ask for a Mercedes Benz? No! How about asking for His character, anointing, passionate prayer, continuing relationship with the Father, continual growth in the calling He has given us…? These are the sort of things He desires us to ask of Him, and these are the sort of things He will give us when we ask.

We all have been anointed. We are all the King's *kohanim* (priests). We need to confess that we have righteousness in God through Yeshua HaMashiach. We need to confess that we have the Shalom of God through Yeshua HaMashiach. We need to confess that we walk in the anointing of God through Yeshua HaMashiach. But, this isn't just a "name it and claim it" kind of a thing, we must walk in it. What we're talking about here is the mentee learns from the mentor, so who is our mentor? Sure, we have people who mentor us in righteousness… But when we spend time with the Lord we are allowing Him to mentor us through the Ruach HaKodesh. The best part is that His mentorship in His character doesn't only pertain to ministry or Body of Messiah stuff specifically, but if we are faithful to His mentorship we will see His characteristics take over every aspect of our lives. By every aspect, I mean how we interact with our families, how we perform and interact at work, how we carry ourselves walking down the street or in the grocery store, or any plethora of other real-life situations we may find ourselves in. It is through all of this that others will see Him in us, not just because the words we speak are anointed, but when everything we do is anointed it gets the world's attention.

Yeshua said we will do greater works. I don't know how many miracles Yeshua performed (and I highly doubt they are all accounted for in the Gospels), but I don't think when Yeshua says we'd do greater things that specifically means individually we will perform greater or even more miracles. But, as a Body, the Bride collectively has done greater works, or even more specifically, Yeshua has done greater works through us. We have to continue as the Body to pass the anointing down and mentor the younger of the Body in the anointing so that as they continue to be brought up, they will desire to walk in the ways of God and continue to strive to do "greater things."

Funnily enough, you can be anointed, and even while walking in sin, see bits of fruit produced from your anointing. Remember, David was anointed and had a fling with a married woman, and is still called a man after God's own heart. But think about how much more God can and wants to do through us for His Kingdom when we turn from our sin and walk in His righteousness. If we are going to move and operate in the power of the Ruach HaKodesh, if we're going to continue as a Body to pass down the anointing and impartation of the Ruach HaKodesh to those coming up behind us, if we're going to continue to be people who allow the Word of the Lord to prosper then we have to spend time with the Lord and allow Him to mentor us. We've got to become people whose character is an emulation of that of our Mentor. We have to be like Elijah who stood firm even in the face of 450 false prophets who wanted to kill him. The way to do that is to have faith and confidence in the Lord, in who He is and what He has done in our lives. We shouldn't allow our hearts to be troubled, as Yeshua said, we should have the faith to walk and believe.

The next thing Yeshua says in John 14 is *15 "If you love Me, you will keep My commandments. 16 I will ask the Father, and He will give you another Helper so He may be with you forever—17 the Spirit of truth, whom the world cannot receive, because it does not behold Him or know Him. You know Him, because He abides with you and will be in you. 18 I will not abandon you as orphans; I will come to you. 19 In a little while, the world will no longer behold Me, but you will behold Me. Because I live, you also will live!*

So, we see in the life of Elijah that he was a great prophet and he performed great miracles. However, even more so, Elijah understood that his job to walk in righteousness and to continue to proclaim the truth, and to continue to mentor Elisha was necessary. He lived in evil and wicked times. Does that sound familiar? We have pleasures of this world available everywhere we turn now. Elisha learned of Elijah and saw his character, and then he modeled that character as he walked in the double portion of the mantle of the Ruach that was on Elijah. Elijah's and Elisha's relationship is a direct comparison and model, a foreshadowing of our relationship with Yeshua. We are Yeshua's disciples and we are called to do greater works. We're called to walk in the double portion of the impartation and anointing that He has given us. And as such, when we live in the model Yeshua has portrayed for us, we can avoid the temptation of the pleasures of the world around us, just as we see Yeshua avoids temptation.

When we look at the life of Elisha we see that he did not walk in the anointing immediately. He was called by Elijah (more specifically by God through Elijah) and he waited patiently for his turn as he learned under Elijah. He did not take on the fullness of his anointing until after the double portion of the mantle was placed upon him. However, you and I have received the Ruach HaKodesh, we are already anointed in the double portion of the mantle Yeshua operated in. I encourage you to continue to push forward in the anointing. Is it easy? Not always. Sadly, we are still here on this broken globe, and we are still human and periodically temptation pops its ugly head up. But, we can overcome and can continue to move forward as long as we walk in the mentorship of Yeshua through the Ruach HaKodesh. As long as we continue to model T'shuvah, as long as we remain faithful to HaShem's ways so that we can continue to shine the Light of Messiah Yeshua in this dark world, the realities of what the Lord can and will do through us is limitless.

CHAPTER 16

As we have now set a solid foundation and groundwork in our study of the Ruach HaKodesh throughout the Tanakh, we are now ready to breach into the Brit Chadashah (New Covenant/New Testament). Albeit we have referenced the Brit Chadashah throughout this book so far, we are now going to dive specifically, intentionally, and thoroughly into it. As is, I believe, absolutely foundational, we will begin with an in-depth look at Yeshua and the Holy Spirit. As believers in Messiah Yeshua, it is important that our lives are modeled after His, that we strive to emulate Him, and to truly operate in the Ruach we must look at His ministry first and foremost to develop a healthy theology and understanding of exactly what that should look like.

So, as we dig into the Brit Chadashah we will be taking great care to deeply examine the example of Yeshua and the mantle of the Holy Spirit. As followers of Messiah, I can't imagine any better way to study the Ruach HaKodesh than to spend a greater amount of time extracting as much as possible from Yeshua's life than we do of anyone else in the Bible. This is because we have, as we saw with Elisha after Elijah, a double portion of the mantle of the Ruach HaKodesh upon us, so we should understand what He did in the Spirit, how the Spirit operated in and through Him, so we can learn how to walk in that same Spirit in our own lives. We will be doing this in two parts: first, we will look at Yeshua receiving the anointing of the Holy Spirit, and second, we will look at how Yeshua operated in the Holy Spirit.

To begin with, we are going to primarily be looking at two passages of Scripture and they are somewhat mirror images of each other. Those two passages are going to be the 3rd and 4th chapters of Matthew and the

3rd and 4th chapters of Luke. As we dig into these passages we recognize this to be a sort of defining moment in which we see the outpouring of the Holy Spirit upon Yeshua. Now, we know Yeshua is God Himself robed in flesh, so the Ruach is a part of who He is already, however, we see this literal activation of the mantle of the Holy Spirit placed upon Him. We recognize Yeshua is 100% God, but He is also 100% man, this is a very complicated concept to wrap our heads around and we likely will never fully understand it until we are sitting at His feet in eternity, but because of this, the mantle of the Ruach had to be placed upon Him as a man in the same way it was placed upon all the men that came before Him who were anointed with the Holy Spirit.

I am sure you are already familiar with the accounts read in Matthew 3 & 4 and Luke 3 & 4 of Yeshua being immersed by *Yochanan HaMatbil* (John the Immerser). As we look at the Gospels we see that this same John is, in fact, the cousin of Yeshua and we see that Yeshua states that John served as the carrier of the spirit of Elijah. The prophecy states that Elijah will come again and will announce the coming of Messiah, which we recognize John did when he proclaimed (my paraphrase of Matthew 3:11), "I am immersing you in water, but the one who is coming after me will immerse you in the Ruach HaKodesh and in fire." We also see in Matthew 17 that Yeshua declared that John came in the spirit of Elijah but that the people were not ready for him. So, we recognize via the Gospel accounts that John served as the one who would announce the coming of Messiah.

When John's mother, Elizabeth, was carrying him in the womb *Miriam* (Mary), Yeshua's mother, walked into Elizabeth's house John began to jump up in down in Elizabeth's belly. Even as an infant still within his mother's womb John recognized the Presence of the Lord within this human container (for lack of a better way

149

of wording it) of Miriam and the Spirit was already upon John in the womb. So as the presence of Yeshua came into the room (again, still in Miriam's womb) the Spirit within John began to leap for joy as he recognized the greatness of the Presence of the Lord in their midst. Through this we see clearly that John already had this unique anointing upon him, his purpose was to be a prophet and he went around calling people to make T'shuvah, to repent. We've already established that when the Spirit of God comes upon someone and they begin to prophesy that their prophecy is not just a foretelling, it is not equivalent to shaking a magic eight ball, prophecy is declaring the Word of the Lord. As we look at Scripture, what we recognize is that the overwhelming Word of the Lord through the prophets is, "Repent and return to the Lord your God." This is the exact message that Yochanan HaMatbil was tasked with bringing to Israel throughout his ministry.

In Matthew chapter 3 beginning with verse 1, we read: *1 In those days, John the Immerser came proclaiming in the wilderness of Judea, 2 "Turn away from your sins, for the kingdom of heaven is near!" 3 For he is the one Isaiah the prophet spoke about, saying, "The voice of one crying in the wilderness, 'Prepare the way of Adonai, and make His paths straight.'" 4 Now John wore clothing from camel's hair and a leather belt around his waist, and his food was locusts and wild honey. 5 Then Jerusalem was going out to him, and all Judea and all the region around the Jordan. 6 Confessing their sins, they were being immersed by him in the Jordan River. 7 But when he saw many Pharisees and Sadducees coming to his immersion, he said to them, "You brood of vipers! Who warned you to flee from the coming wrath? 8 Therefore produce fruit worthy of repentance; 9 and do not think that you can say to yourselves, 'We have Abraham as our father'! For I tell you that from these stones God can raise up children for Abraham. 10 Already the axe is laid at the root of the trees; therefore every tree that does not produce good fruit is cut down and thrown into the fire!*

Let's pause here for a moment and recognize one very important reality, this is not a message specifically to the Pharisees or Sadducees… This is an equally important message for us as believers today as well. If we as believers are not producing fruit, we will be cut down also. The Brit Chadashah tells us that we know those bought by the Blood of the Lamb by the fruit that they produce, so if we are not producing fruit we are no better than the Sadducees or Pharisees.

The text continues *11 "As for me, I immerse you in water for repentance. But the One coming after me is mightier than I am; I am not worthy to carry His sandals. He will immerse you in the Ruach ha-Kodesh and fire. 12 His winnowing fork is in His hand, and He shall clear His threshing floor and gather His wheat into the barn; but the chaff He shall burn up with inextinguishable fire."*

After this the very next thing we read (as to whether this happened immediately after in real life we don't know) in the text is: *13 Then Yeshua came from the Galilee to John, to be immersed by him in the Jordan. 14 But John tried to prevent Him, saying, "I need to be immersed by You, and You are coming to me?" 15 But Yeshua responded, "Let it happen now, for in this way it is fitting for us to fulfill all righteousness." So John yielded to Him. 16 After being immersed, Yeshua rose up out of the water; and behold, the heavens were opened to Him, and He saw the Ruach Elohim descending like a dove and coming upon Him. 17 And behold, a voice from the heavens said, "This is My Son, whom I love; with Him I am well pleased!"*

As we look through every account in the Bible, whether Abraham, Isaac, Jacob, Moses, Joshua, David, etc., any account of anyone used by God in Scripture there is a defining moment in their life in which you know the Lord called them. This is a moment in which you know the individual has succumbed to the leading of the Lord, in which they laid their personal will down to follow the Will of the Lord. With Abraham, it was when God said, "Get up and go…," and Abraham got up and went. He didn't ask questions when the Lord said, "I am going to take you somewhere away from your family, to a land you haven't seen before, away from your father's household and his gods, and you'll serve Me there and I will give the land to you and your descendants for eternity." When this call came Abraham got up and left with no questions, he just listened and moved.

I believe Isaac's moment was during the *Akeidah*, the Binding of Isaac, on Mt. Moriah when he was tied down on the altar and his father was prepared to offer his life as a sacrifice. It is often viewed as though Isaac was a young boy when this occurred, but it is more likely he was in his late twenties to early thirties (I think it would be awesome if he was 33 when it happened just because of the correlation between these events and Yeshua's Sacrifice, but I digress...). Isaac was a young man, not a young boy, but just for the sake of discussion let's assume he was 30 at the Akeidah, which means that Abraham (who was 100 years old when Isaac was born) was 130 years old at this time. A 130-year-old man is not putting a 30-year-old man down on a slab of stone and tying him down without a fight if the younger does not allow it. My father is only twenty years older than I am and I can tell you right now he couldn't pull this off with me unless he knocks me out, kills me first, or I allow it. Isaac allowed Abraham to tie him down, I believe he was well aware of exactly what was going on. He asked Abraham on the journey to Moriah, "I see we have the wood and the fire, but where is the offering?" I think he knew what was going on, what was about to happen, and I think he knew the burden on Abraham's heart. Abraham tells him, "Don't worry son, God will provide Himself a lamb..."

This statement from Abraham, I believe, was a prophetic declaration of what would happen through Yeshua HaMashaich. Yeshua did, in fact, come as a Sacrifice Lamb provided by HaShem, just as Abraham says. When they looked to the thicket after Abraham was told to stop they didn't see a lamb caught, they saw a ram. What we see in this account is Isaac allowed himself (just as Yeshua allowed Himself to be hung on the cross) to be tied down to the altar to be an offering. Interestingly enough, notice that, other than the Akeidah, we never read of another defining moment in Isaac's life as we do with Abraham or Jacob. The defining moment for Isaac was the Akeidah, which was a foreshadowing of Yeshua on the cross. Yeshua had to willingly lay His life down in order to be our Sacrifice Lamb provided by the Lord. This was an act of the Ruach HaKodesh leading Yeshua and Him willingly setting Himself aside.

With Moses, we see the defining moment is the first account we read of him on Mt. Sinai. He's out herding his father's-in-law sheep along and all of a sudden he comes across this bush awkwardly on fire and not being consumed. So he walks over to check out this oddity of a burning bush not being destroyed. We know Scripturally that fire is often an image of the Holy Spirit, throughout Scripture, we see this image of fire in the Holy Spirit, the Presence of the Lord. So here stands a man before the Presence of the Lord (the fire, the Ruach HaKodesh) hearing the Voice of the Lord calling him forward.

Yeshua experiences and John witnesses the heavens open up and the Spirit descends upon Yeshua like a dove. I don't think they literally saw a dove, but something that gracefully came down like a dove. Often God uses language in finite human terms that are as beautiful as we can qualify in human language to explain things that are infinite and beyond what human language can explain. So God tells us about heavenly things in the most beautiful terms available in finite language. This is not unlike what we see in the description of streets paved with gold; this doesn't mean they are necessarily paved in gold (Can they be? sure… but I doubt it is literal) but that this is one of the most beautiful things available in human language to describe it. In essence, God is telling us we can't understand (as of yet), the infinite, so He'll explain it to us as best He can in the finite.

At the immersion of Yeshua, they see the Spirit of God descend on Yeshua like a dove and then they hear the voice of the Lord speak. Yeshua is having a Mt. Sinai type experience here, this man (Yeshua) standing before the Presence of the Lord and hearing the voice of the Lord call Him forward. He is having an experience like that of Moses the first time on Mt. Sinai with the burning bush, like that of Israel as a whole standing at the base of Mt. Sinai seeing the Presence of the Lord like fire upon the mountain and the heavenly shofar blast followed by the Voice of the Lord speaking forth. This encounter we read at the end of Matthew 3 was Yeshua's "Sinai experience" and everyone present saw it.

Not only did those present see the events taking place, but they heard the Voice of the Lord as He proclaimed from heaven, "This is my son with whom I am well pleased!" Notice how similar the words spoken here over Yeshua are to the words we long to hear spoken from the judgment seat by HaShem, "Well done my good and faithful servant!" The reality is, this account is the defining moment of Yeshua's earthly life in human form where He receives the Mantle of the Ruach HaKodesh, this is the beginning of His ministry. For the next three years, Yeshua wanders around Judea and Samaria and

He is ministering, healing, bringing deliverance, and prophesying of what is to come. Ultimately, He is also drawing into His following those who would be the first to be saved once His earthly ministry was complete and who will receive the Great Commission and go out to impact the world for His Kingdom, those who receive the double portion of the mantle that is now upon Him. This is that defining moment in His life.

CHAPTER 17

The very next thing we read is in Matthew chapter 4 beginning with verse 1: *1 Then Yeshua was led by the Ruach into the wilderness to be tempted by the devil. 2 After He had fasted for forty days and forty nights, He was hungry. 3 And when the tempter came to Him, he said, "If You are Ben-Elohim, tell these stones to become bread."*

Was the enemy saying anything untrue? In order for it to be tempting, it's gotta have at least some truth to it. The enemy says to someone, "Hey, go fornicate, it will feel good!" It's tempting… Why? Because it could be true, perhaps it will feel good. But it's a temptation, that doesn't mean it is real, that doesn't make it right, but it could be true. If he says, "Take these drugs, it will feel really good!" It might, for a few minutes, but it could also ruin the rest of your life.

Here in Matthew 4, the enemy is tempting Yeshua. He's not specifically saying anything untrue, God does have the power to turn stones into bread. God says if we're not going to worship Him He'll make the stones cry out. John says that if the Pharisees aren't going to serve God right, then it doesn't matter if they think they're the sons of Abraham, the Lord will make the stones rise up as the sons of Abraham.

So the enemy says, "If you are *Ben Elohim* (the Son of God) tell these stones to become bread." He has the authority to do so. God can very well perform exactly such a miracle should He choose. This temptation was not untrue, it is just not godly.

We continue *4 But He replied, "It is written, 'Man shall not live by bread alone, but by every word that comes from the mouth of God.'" 5 Then the devil took Him into the holy city and placed Him on the highest point of the Temple. 6 "If You are Ben-Elohim," he said, "throw Yourself down. For it is written, 'He shall command His angels concerning you,' and 'upon their hands they shall lift you up, so that you may not strike your foot against a stone.'"*

Was it untrue? No, not at all… It was absolutely true, or at least just enough truth to be tempting. But it was not within God's will, it was not what Yeshua was supposed to do. Just like when the enemy tempts us, is what he is saying untrue or flat-out wrong? Not necessarily, but that doesn't mean it is God's will for our lives, nor does it mean it is in accordance with the image and likeness of God in which we were created and restored. True, or even partially true, doesn't suddenly make it right though. In this temptation, the enemy quotes Scripture. The enemy knows Scripture, and he knows it very well, and he knows how to contort it and make it say whatever he wants.

So Yeshua responds to the enemy: *7 Yeshua said to him, "Again it is written, 'You shall not put Adonai your God to the test.'" 8 Again, the devil takes Him to a very high mountain and shows Him all the kingdoms of the world and their glory. 9 And he said to Him, "All these things I will give You, if You fall down and worship me."*

Is that entirely untrue? Does the enemy have the authority to give that over? Sadly, absolutely… Why? Because we gave that authority over to him, as we have discussed earlier. We gave the authority and dominion over things of this world that God gave to mankind over to the enemy when we gave in to the temptation of sin. So, yes, at least to some degree, that authority was his, because we gave up our authority when we chose to allow sin into our lives. And here is Yeshua, God himself robed in flesh correcting our mistake. He's hearing the enemy's temptation just like Adam and Eve in the garden, but contrary to Adam and Eve (and contrary to some of our own choices in our lives today) Yeshua doesn't give in. He responds to the enemy's contortion of the Word of the Lord with the full truth of the Bible, with the definition of a righteous life before the Lord.

Matthew's account continues: *10 Then Yeshua says to him, "Go away, satan! For it is written, 'You shall worship Adonai your God, and Him only shall you serve.'" 11 Then the devil leaves Him. And behold, angels came and began to take care of Him.*

Notice, we go back to the second temptation, *6 "If You are Ben-Elohim," he said, "throw Yourself down. For it is written, 'He shall command His angels concerning you,' and 'upon their hands they shall lift you up, so that you may not strike your foot against a stone.'"* In other words, the angels will come and take care of you. Was it untrue? Not at all, and as a matter of fact, that is exactly what they did. But it took Yeshua following the will of God and denying the enemy's temptation.

See, the overwhelming problem with sin is that sin begins with temptation. When we give in to that temptation that sin produces a barrier between us and the Presence of God. The Presence of God cannot dwell within the midst of sin. So, when we have spiritual oppression in our lives, when we are in need of deliverance, it prohibits the work of God in us because we are so buried in this sin, in this temptation, in this thing that is contrary to the very image and likeness of God that we are unable to see the Presence of God in our lives.

This concept is exactly what HaShem is speaking about in the Blessings and Curses of Deuteronomy 27-30. If we pay attention to them, we'll notice that the blessings say if you follow Me and obey My Word then I will provide for you, take care of you, protect you, nourish you, keep sickness away from you, etc. But, to the contrary, He says if you do not follow and obey My Word then all of these things will occur in reverse. The thing we often don't realize is that God is still providing for us, He is still caring for us and protecting us, we are just unable to see it because of the sin in our lives. When we are walking in sin, we are outside the will of God. As believers, if we're honest about it, when we look back at our lives where we have found ourselves outside the will of God, oddly enough our bills are still getting paid, food is on the table and a roof is over our heads. We may not recognize God's blessings in these times, we may stress over things a lot more, but He is still caring and providing for us, but our perspective is thrown way off because of our walking outside His will. The problem with our perspective at these times is that the sin in our lives has caused a barrier that prohibits our seeing Him and His blessings in our lives. But, trust that He is certainly taking care of us even when we don't see it because He has promised He will never leave us or forsake us. He is taking care of us, we are still bought by the Blood of the Lamb, we are still His, sin simply limits our seeing Him in our lives (and others seeing Him in our lives as well). But, when we reject sin, we see everything He is doing and it all seems even greater than we could have imagined.

Here the enemy tries to tempt Yeshua by saying, "If You throw Yourself off of here at this height the angels will protect You." But Yeshua counters the enemy's temptation with God's truth and He throws off the enemy's assault on what God is trying to do. What ends up happening next? The angels do in fact come and take care of Him, they provide for Him.

When Yeshua returns from the wilderness, the first thing He does is return to His home synagogue in the Galilee and He is called forward for an Aliyah to read from the Haftarah Scroll. He reads the very prophecy that speaks specifically of His coming and He proclaims, "Here before your very eyes this has happened!" Those hearing Him speak are shocked at the authority with which He is speaking and are left trying to process exactly what just happened. Yeshua then spends the next three and a half years ministering to the hearts and lives of Israel.

This is a powerful reality. Yeshua receives this mantle of the Ruach HaKodesh and it changes everything. The reason it is so important for us as believers to understand and wrap our heads around this is that we have been promised a double portion of this exact anointing, just as we see with Elisha following Elijah. As we said previously, Elijah had the anointing of the Ruach HaKodesh upon him and Elisha, his mentee, received a double portion of the anointing and does even greater things than his mentor did. Yeshua, God Himself robed in flesh, tells us that when the Comforter comes (speaking of the Holy Spirit) as it did in Acts chapter 2, that we will be able to do even greater things than He did. In other words, we will receive a double portion of the mantle of the Holy Spirit. So if in the power of the Ruach HaKodesh Yeshua was able to deny the temptation of the enemy and we are told we have a double portion of the Ruach as believers in Messiah and receivers of the Blood of the Lamb, then why do we fall prey to his temptation so often? Why do we not walk in the power, authority, and dominion we have over things of this world that God has now restored?

What we see in Matthew and Luke 3 and 4 is Yeshua undoing, or redeeming, the mistakes that Adam and Eve made, the problems that they left for us. Adam and Eve were tempted by satan, and that what he spoke to them was not entirely untrue words. He said, "Did the Lord really say you would die?" (By this what he was asking was, "Did He really say you'd drop dead immediately?") The temptation he posed to them was one founded upon a simple question. The Lord did say that if they ate of the fruit they would die, but He didn't say they would die instantaneously, He didn't even say when they would die due to such an action, and the enemy knew this. To which Eve said, "Well, I guess He didn't say we would just drop dead right now… The fruit does look really good, so let's eat it and see what happens." The enemy was right, he may have twisted the truth, but he was right in that they didn't just die right then and there. However, death did enter their lives because death is the consequence of sin.

As believers, we speak a lot about avoiding sin, and truthfully, for the most part, we tend to have horribly weak definitions of what sin is. My base definition of sin is pretty simple, it is also very surreal, and that is that sin is anything in our lives that damages the image of our Creator within us. We were made in His image and likeness, if someone looks at our lives and they don't see His image and likeness, then there is sin hindering our lives. If the world around us looks at our lives and they don't see the Holy Spirit, there is sin in our lives. This sin prohibits God's Presence in our lives, and it is as simple as giving in to the temptation of the adversary, which is what the Hebrew word hasatan (where we get the name satan from) means.

CHAPTER 18

By receiving the mantle of the Holy Spirit and walking in it in the midst of temptation for forty days, Yeshua redeemed our dominion and authority over things of this world. This is the authority given to us by God that we handed over to the enemy when we chose to walk in sin. However, as a human empowered by the Ruach HaKodesh, He took our authority back and He said now a double portion will be given unto you. He told us we would do even greater things than He did.

If you notice (and we'll deal with this in greater depth a little later) when Yeshua and His Talmidim (disciples) prayed for healing, it sounded very different from how we tend to do it now. Think about it, have you ever read, in the Gospels, Yeshua praying for healing and sounding like this, "Oh Lord, Johnny has this bad lump on his arm and the doctors are afraid it might be cancer. He has to go in for tests on Monday and it could be this or it could be that. If it is cancer it will definitely affect his family because he'll have to go through chemo and radiation and it will affect his ability to work, which will affect his ability to provide for his family. But, if he dies, Lord, it will affect so much more. Lord, if You would just heal him then none of this would happen..." Have you ever read about Yeshua or His disciples praying like this?

When Yeshua prayed it was entirely different, He simply declared healing. Yeshua said, "Get up and walk!" He said, "Lazarus, come out the grave!" He said, "Open your eyes and see!" Why do we not pray as He did? Why do we not pray in the authority He has given us? When we pray as though we are trying to express to HaShem how bad things are and why it's bad, and what's going to happen if it gets worse, and so on, really what we're doing is trying to talk up our own faith in God's ability to heal. We're trying to boost our faith in the power and authority given to us. But, Yeshua calls us to emulate Him, He says we have a double portion of what He has, He says we will be able to do even greater things than He did.

So, why is it that believers today don't walk up to people, lay hands on them, and declare, "Be healed! In the Name of Yeshua and the Blood of the Lamb! Be healed!"? Why are we so afraid? Why do we not operate in faith in the mantle of the Holy Spirit that is upon us? Why are there so many believers that, rather than reevaluate the way we walk in faith in the Lord, we try to explain away the lack of the presence and power of the Spirit in our lives by saying the gifts of the Spirit are just not for today? That's not at all what the Word of God says, it never says the gifts or the move of the Spirit would cease. The Word of God says that we as believers would receive a double blessing of His Ruach. That wasn't just said to Peter and the other disciples, that was a promise meant for every single believer that would follow them, that would hear their testimony and find Yeshua through it. And 2000 years removed from Peter, that promise is as much true today for you and me as it was for anyone in the Bible.

In Luke 4 Yeshua receives the mantle of the Ruach HaKodesh and goes into the wilderness to be tempted by the enemy and He overcomes that temptation. Why? Because the mantle of the Ruach was upon Him. I wonder, had Yeshua not received the Holy Spirit when He did, would He have been as successful in rejecting the enemy's temptation? (Obviously, as much as Yeshua was 100% man He was also 100% God, so anything's possible.) As humans called to emulate Yeshua, we have to look at this passage and ask ourselves, if we were in that situation without the Holy Spirit, would we have been able to respond as Yeshua did? As a matter of fact, and in all reality, we DO have the mantle of the Ruach and we still falter from time to time when faced with temptation, and if we're honest with ourselves it happens more often than we'd like to admit...

Yeshua reestablished the dominion and power that was given to us at creation so that we can make things of this world be in alignment with the will of God. What's often called "the Lord's Prayer" says, "May Your will be done on earth as it is in heaven..." Does God want people to be healed? Yes, in heaven and on earth. Does God want people to be saved? Absolutely! Because to be in heaven you've got to accept salvation on earth first.

We have been given a double portion of the Holy Spirit that was upon Yeshua. You think that Elijah did was powerful? Read more about what Elisha did after him as he operated in a double portion. Yet Yeshua was even greater than both Elijah and Elisha, and He tells us we'll do even greater than He did... Why do we not faithfully walk in it? Why do we not work in it? Why do we not truly believe in it? Why do we not declare it over ourselves every single day? We should be asking the Lord every day to build our faith in His Holy Spirit within our lives. We ask Him to give us patience and His answer is we end up finding ourselves in situations where we have to be patient. I wonder if the reason we don't ask the Lord to build our faith in His Ruach every day is that, likewise, we know He will give us opportunities where we'll have to use it. But, imagine how much stronger our faith will become if we jump at those opportunities to operate in faith in His Spirit which is in us. And if we realize we aren't doing so for our own good, or even the good of those being blessed by it, but for the sake of this lost world seeing His Presence actively among them. When we walk in this kind of power we will see the world around us open their hearts to Yeshua's Salvation.

You'll notice when Yeshua walked up to John John knew immediately who He was and recognized who was actually standing before him. I worked for years in restaurants, the better part of two decades. Some of my favorite experiences when I waited tables was when people would call me over to their table to talk to me. They'd see my Kippah on my head and would often ask me, "Hey, are you an Orthodox Jew?" I'd respond, "No, I'm actually a Messianic Jewish rabbi." And then I'd explain a little further about what that means, particularly if they hadn't heard the terminology before. They'd follow that with something like, "Oh, see, I could sense there was something different about you." The conversation would usually follow with them asking me to tell them more about what I believe, or to answer some questions about the Bible, etc. Then there would almost always be the following question to close out the conversation, "Would you pray for us…?"

You can't even begin to imagine the number of people I've had the opportunity to minister to while waiting tables. Oddly, there are two main rules that servers and bartenders in restaurants and bars try to uphold while on the clock: #1 Don't talk politics! #2 Don't talk religion! Yet, the Lord regularly put opportunities to share my faith with my guests, with other servers' guests, and with coworkers over and over again and every opportunity I had, I walked faithfully in it. Not because of any other reason than I didn't want to throw away these opportunities the Lord gave me. He placed these people in my path for His purpose, and if I am going to truly walk in the "greater than" that has been given to me, then I have to walk in it faithfully in every situation, day in and day out.

Have you ever been in the grocery store standing in line at the register and felt the Lord tug at your heart to talk to the person behind you? More often than not, most believers are either too shy, too afraid, or just flat-out unwilling to spend their time on these divine appointments. We're busy people, we've got this thing to get to, or that person waiting on us, or whatever other excuses that arise… But, unfortunately, too often we refuse to take the time to stop, breathe, and listen to the Lord.

The Lord hit me with this reality a few years back. At that point in time (and thankfully we don't read about it as much anymore, doesn't mean it isn't happening, it just isn't as pervasive in the media now) it seems like every day when you'd look at the news there was a story that goes something like this: a middle-aged guy had just been laid off at work. He wasn't sure he'd ever be able to find a job again and doubted he'd be able to provide for his family. He was too ashamed to deal with what was going on and had no hope for a future and he'd go home and kill his family and himself. He saw murder-suicide as his only solution. The Lord woke me up to this realization… That person behind us in the grocery store line that He is tugging at our hearts to minister to, how do we know that this isn't the last chance for them to hear that there is Hope before they go home and kill themselves? What makes us think that, as believers saved by the Blood of the Lamb and called to the Great Commission, we have the right to waste the opportunity the Lord has put in our path to touch somebody's life? Who do we think we are to take that risk…? We have been given a double portion. Truthfully, Yeshua says in Luke 12:48, "From everyone given much, much will be required…" We've been given a great calling and an even greater anointing, we must operate in it. We complain because we don't see as many people come to faith as we'd like, but it is often because we don't walk in faith in our lives.

Truthfully, this book was birthed out of a study on the same subject that we did in our synagogue. We are a congregation that believes fervently in the outpouring of the Ruach HaKodesh, we believe enthusiastically in the move and gifts of the Spirit. We believe passionately that we are living in the Latter Rain days and that we are seeing revival happen. We have seen people healed, we have seen people delivered, we have seen lives changed dramatically. We've seen all of this and more happen in our congregation, and we believe there is so much more in store. But, as a congregation that believes in all of this, we are also a Messianic Jewish synagogue, which means that we have people coming from all sorts of faith backgrounds. Some are coming from traditional Jewish backgrounds without much experience or connection at all to the move of the Spirit, or what idea they may have about it is some connection to Kabbalah/mysticism. Some are coming from charismatic, Pentecostal backgrounds where this is nothing new (and we're probably pretty tame compared to what some may have experienced in those environments). There are still others coming from backgrounds rooted in cessationism and aren't even certain that the Ruach operates among us today. Yet the Lord has called us all together as a community for a purpose, and if we believe fervently in the power of the Spirit of God, that the Spirit is active today, and that we are called by God to be used by His Spirit for His purposes today then we need to understand this stuff. We need to understand how to walk in it.

There are examples in the Bible that we read and talk about every day that we have failed to learn how to live by. There are examples in the Bible of how to walk out a life fully encompassed in the power of the Ruach HaKodesh. This book, and the study it was birthed from, was developed because if we are going to walk in the Ruach HaKodesh and the revival that He is birthing, then we must examine Scripture for what that walk looks like. The mantle of the Holy Spirit is upon every one of us who call on the Name of Yeshua. We may not know exactly what to do with it, we may get a little freaked out by it when it moves, but the Holy Spirit is there. It is our responsibility to give Him free-reign in our lives. It is our responsibility to let the anointing that was upon Yeshua that is now a double anointing upon us operate through us looking to Messiah Yeshua and the anointed ones of the Bible as our example.

We also have to be cautious not to develop some hard-pressed theology (like everyone has to speak in tongues) because it is just not biblical. Honestly, I am not confident at all that the list Paul gives of the gifts of the Spirit is a comprehensive list. I think it is a foundation, the beginning of what's available. But, who are we to limit God? I also don't think the Bible specifically says anyone single person will only operate in any single gift. I think, if we are willing, the Holy Spirit will operate through us in any way He sees fit in the situation He places us in depending on the situation. Ultimately the move of the Spirit is for God's purposes and we shouldn't try to limit what He wants to do through us and for His Kingdom. No matter the situation though, it is our responsibility as being blessed with the anointing of the Holy Spirit to operate in the authority and power that has been given to us. This is not for our own purposes or our own gain, it is not to stroke our own egos, it is for the purposes of God, it is for the purpose of furthering His Kingdom. And we need to submit our will to His ways and allow Him to operate freely through us.

As believers we are called to emulate Yeshua, living our lives in the example of Yeshua. Yeshua overcame temptation through the power of the Ruach HaKodesh in His life. He operated in the restored authority and dominion that was given to mankind over things of this world. We have a requirement by the Word of God and the will of God to walk in that same calling, in that example. When the enemy throws temptation in our face it is our duty and responsibility to reject that temptation through the empowerment of the Holy Spirit, to declare the word of the Lord against that temptation. Every sin begins first and foremost with temptation.

I think that's the beauty of Matthew 5 and Yeshua saying (my paraphrase), "You've heard it said it's a sin to commit murder and adultery, but I tell you if you've even hated or lusted in your heart you've already committed these sins." All four of these issues are dealt with in the Torah, there are already existing commandments against each of them individually. But, what Yeshua is telling us is, "for every external sin there is an internal sin, and if you let Me take care of the internal letting My presence block the internal temptation the external temptation will never win."

If we reside in the presence of the Lord every waking moment of our lives then it doesn't matter what the temptation the enemy throws our way is, the reality is the Presence of the Lord is strengthening and uplifting us and will win the victory if we submit our will to Him. Sometimes we go through some of this mess just so the Lord can show His strength in these situations, so He can teach us how much we need to lean on Him. The problem is that far too often we never figure out the lesson He is teaching us because we end up just giving in, we just let the enemy have his way with us.

Yeshua showed us that temptation can be overcome and He showed us in His humanity. Sure, He was fully man and fully God, but I don't think He overcame the temptation because He's God. He overcame it in His humanity by the power of the mantle of the Spirit of God that was upon Him so that He could show us that it is possible for us because the same Spirit resides within us, and in a double portion. There is no temptation the enemy could throw at Yeshua that would throw Him off track and likewise there is none he can throw at us that should be able to throw us off either. The only way the enemy can have his way in our lives is if we are not walking in the renewal of the Holy Spirit every single day as has been given to us. With that, Yeshua has also shown us that He has restored the authority and dominion given to us over things of this world, and through that, we can, in fact, declare healing, broken chains and deliverance and in turn bring hope and light into this dark world because the power and authority of the Holy Spirit have been given to us through the Blood of the Lamb.

What happens when we choose to walk faithfully in His ways and His Spirit? Lives are changed and souls are saved. Look at how many people came to faith in Messiah because He spoke healing over them. Look at how many people came to faith in Messiah because the disciples spoke healing. Thousands were saved in one day just from seeing the tangible Presence of the Ruach HaKodesh fall in Acts 2, and hundreds were being added daily from then on. How awesome is that? And we've been given a double portion of that, we just have to submit to His will and allow Him to operate in our lives.

CHAPTER 19

As we move forward, we are going to take a look at Yeshua as He goes from receiving the mantle of the Holy Spirit to modeling how His followers are to operate in it. We also see powerful examples beyond Yeshua throughout the *Besorah* (Good News) of Yeshua doing exactly that. As believers, this is a big part of who we are supposed to be, people empowered in the Holy Spirit and living our lives in the Power as modeled by Yeshua, emulating Him. Realistically, this is the purpose of this book as a whole, not for the sake of consuming knowledge just to have it, but to learn how to walk in the power of the Ruach by examining the examples we see throughout the Scriptures. We as the people of God need to learn to walk in this mantle which is as much available for us today as it was in Yeshua's day, as it was in Elisha's day, as so on.

There is a powerful restoration available in the Ruach HaKodesh, and we've seen it throughout this study. We've seen healing, deliverance, the outpouring, dominion, etc. These are all things that Yeshua redeemed for us through His death, burial, and resurrection, through His ascension to pour out His blood as an offering upon the Mercy Seat in Heaven for our sins, and then through the outpouring of the Ruach HaKodesh upon His bride. I fear that the bride of Messiah is selling herself short by not taking up the mantle and letting the Presence of the God of all creation be known throughout His creation by letting His Ruach move freely and mightily through us. How many more lives could we see come to the saving knowledge of our Messiah if we simply allow Him to work through us, if we stop cowering in fear and lack of knowledge in the truth of the Ruach HaKodesh? How many lives can be changed if people see His Presence in their midst in our lives before they hear us speak? This is the example that Yeshua shows us in the Besorah, and it is vital that we begin to let His life be a mentor to ours.

Didn't Yeshua say we would do even greater things when the Comforter comes? Yes, He did, and there is a learning, a mentoring that has to take place. This will come through our willingness to be able to humble ourselves and say, "Lord, we need Your help. Teach us how to walk in Your ways." Yeshua says, "Ask and it will be given to you," and if we ask He will show us. And the primary way He will show us, truthfully, is through His Word.

As mentioned before, Yochanan HaMatbil (John the Immerser) said, "the One who is coming after me will baptize you with Ruach and with fire." Shouldn't we be the burning ones, the light on the hill? If the Ruach and fire are raging within us, shouldn't people see that Light raging WITHIN us? Shouldn't they recognize a difference in those representing the Kingdom of Mashiach from those representing the world? Shouldn't they see something within us that they desire for their own lives? Shouldn't they see something that grabs ahold of them and draws them to us?

We do tend to overlook sometimes that Divine wisdom, love, grace, mercy, compassion, etc., are all miracles that can happen within the working of the Ruach in and through our lives. These tend to be overlooked because they aren't as "showy" as people being healed and climbing out of a wheelchair, or the sight being restored to the blind or something of these sorts. However, they are absolutely miracles and are absolutely moves of the Ruach HaKodesh, and as Paul says, the greatest of these is love. Have you experienced times where you prayed for divine wisdom in a situation in your life and all of a sudden you knew what to do, or someone else immediately afterward speaks into that situation the exact answer you'd been looking for? These are miracles that happen on a daily bases and are often overlooked because we are almost always looking for big, showy miracles instead.

So, let's go ahead and dig into the example we see of Yeshua operating in the mantle of the Ruach as a basis of mentorship for our own walks. As we discussed earlier, in Matthew 3 & 4 (and Luke 3 & 4) we read of Yeshua's immersion by John, His empowering of the Ruach HaKodesh, and His journey of temptation in the wilderness which He overcame through the Ruach HaKodesh. As a matter of fact, Matthew 4 is an excellent lesson for believers to learn how to overcome the temptation of the enemy, which is only possible through the indwelling of the Holy Spirit. Yeshua served in Matthew 4 as an example that through the indwelling of the Ruach we can overcome the temptation of the enemy. This is one of the first lessons He modeled for us as His followers.

As we look at the narrative of Yeshua in the Gospels we notice that once He is empowered with the Ruach, He doesn't immediately run out and start speaking over everyone, laying hands on everyone, slaying people in the Spirit, making folks drunk in the Spirit, etc... To the contrary, here are some of the things we begin to see in Yeshua's example of the mantle of the Holy Spirit, beginning with Matthew 4:17, after His temptation and after reading the Word in His home synagogue—*17 From then on, Yeshua began to proclaim, "Turn away from your sins, for the kingdom of heaven is near."* Yeshua had the boldness of the Holy Spirit as a prophet to proclaim the favorable year of the Lord, to call people to turn from their sins, and to see the Kingdom of Heaven draw near.

Immediately after we continue to read, *18 Now as Yeshua was walking by the Sea of Galilee, He saw two brothers, Simon who was called Peter and Andrew his brother. They were casting a net into the sea, for they were fishermen. 19 And He said to them, "Follow Me, and I will make you fishers of men." 20 Immediately they left their nets and followed Him.* Something else Yeshua did is that He continually pursued the calling that He saw in other people's lives. He then built them up and discipled them to believe in and follow His example. Yeshua saw the calling, the divine purpose for the lives of others, such as the disciples, and He called them to walk in that.

In Mathew 5 we see that He preached the truth regarding the inward motives of man, as opposed to blindly following traditions of man, He spoke specifically to the inward man. In the "Sermon on the Mount" He said that we are to be salt and light and He began to share what our purpose was in Him. He continues by teaching not to toss away the guidance of the Torah, but to recognize He came to bring fullness to the Torah, as we read in Matthew 5 beginning with verse 17: *17 "Do not think that I came to abolish the Torah or the Prophets! I did not come to abolish, but to fulfill. 18 Amen, I tell you, until heaven and earth pass away, not the smallest letter or serif shall ever pass away from the Torah until all things come to pass. 19 Therefore, whoever breaks one of the least of these commandments, and teaches others the same, shall be called least in the kingdom of heaven. But whoever keeps and teaches them, this one shall be called great in the kingdom of heaven. 20 For I tell you that unless your righteousness exceeds that of the Pharisees and Torah scholars, you shall never enter the kingdom of heaven!*

We're talking here about how Yeshua modeled the mantle and this is exactly what He teaches all through Matthew 5. He discusses the fact that there are both internal as well as external Mitzvot in the Torah (murder/ hatred and adultery/lust) and teaches that if we allow Him to reside on the inside and to write His covenant upon our heart (Jeremiah 31:31) then He will handle the inward so that the outward can't fall prey to sin. Think about it for a moment, sin is lead into by temptation. Temptation is, in essence, an inward draw to an outward sin and Yeshua first shows us through His life in Matthew 4 that it is possible to overcome temptation, then in Matthew 5, He goes even deeper in teaching us the reality of how we overcome temptation practically in Him so as not to sin outward. The answer is simple, if our Messiah who is the Word made flesh (John 1) resides within us and we are empowered with His Ruach HaKodesh and we completely submit ourselves to Him then He will care for and guard our heart and fight for us against the temptation of the enemy so that we can stand against temptation inwardly and not sin outwardly.

In Matthew 6 Yeshua teaches us to trust the process of God. He begins with verse 1 talking about being humble in our service before the Lord—1 **"Beware of practicing your righteousness before others to be seen by them; otherwise you have no reward from your Father in heaven. 2 So whenever you do *tzadakah*, do not sound a trumpet before you as the hypocrites do in the synagogues and on the streets, so that they may be glorified by men. Amen, I tell you, they have their reward in full! 3 But when you do *tzadakah*, do not let your left hand know what your right hand is doing, 4 so that your *tzadakah* may be in secret; and your Father, who sees in secret, shall reward you.** And He continues through the next several verses giving more examples of this.

As we continue to read through chapter 6, we see Yeshua speaks on living in the secret place of the Most High and longing to be in that secret place. He discusses the great virtue of forgiveness, which is a necessary foundation for building community and relationships. He then talks about building a firm foundation through understanding and walking in the teachings and direction that the Torah has given us. He encourages us to not compare ourselves to other people because He has called each one of us equally in our own unique characteristics, gifting, and talents for His own purpose.

To that point, we need to learn, and I think this is one of the ultimate lessons we can and should learn from Yeshua's example, to be who we are supposed to be, who we are created to be. When we walk faithfully in who God has created us to be, humbly being willing to use our divinely given talents and gifts for His Kingdom, then we will recognize that we cannot compare ourselves to others because no one else is built to be who we are. God has specifically and intentionally given each of us talents, giftings, callings, strengths, etc… Who cares if someone has opportunities to preach to thousands and you don't? Who cares if someone has a bigger or better house than you do? Who cares if someone has a better education? Who cares if someone leads a large congregation and you don't? What difference does any of this make? Is it about our kingdom or Yeshua's Kingdom? Comparing ourselves to others undermines the work of God in our own lives and diminishes the ministry He wants to use us in. We should learn to be who we are in Yeshua and in the Ruach HaKodesh. Comparing ourselves to others also undermines the image and likeness of God in which we as individuals were created.

In what other ways do we see Yeshua modeling the mantle of the Ruach throughout the Gospel? He taught and preached the Word of God with the authority of God. He proclaimed the call to *T'shuvah* (repentance). He worked miracles, signs, and wonders. He uplifted the broken and downtrodden. He boldly opposed those who opposed or twisted the Word of God.

In Matthew 8 beginning with verse 5, we see that with the mantle He brought healing—*5 Now when Yeshua came into Capernaum, a centurion came begging for help. 6 "Master," he said, "my servant is*

lying at home paralyzed, horribly tormented." 7
Yeshua said to him, "I'll come and heal him." 8 But
the centurion said, "Master, I'm not worthy to have
You come under my roof. But just say the word and
my servant will be healed. 9 For I also am a man
under authority, with soldiers under me. I say to this
one, 'Go!' and he goes; and to another, 'Come!' and
he comes; and to my servant, 'Do this!' and he does
it." 10 Now when Yeshua heard this, He marveled and
said to those who were following, "Amen, I tell you, I
have not found anyone in Israel with such great
faith!... 13 Then Yeshua said to the centurion, "Go.
As you have believed, let it be done for you." And the
servant was healed in that same hour.

Yeshua healed not only through His faith but also because of the faith of those asking. Sometimes when we pray for people it's not just our own faith or understanding of the word, but those needing healing may also need faith in God's ability to heal. When we gather together in worship, there is a divine synergy that happens among us. When we pray in faith, there is a mingling of this same synergy coming together in agreement in faith, a mingling of the Presence of the Lord. When we are praying with others in faith, there is a coming together in agreement that plays a part in bringing about the necessary miracle. However, and this is very important, do not confuse whether or not we have "enough" faith with there being any sort of limitation to God due to our faith, He can and does heal—sometimes despite our lack of faith.

Under the mantle of the Ruach Yeshua produced healing and freedom through deliverance, as we see exemplified beginning in verse 28—**28 When He came to the other side, into the region of the Gadarenes, two demon-plagued men coming from the graveyard met Him. They were so violent that no one could pass by that way. 29 And they screamed, "What's** between You and us, *Ben-Elohim*? Have You come here to torment us, before the appointed time?" 30 Now a large herd of pigs was feeding some distance away from them. 31 The demons kept begging Him, "If You drive us out, send us into the herd of pigs." 32 And He told them, "Go!" So they came out and went into the pigs, and the whole herd rushed down the cliff into the sea and drowned. 33 The herdsmen ran away, went into the town, and told everything, including what had happened to the demon-plagued men. 34 The whole town came out to meet *Yeshua*. And when they saw him, they begged Him to leave their region.

Isn't it interesting the way the human mind works? Think about it, here are these two men plagued with demons that are viciously violent because of it. Yeshua approaches and they are fearful and beg for him to cast them into the pigs. When He does so, the pigs run into the sea and drown to death. Albeit Jews wouldn't eat pork, and they realized pigs were fantastic garbage disposals, as a matter of fact, this is exactly what God created them to do. So, the pig herders lost their herd of pigs and they also lost whatever revenue stream they represented. So, now the pig herders likely view Yeshua's actions, rather than rejoicing over the deliverance the two men experienced, as having been detrimental to their livelihood. The townspeople likely anticipated the possibility that Yeshua could ruin even more business ventures if He stuck around long enough, so, they then urged Him to leave the area. The good He had just done, the miracle He had just performed was not part of their thought processes at all. The presence of the Ruach HaKodesh in Yeshua was so strong that these demonic spirits begged to be cast out to get away from Him, yet the townspeople couldn't wait to get rid of Him. Unfortunately, within the Body of Messiah at times we act just like this, we don't understand the way God is working, so we opt to just shut what He's doing down as a means of a risk aversion.

Yeshua provided healing and freedom through deliverance because both happen when being set free from the enemy's grip. This reality was a part of what Yeshua was modeling for His followers in the mantle of the Holy Spirit. This is a part of the way of life and personal ministry that we as believers empowered with the Ruach should be walking in. Many believers today are scared to death of spiritual warfare, many more don't even believe in it, but whether we like it or not spiritual warfare is a very real thing. The enemy hates us, he hates Who is in us, and he hates what the Ruach wants to and can do through us. This is even more true in that with the power of the Ruach and the authority given to us we can bring deliverance just as we see Yeshua did. This, in and of itself, is a tremendous threat to the enemy.

CHAPTER 20

Next, we look at the way Yeshua modeled forgiveness through the Ruach HaKodesh in His life. Matthew 9 beginning with verse 1 — *1 After getting into a boat, Yeshua crossed over and came to His own town. 2 Just then, some people brought to Him a paralyzed man lying on a cot. And seeing their faith, Yeshua said to the paralyzed man, "Take courage, son! Your sins are forgiven."*

In our own lives, how difficult is it for us as human beings to forgive a wrong that has occurred against us? Yeshua speaks directly to the necessity of forgiveness in our own lives just a few chapters back in Matthew 6 with what is often called "The Lord's Prayer." The passage reads, *9 "Therefore, pray in this way: 'Our Father in heaven, sanctified be Your name. 10 Your kingdom come, Your will be done on earth as it is in heaven. 11 Give us this day our daily bread. 12 And forgive us our debts as we also have forgiven our debtors. 13 And lead us not into temptation, but deliver us from the evil one.' 14 "For if you forgive others their transgressions, your heavenly Father will also forgive you."* As believers we regularly quote this, it is a part of the liturgical practice of many denominations, however, how often do we really pay attention to exactly what Yeshua is saying? He says, *"12 And forgive us our debts as we also have forgiven our debtors. 13 And lead us not into temptation, but deliver us from the evil one.' 14 "For if you forgive others their transgressions, your heavenly Father will also forgive you."* So there is a direct connection to our forgiveness and how we forgive others, yet so often we run around with severe un-forgiveness in our hearts and give the enemy more ground in our lives than he deserves because of it.

This isn't to say forgiveness is an easy task either. It can be tremendously difficult, especially depending on the wrong, or abuse, or whatever else was done. This becomes even more difficult when our lack of forgiveness allows for bitterness and hatred to take root in our hearts. Then there's the reality of the fact that forgiving ourselves when we mess up is even harder to do than to forgive others. We beat ourselves up and tear ourselves down over our own mistakes and sins and wallow in un-forgiveness over ourselves all while crying out for God's forgiveness.

Yeshua had the power to forgive sin and He clearly spoke in that power over the paralyzed man in Matthew 9. It is in the same power to forgive sin that Yeshua spoke over this man that He forgives our sins as well. When the Ruach HaKodesh is inside of us, He will dig up roots of bitterness inside of us (if we allow Him too) and set us free so that we can become experience the joy of letting those wrongs go.

Yeshua has authority over evil spirits, disease, and sickness and He operated in that authority. He told His Talmidim to operate in this same exact authority as we read in Matthew 10—*1 Yeshua summoned His twelve disciples and gave them authority over unclean spirits, so they could drive them out and heal every kind of disease and sickness.* There are people who are specifically called to deliverance ministry, but Yeshua has given all His followers the ability to drive out evil spirits. He has given all of us the ability to set free the captive, to break the chains of bondage, to release those in spiritual prison in Yeshua's Name. Yeshua modeled the authority of the mantle of the Holy Spirit for us as His followers throughout the Gospels.

We move to Matthew 12:22—*22 Then a demon-plagued man, who was blind and mute, was brought to Yeshua; and He healed him, so that he spoke and saw. 23 All the crowds were astounded and saying, "This can't be Ben-David, can it?" 24 But hearing this, the Pharisees said, "This fellow drives out demons only by beelzebul, the ruler of demons." 25 Knowing their thoughts, Yeshua said to them, "Every kingdom divided against itself is destroyed, and every city or house divided against itself will not stand. 26 If satan drives out satan, he is divided against himself; how then will his kingdom stand?*

This is one of the keys for us as disciples of Yeshua to walking in dominion. If we are divided in ourselves, in our thoughts and beliefs of Yeshua, if we're divided in our belief in the Word of God, if we're divided in our confidence in Salvation or our own freedom, then how are we going to have the power to even stand and say, "As for me and my house, we will serve the Lord"? Now take that concept from a personal and independent discussion and consider it from the aspect of division in the Body of Messiah.

Yeshua tells us in John 17:20-23, *20 "I pray not on behalf of these only, but also for those who believe in Me through their message, 21 that they all may be one. Just as You, Father, are in Me and I am in You, so also may they be one in Us, so the world may believe that You sent Me. 22 The glory that You have given to Me I have given to them, that they may be one just as We are one—23 I in them and You in Me—that they may be perfected in unity, so that the world may know that You sent Me and loved them as You loved Me.* The greatest tool we have available to us as followers of Messiah is unity, being *Echad* (one/united) in Yeshua. Contrarily, the greatest tool the enemy has available to him is division, and the Body of Messiah is letting the enemy have his way dividing us. There are thousands of denominations that exist within the Body of Messiah, many of these have absolutely nothing to do with each and go as far as to believe that if you aren't their flavor of believer then you aren't really saved at all. So, we are blissfully and ignorantly divided and typically over issues that don't matter at all in the grand scheme of things, or at the least aren't salvational issues. Instead of this, we should be coming together united in what we can agree on which is Yeshua and experiencing His true power. More dramatically, if Yeshua says through our unity the world will know Who sent us, then who do they see when they see us divided and continually infighting among the family...?

We are truly not as powerful a people for the Kingdom of Messiah today because we are so drastically divided. So, the questions we have to ask, as per the example of Yeshua, is why are we so divided? Why are there so many denominations? What does the world actually see and think when they see us? And what are we going to do to change that? Because division is not what God has called us to, Yeshua makes it very clear (albeit talking about the enemy) in Matthew 12 that a house divided cannot stand, and we wonder why the Body of Messiah is losing ground in the world around us. If we as the people of God will come into agreement with the entirety of the Word of God and come into agreement as ONE people, we will not be a powerless kingdom! We will walk in the authority and power of God because we will truly be ONE in Him. We have to begin with what we can agree on, which is the Blood of the Lamb, stand on what we can agree on, and then build our unity from there. Then we can march as ONE toward the common goal of making disciples of all men, bringing freedom and hope to the bound and lost, and awakening a powerful revival that will shake the foundations of the world. And when we are united the gates of hell can not/will not prevail against the Kingdom of the Lord.

We're talking in this section about Yeshua's modeling the mantle of the Holy Spirit for us, and what better way could He have done this than being united? He discusses in Matthew 12 about how a kingdom divided cannot stand. He was able to do what He needed to do, He was able to bring healing and deliverance, He was able to bring Salvation and hope because He was united with our Heavenly Father. It is in this same way, as we see Yeshua mention in His prayer in John 17, that we are called to be united with Yeshua, and through Yeshua with our Heavenly Father. This unity is bound in the Ruach HaKodesh and through this unity and the interweaving of the Ruach HaKodesh we can do even greater things than Yeshua did, not for our own sakes, but for the purposes of His Kingdom here on earth.

This concept of unity is both a macro- and micro-issues. As we mentioned previously, this is a task the Body of Messiah as a whole has to take up. But, it also must begin with the individual (the micro-) first. In Matthew 5 Yeshua says that if we've hated someone then we've already committed murder in our hearts, and if we've lusted after someone then we've already committed adultery/fornication in our hearts. This is a house divided… If our hearts are not truly in alignment with the Word of God then we are divided against the work of Messiah (the Word made flesh) within us. Does this mean we won't be tempted? No! Does temptation mean that we are in sin? No! We have been given the power to overcome temptation. Paul says in 2 Corinthians 10—*1 Now I, Paul, appeal myself to you by the meekness and gentleness of Messiah—I who am humble when face to face with you, but bold toward you when far away. 2 I beg of you that when I am present I won't need to be bold with the courage I consider showing against some who judge us as walking in the flesh. 3 For though we walk in the flesh, we do not wage war according to the flesh. 4 For the weapons of our warfare are not fleshly but powerful through God for the tearing down of strongholds. We are tearing down false arguments 5 and every high-minded thing that exalts itself against the knowledge of God. We are taking every thought captive to the obedience of Messiah — 6 ready to punish all disobedience, whenever your obedience is complete.*

So, if a house divided cannot stand, what happens if temptation comes into our minds and thoughts that go against the Word of God? We stand boldly against the work of the enemy and we badly proclaim the Word of the Lord, just as we see the example of Yeshua in the wilderness in Matthew 4. We declare that we are bought by the Blood of the Lamb, we declare that the enemy has no ground in our lives, we declare, "Greater is He who is in me than He who is in the world!" And we recognize that this is a spiritual battle, not one against flesh and blood. It is the enemy trying to tear down the Kingdom of Messiah, and it is a battle the enemy will not win and we should not give him a stronghold in our lives through. Remember, the reality is the enemy only has ground in our lives in areas we allow him, so if we stand on the example of Yeshua in Matthew 4 and don't give him any ground then the temptation can have nothing over us.

CHAPTER 21

This idea of not being a divided house goes even farther than just looking at the individual as well. This is a necessary concept within our congregations. Unity in the Body is one of the most important pieces to the puzzle, which I believe is why Yeshua prays the way He does in Matthew 17 as we discussed previously. However, we know as humans that when we operate within a community there will be times in which our humanity will get the best of us, whether that is hurting others or others hurting us. How exactly do we handle these situations as *kedoshim* (holy ones)? Yeshua tells us exactly how in Matthew 18—*15 "Now if your brother sins against you, go and show him his fault while you're with him alone. If he listens to you, you have won your brother. 16 But if he does not listen, take with you one or two more, so that 'by the mouth of two or three witnesses every word may stand.' 17 But if he refuses to listen to them, tell it to Messiah's community. And if he refuses to listen even to Messiah's community, let him be to you as a pagan and a tax collector. 18 "Amen, I tell you, whatever you forbid on earth will have been forbidden in heaven and what you permit on earth will have been permitted in heaven. 19 Again I say to you, that if two of you agree on earth about anything they may ask, it shall be done for them by My Father in heaven. 20 For where two or three are gathered together in My name, there I am in their midst."*

So, we see Yeshua's desire is always restoration, this is what we see Him model post-resurrection as He restores Peter. I am a fervent believer that there wasn't a real difference between what Peter did in denying Yeshua before the cross and what Judah (Judas) did. The real difference is what happened after, Peter repented and was restored, Judah was swallowed up in the guilt and despair of his sins and took his own life. But I believe, without a doubt, that had Judah repented and waited for Mashiach's resurrection that Yeshua would have restored him just as He did Peter. And this is ultimately the beauty of the Besorah, the reality that despite how we have turned our backs on HaShem, He has provided a means of redemption and restoration through the atonement of Yeshua for all who should choose to accept. So, in our own communities it is necessary that we model through the Ruach what we see in Yeshua and always work toward restoration when someone wrongs us or vice-versa. Especially considering the wounds from being wronged by a brother or sister in faith are prime fertile soil for the enemy to plant the seed of temptation for that pain to fester into something that will destroy us, our reputation, our relationships, and our witness for the Kingdom. If we follow the formula for successful restoration that Yeshua lays out in Matthew 18 we will either see restoration and thus unity grow or we will remove the opportunity for festering temptation in anger and emotional wounds.

Joshua says, "As for me and my house we will serve the Lord!" This goes for our own lives, homes, and congregations, we must take a stand for seeing our house serve the Lord. What has Yeshua taught us to do to see this come about? He's taught us to stand on His promises and provision. He's taught us to be steadfast and persistent in prayer. He's taught us to walk in, retain and stoke the Holy Spirit in our own lives, just as the mantle has been placed upon us we are in charge of being managers of our own lives and making sure we are a holy dwelling place for His Presence. We must rely on the Ruach for strength to stand against and overcome temptation.

With that said, what about when we face temptation while in persecution? Let's look at Matthew 26 — *59 Now the ruling kohanim and all the Sanhedrin kept trying to get false testimony against Yeshua so they could put Him to death. 60 But they found none, though many false witnesses came forward. At last two came forward 61 and said, "This fellow said, 'I'm able to destroy the Temple of God and rebuild it in three days!'" 62 The kohen gadol stood up and said to Yeshua, "Have You no answer? What's this they're testifying against You?" 63 But Yeshua kept silent. The kohen gadol said to Him, "I charge You under oath by the living God, tell us if You are Mashiach Ben-Elohim!" 64 "As you have said," replied Yeshua. "Besides that, I tell you, soon after you will see the Son of Man sitting at the right hand of power and coming on the clouds of heaven." 65 Then the kohen gadol tore his clothes and said, "Blasphemy! Why do we need any more witnesses? Look, you've heard the blasphemy. 66 What's your verdict?" "Guilty," they answered. "He deserves death!" 67 Then they spat in His face and pounded Him with their fists. Others slapped Him and demanded, 68 "Prophesy to us, you Messiah! Which one hit You?"*

Right away we notice that Yeshua kept silent. Keep in mind, this is God in flesh, if He really wanted to make a scene and prove the validity of His Messiahship right then and there He absolutely could have. However, He stared the temptation in the face even in the midst of persecution and facing the reality of death itself and remained silent, He waited for the right time to say the right words. Shortly after this, we see Yeshua is handed over to the Romans and is ultimately punished via capital punishment upon the stake.

We have been given the power to overcome temptation, just as we see Yeshua do while facing persecution itself. As believers, we need to recognize the value of this lesson in the days that lie ahead for us. We are drawing closer and closer to the end, and as we do, persecution of the Bride of Messiah will only continue to grow. Think about how many times we see in the Besorah as the religious leadership of Israel tried to catch and/or trap Yeshua in a snare, trying to get Him to slip up and say something for which they could punish Him… He always knew exactly what to do and say in these moments of temptation. Through the Holy Spirit, we can operate in the same restraint. As believers when the outside world assaults us for our faith it is all too easy to jump on our soapboxes or to burst into a vehement tirade in the face of crushing pressure. However, we are instructed biblically to operate in love, to be a witness of the Kingdom with our lives before our mouths. So, when these moments arise we must rise to the occasion and model the restraint and timely words of Yeshua, we must lean upon the Ruach for the strength to withstand both the temptation to "defend" our faith and the persecution the enemy is trying to throw at us.

Recognize that Yeshua said that if we follow Him we WILL BE persecuted. However, often we run from it, or we try to hide or soften the message for the sake of avoiding persecution. But the truth is we can't hide from it if we are truly Yeshua's, as we see in His words in John 15—*18 "If the world hates you, know that it has hated Me before you. 19 If you were of the world, the world would love you as its own. But you are not of the world, since I have chosen you out of the world; therefore the world hates you. 20 "Remember the word I spoke to you: 'A servant is not greater than his master.' If they persecuted Me, they will persecute you also.* So, it is not only important to explore the example Yeshua has set for us in standing in faith against persecution, but also in recognizing that if we are truly His, we cannot avoid it either. Trust that it isn't you that the world hates, but instead it is He who is in you that they hate. And trust that He has not only given us the ability to stand in the face of temptation, but He has empowered us with His Ruach HaKodesh specifically so we can.

Do we really believe that the same power that raised Yeshua from the grave resides within us? Think about how Yeshua raised Lazarus from the grave, he had been in the tomb for three days already. All of those there that morning were upset at the loss of this man, but despite the emotional despair Yeshua's word to the crowd was, "Don't you know that I am the resurrection and the life?" Then He calls Lazarus forth from the tomb, He didn't beg for the restoration of life, He didn't say this with any doubt in the possibility. Yeshua declared in perfect faith, "Lazarus come out!" That same resurrection power to raise the dead exists still, it is real, and it is available to us in the Holy Spirit. We're not simply talking about the typical "dead things in our life…" type of stuff either. Don't get me wrong, the power of the Holy Spirit can revive the dead things and areas in our lives as well. However, there is a very real resurrection power that lives in us, and just as He raised Lazarus from the dead, we also have the power in the Ruach to do the same. I am talking about a literal rising from the dead. Yeshua had the power to operate in the miraculous, bringing death to life, giving sight to the blind, giving mobility to the lame, etc, and that same miraculous power is flowing within our bodies as followers of Messiah today! The question is, do we truly believe in the power that is fully available to us?

Yeshua operated in the power of the Ruach HaKodesh to produce disciples. We may not think of this as something miraculous or something that is of the Ruach, but when people see the Presence of God in our lives and want what we have and desire to learn how to walk in His ways as we do, this is miraculous. Think about how swiftly the Talmidim dropped everything they were doing to follow Yeshua as He walked through Israel calling them forth. Yeshua calls us to pick up our cross and follow Him, He calls us to not just follow Him in Salvation but also in the reality of making disciples of all men as we see in the Great Commission.

When we walk in the mantle of the Ruach there is a profound desire to walk in communion with the Lord daily. When we walk in this reality, we begin to see the Word of God becoming a tangible part of our life, we begin to hear and recognize the voice of God speaking in our hearts. We begin to see, through that communion with Him, how He draws our attention to His desires, to His ways in our every day lives. As an example, when you see someone drop a $5 bill on the sidewalk, the natural desire is to pick it up and pocket it. But when we walk in the Ruach in communion with HaShem as we see modeled in Yeshua's life, we hear the Lord leading us to instead be honest, pick up the money and hand it to the person who it belongs to. In doing so, in being able to hear and recognize His still, small voice and respond to it, we can not only be a blessing in others lives, but we are also able to stand as a witness to the Kingdom of God in a way that can profoundly change someone else's life. Instead of destroying the testimony of God in our lives by potentially stealing that money, we can present a witness of His love in a tangible way. When we walk in the Ruach HaKodesh, we can hear the voice of the Lord leading us to respond to His Word.

The baptism of the Holy Spirit and the fire that is revealed in it produces the power to proclaim and walk in our divinely given purpose, which is to dwell in the Presence of God. When we submit to this, we will see the Spirit pursuing and pushing us to produce good fruit. This good fruit is ultimately love—in the Ruach, we can love God, love others, and love ourselves.

To understand the power of the Holy Spirit, we must understand that it isn't just about these huge, mind-blowing miracles and signs and wonders. We must understand that many things that we don't even begin to consider as miraculous really are. Sure, there is a potential for seeing God use us to bring sight to the blind or to raise the dead, but it is even more likely to see God use us miraculously in ways we could have never considered simply through love. Yeshua performed fantastic miracles and we can as well, but there is so much more.

Everything that Yeshua did—from the miraculous healings and casting out demons, to teaching a greater depth of understanding of God's Word, to offering His own life for the sins of the world in His death, burial, and resurrection—was done solely because He loves us. God created humanity to experience His love, we were created to exist in His Presence, and we chose to fall to sin and to live in separation from His Presence instead. God loves us so much that even though He foreknew we were going to sin and fall short of glory He still created us specifically to receive His love. He loves us so much that before He ever created us He had already put into play a plan for redemption, salvation, and restoration. He loves us so much that He gave His only begotten Son so that whoever may believe in Him would have everlasting life in His Presence (John 3:16). It is in this same depth of love that God has placed His Ruach HaKodesh within us to empower us to see the world through His merciful eyes and to show the world His love.

In 1 Corinthians 12 Paul discusses the gifts of the Spirit, and then in chapter 13 he goes on to discuss the greatest gift—*1 If I speak with the tongues of men and of angels but have not love, I have become a noisy gong or a clanging cymbal. 2 If I have the gift of prophecy and know all mysteries and all knowledge, and if I have all faith so as to remove mountains but have not love, I am nothing. 3 If I give away all that I own and if I hand over my body so I might boast but have not love, I gain nothing.* He goes on to close out this same chapter with the following words—*13 But now these three remain— faith, hope, and love. And the greatest of these is love.* Love is at the core of everything that Yeshua has done for us, and if His Ruach is in us then the world must see His love coming through us. Yeshua and Paul both make it very clear that the Love of God in us is far greater a gift of the Ruach in us than any act of speaking in tongues or prophecy or healing. If people hear us talking about revival and the gifts of the Spirit but they don't see the pure love of God in us, then what difference does it make…? This is the greatest example we can and should model of Yeshua's life in the Ruach HaKodesh in our own walk day in and day out. Everything God has done for us and everything He wants to do through us is for the purpose of His love being known and for Him to be seen in us so that the world will have a guiding light to find their way to Him in this dark and gloomy fallen world.

To this point, it is vital for us to grasp the power of the words of Yeshua in Matthew 7—*21 "Not everyone who says to Me, 'Lord, Lord!' will enter the kingdom of heaven, but he who does the will of My Father in heaven. 22 Many will say to Me on that day, 'Lord, Lord, didn't we prophesy in Your name, and drive out demons in Your name, and perform many miracles in Your name?' 23 Then I will declare to them, 'I never knew you. Get away from Me, you workers of lawlessness!'"* May the Lord grab ahold of the hearts of His bride and make us a greater example of what His heart truly is because this world needs His love and power in a far greater way and the Body of Messiah as a whole has done a pitiful job at living the example of Yeshua in His Ruach HaKodesh.

CHAPTER 22

Up to this point, we've been talking about the Ruach HaKodesh from a perspective primarily of how we see things in the Tanakh and the Gospels, and in this section, we will be focusing on the Book of Acts and how the Ruach moved upon and through the early Body of Messiah. As we've seen thus far, the Ruach HaKodesh was as active in the Tanakh as we see it in the Gospels and now the Book of Acts, but what we notice is different is that the mantle of the Holy Spirit in the Tanakh was primarily on an individual basis from one person to another for a time and a purpose. However, as of Acts 2, the table flips and the mantle of the Ruach HaKodesh is available for the masses, for the Body of Messiah as a whole. What we see as of Acts is that what God intended for His people from the foundations of creation itself was for us to be in His Presence at all times and we walked away from that because of sin, however now we can experience His Presence within us and can be used by God through the Holy Spirit for His purposes.

That's the most important thing about the Holy Spirit in our lives also, we don't just have it for kicks and giggles. We don't get to prophesy and perform miracles through the Ruach as though we're a part of a parlor show or carnival act. His Ruach moves in our lives for His purposes, particularly for impacting those around us for His Kingdom and for them to encounter His Presence. Every time there was a move of God throughout Acts (and we see this right out the gate in Acts 2) we see there was a major increase in those being saved.

In Acts 1 we see the ascension of Messiah. Yeshua is on the Mount of Olives and ascends into Heaven and as He does we read beginning in verse 8: *8 But you will receive power when the Ruach ha-*

Kodesh has come upon you; and you will be My witnesses in Jerusalem, and through all Judah, and Samaria, and to the end of the earth. So—as per Yeshua's words—we receive the Ruach HaKodesh for what purpose? To be witnesses of His Kingdom to Judea, Samaria, and to the ends of the earth… Not for our purposes, but solely for His Kingdom.

Interestingly enough, the disciples were there when Yeshua ascended, they witnesses this amazing event happen before their eyes. Yet, when we read the end of Acts 1 in juxtaposition against the end of Acts 2 there wasn't any significant difference between the way the disciples acted between the two. After Yeshua's ascension, they gathered together in Jerusalem as they normally did, they prayed together, they studied together, they taught and encouraged each other and those that came in, they ate together, fellowshipped, and spent time as a community. At the end of Acts 2, after the outpouring of the Ruach HaKodesh, they did the exact same thing… The only difference is that the power and presence of the Ruach HaKodesh is upon them and there are those being added to their numbers daily that are being saved. Whereas at the end of Acts 1 they were simply giving a "promotion" to someone from within their ranks, not necessarily making disciples throughout the world…

Let's take a look at Acts 2 now:

1 When the day of Shavuot had come, they were all together in one place.

Real quick, let's pause here and take a moment to discuss where exactly this went down… Where was that "one place"? Jerusalem, at the Temple. It wasn't in some random upstairs apartment somewhere down the street. Far too often people confuse what is going on in chapter 1 with what is going on in chapter 2. In chapter 1 it talks about the believers gathering in an upper room, however, in Acts 2 this upper room is never mentioned at all. It talks about how there were Jews and proselytes to

Judaism from all over the known world gathered together there to celebrate Shavuot. Where would they be going to do so? To Jerusalem, to the Temple, as the Torah specifies as Shavuot is one of the *Shalosh Regalim* (Pilgrimage Feasts). There is no way possible for the events of Acts 2 to have occurred in some obscure room upstairs somewhere in Jerusalem and thousands of people have been able to see it all at the same time, but this would be possible at the Temple, where thousands upon thousands would have been gathered already.

We continue in Acts 2: *2 Suddenly there came from heaven a sound like a mighty rushing wind, and it filled the whole house where they were sitting. 3 And tongues like fire spreading out appeared to them and settled on each one of them. 4 They were all filled with the Ruach ha-Kodesh and began to speak in other tongues as the Ruach enabled them to speak out.*

Notice, they didn't begin speaking in tongues as they wanted or desired. But, instead, they did so solely as the Ruach enabled them to speak.

5 Now Jewish people were staying in Jerusalem, devout men from every nation under heaven. 6 And when this sound came, the crowd gathered. They were bewildered, because each was hearing them speaking in his own language.

They weren't speaking in random noises or sounds that have never been heard before. They were speaking languages that were unfamiliar to them as the Spirit of God led them, these were, however, languages those in the crowd would be able to understand but the disciples would not. I believe what they were speaking in all of these various languages was the Gospel.

6 And when this sound came, the crowd gathered. They were bewildered, because each was hearing them speaking in his own language. 7 And they were amazed and astonished, saying, "All these who are speaking—aren't they Galileans? 8 How is it that we each hear our own birth language? 9 Parthians and Medes and Elamites and those living in Mesopotamia, Judea and Cappadocia, Pontus and Asia, 10 Phrygia and Pamphylia, Egypt and parts of Libya toward Cyrene, and visitors from Rome 11 (both Jewish people and proselytes), Cretans and Arabs—we hear them declaring in our own tongues the mighty deeds of God!"

Again, the disciples are not just randomly making noises, they are speaking in foreign languages that are not familiar to them. Specifically, they are speaking of the mighty deeds of God as Acts 2 says—which is why I believe they are preaching the Gospel in these foreign languages. Most importantly to this point is that those in the crowd of thousands from every tribe and tongue were able to understand what was being said by the disciples, even though the disciples had no clue what they were saying themselves.

After all of this, the people begin to ask, "Are these guys drunk…? What in the world is happening…?" Peter begins to preach and goes back to the beginning, back to the message of the Tanakh. He says what you are witnessing is exactly what the Lord has been saying through the prophets of old would happen. This is exactly what Messiah said would happen… And at the end of Peter's response to the crowd's curiosity Acts 2 continues *38 Peter said to them, "Repent, and let each of you be immersed in the name of Messiah Yeshua for the removal of your sins, and you will receive the gift of the Ruach ha-Kodesh. 39 For the promise is for you and your children, and for all who are far away—as many as Adonai our God calls to Himself." 40 With many other words he warned them and kept urging them, saying, "Save yourselves from this twisted generation!" 41 So those who received his message were immersed, and that day about three thousand*

souls were added. If we take the time to pay attention to what is happening here in Act 2, it is mind-blowing how this all transpires.

I'll give you a bit of an idea of what I believe the gift of tongues is (and we'll talk more about this later on in this book as well). We hear people talk about the personal prayer language and also of that which is for the edification of the Body and so on. However, right now I am solely talking about that which is to be heard by all which is for the edification of the Body and of which the Bible tells us requires interpretation. If we go back to Genesis we read about the Tower of Babel. At the Tower of Babel God says that if we as humans, as messed up as we can be, if we all agree on something together then nothing is impossible. So, Genesis says God confounded the languages, He didn't create new languages. I believe what God did is that He confused the way we hear languages. I wouldn't be surprised if there is still only one language being spoken realistically and this is what God hears when we all speak, but that we hear different and we perceive as being various languages because He has confounded or confused the languages.

When we go to Acts 2 it says there were men from every nation and language who heard the disciples from the Galilee speaking in their own languages. And those hearing them said, "Wait, aren't these guys from the Galilee...? Don't they speak Hebrew...? How in the world are we hearing them in our languages right now?" I believe that when the power of the Ruach fell in Acts 2 it un-confounded the language of those who were there that day and this is why they were able to hear the message the Lord wanted to be spoken in what appeared to be their own native tongues.

So, as we see in Acts chapter 2 we see this outpouring of the Holy Spirit that allows it to be given to all who believe in Messiah Yeshua, no longer just for a particular person for a particular purpose for a particular time. The mantle of the Holy Spirit is now available for all who would believe in Messiah, be repentant of sin, and be immersed for the remission of sin. The power and the presence of the Ruach is available for all for His purpose, for mass availability. Why? Because what God always intended was for us to be in His Presence anyways, this desire isn't anything new. We were created to be in His Presence, we sinned; He removed us from His Presence and put His Presence in our midst to lead us; then He put His Presence inside of us; so that ultimately we can be restored to being in His Presence again. As we investigate all of this, what we now see is that the Ruach HaKodesh now dwelling within us is literally His Shechinah, His Divine Glory within us, allowing us to follow His lead.

On Shavuot in Acts, 2 we see this fantastic event that occurs, but we must realize that it mirrors what occurred on Shavuot in Exodus 19 & 20 at Mt. Sinai. There is fire, quaking of the ground, heavenly sounds (heavenly shofar blast if you will). There is even the message of God being spoken boldly and loud for all to hear, just like Israel experienced at Sinai with the Bat Kol speaking forth the Aseret HaDibrot (the Ten Words). So we see the events of Acts 2 are mirror images, they are a correlating account of what Israel experienced in Exodus 19 & 20.

Unfortunately, for most of the past 1700 years of the history of the Body of Messiah the church has been removed almost entirely from our Jewish roots. So, what most believers reading Acts 2 do not realize is that the events of Yeshua's Sacrifice and that of Acts 2 are actually prophetic fulfillments of the Appointed Days of Leviticus 23. Because we have found ourselves as the Bride of Messiah devoid of a Jewish contextual understanding of the events that take place in the Brit Chadashah we find ourselves looking at it from a 21st-century Christian perspective rather than from a 1st-century Jewish perspective. But we gain such a deeper understanding of His Word when we strive to look at the Word in the true Jewish context in which it was written.

CHAPTER 23

Now one big thing that stands out in Act 2 at the Temple in Jerusalem is that this Ruach experience was only for Jews or converts to Judaism. At that very moment, only those within the context of Judaism already had access to the Holy Spirit. But as we move forward to Acts 10, we read an account that many believers are already aware of, however for all the wrong reasons. Most of the Body of Messiah seems to take Acts 10 out of context, contort it and make it say what they want it to say, rather than focus on the powerful message that is readily available from God in the text itself. People like to look at this account and say, "Peter says we can eat whatever we want to eat now!!!" However, to come to that conclusion, we have to ignore that there was a greater message being given. Peter's vision was merely the "fixings" of a sandwich and it is the bread of the sandwich that matters most.

What we see at the beginning of Chapter 10 is a gentile man named Cornelius that has this encounter with the Lord. The Lord tells him, "I want you to send some men to get Peter and ask Peter to come to speak to you, he has a powerful message for you." Peter (#1) has no clue he is supposed to bring a message to them and (#2) hasn't even received said message from the Lord yet. On top of that, Peter is a 1st century Jew's Jew, he doesn't like gentiles… Well, more specifically he doesn't interact with gentiles. They were considered unclean at the time because of idolatry, and a Jew interacting with them would mean that they have become unclean and couldn't go into the Temple. Even more so, God was well aware of this about Peter long before He told Cornelius to send for Peter. God was well aware of Peter's heart, I know it is hard to believe, but God knows our hearts even better than we think we do. God had to get Peter's attention because of what He had in store for Peter's ministry for the Kingdom. God had a divine purpose and task for Peter that he was not yet aware of and would, left to his own vices, refuse otherwise.

Peter falls into a deep trance on this roof and has this crazy dream. In the dream, this sheet comes down from heaven with all this *treif* (unkosher food) upon it and God says, "Peter, get up and eat..." To which Peter responds in protest, "Not gonna happen, I've never put anything unclean in my mouth and I'm not starting now, I don't care Who You are..." This happens three times, the sheet vanishes, and the Lord tells Peter, "Do not call anything I've made clean unclean."

Have you ever argued with God? Have you ever won any of these arguments? I know I haven't. I've never won an argument with God (and unfortunately I've tried way more than I'd like to admit...). It would appear that Peter has won this argument with God... He tells God he isn't eating anything on the sheet and the sheet vanishes. But it was never about the unclean meat on the sheet in the first place, it had to do with what God said at the end of the vision. If God wanted Peter to eat of the unclean meat, God would have made Peter eat... But He didn't, which means it wasn't ever the purpose of this passage in the first place. The sole lesson God was teaching Peter was to not call anything that He has made clean unclean, and the very next thing that happens is a knock at the door. Peter finds a couple of gentiles at his door inviting him to come to speak to their gentile master at his house about the Jewish Messiah. And as soon as Peter heard them speak, the text says Peter understood the vision, and it wasn't about food, it meant the same salvation available to Jews is available also to gentiles, and the same Ruach available to Jews is also available to gentiles. And Peter would have never left with them had he not had that vision from the Lord in advance.

We continue reading in Acts 10:24— *24 The following day he entered Caesarea. Cornelius was waiting for them and had called together his relatives and close friends. 25 As Peter entered, Cornelius met him and fell down at his feet and worshiped him. 26 But Peter pulled him up, saying, "Stand up! I too am just a man." 27 Talking with him, Peter went inside and found many people gathered. 28 He said to them, "You yourselves know that it is not permitted for a Jewish man to associate with a non-Jew or to visit him. Yet God has shown me that I should call no one unholy or unclean. 29 So I came without objection when I was sent for. I ask, then, what is the reason why you sent for me?"*

Notice Peter says, "*God has shown me that I should call no one unholy or unclean.*" He didn't say God showed me it's ok for me to eat a ham sandwich, or that God has made shellfish suddenly clean for human consumption. Although the vision was of a sheet of unclean meat coming down, Peter realized that this was a symbolic vision, it was symbolic of gentiles being made clean, and nothing else.

Picking up again in verse 30— *30 Cornelius declared, "Four days ago at this hour, I was praying minchah in my house. Suddenly, a man stood in front of me in shining clothes. 31 He says, 'Cornelius, your prayer has been heard and your tzadakah remembered before God. 32 Therefore send to Joppa and ask for Simon, who is also called Peter. He is staying in the house of Simon the tanner, by the sea.' 33 So I sent for you immediately, and you have been kind enough to come. Now then, we are all here before God to hear all that you have been commanded by the Lord."*

So then Peter begins to preach and tell them about everything the Lord had done. He laid out for Cornelius and his friends and family all about what happened in Jerusalem, what happened when Yeshua died, was buried, and then resurrected. He relayed all about what happened at the Temple on Shavuot in Acts when the Ruach HaKodesh was poured out in might and power upon the Believers there. He told them all about the thousands coming to faith that one single day because they saw the Presence of God in their midst.

Picking up again in verse 44—*44 While Peter was still speaking these words, the Ruach ha-Kodesh fell on all those hearing the message. 45 All the circumcised believers who came with Peter were astonished, because the gift of the Ruach ha-Kodesh had been poured out even on the Gentiles. 46 For they were hearing them speaking in tongues and magnifying God.*

How did they know they were magnifying God? These were not native Hebrew or Aramaic speakers. Yet, in almost an inverted reality of what was seen in Acts 2, all of the Jewish believers from Jerusalem and the Galilee were hearing these men of the nations speaking the truths of God in their own language. They were speaking to men who had unconfounded hearing and were able to understand Cornelius and his friends and family as they began to speak in tongues as the power of the Ruach came over them.

Then Peter answered, 47 "Can anyone refuse water for these to be immersed, who have received the Ruach ha-Kodesh just as we did?" 48 So he commanded them to be immersed in the name of Messiah Yeshua. Then they asked him to stay for a few days.

In other words, they realized that the same manner in which the Ruach HaKodesh was made available to the Jewish believers in Acts 2 it had been made available to believers from the nations as well.

What we see here, and it is in connection to Romans, the outpouring of the Ruach HaKodesh came to the Jews first, and then from the Jews, it went to the nations. Who is it that encamped around the Tabernacle in the wilderness? Israel, the Jewish people. We pray all the time quoting Yeshua, "*may Your will be done on earth as it is in Heaven…*" So the Tabernacle was the temporary dwelling place for the Presence of the Lord here on earth, so anything that happened in the Tabernacle in Heaven happened in the Tabernacle on earth. Scripture tells us that Moses built the Tabernacle on earth exactly as he saw the Tabernacle in Heaven. So, when the Presence fell in the Temple, who was it that would normally be living around the Temple? The Jewish people. With that, notice that in the Second Temple (which was destroyed in 70 c.e.) the Aron HaBrit (Ark of the Covenant) was not there. When the Temple was rebuilt the Ark was never brought back (we still have no clue where it is…). So, if the Torah tells us the Presence of God resided upon the Mercy Seat upon the Ark of the Covenant and the Ark of the Covenant wasn't in the Second Temple, then that means the Presence of God didn't reside in the Second Temple. There was no column of fire and cloud in the Second Temple. But why…? Because God was preparing through the Second Temple a way for His Presence to no longer be trapped inside a permanent structure anymore, but to return to temporal dwelling places again (i.e. the Body of Messiah). So His Presence came down through the Holy of Holies in the Temple and burst out through the curtain that was split at the sacrifice of Yeshua and this allowed for all to have access to the Presence of God. The Ruach HaKodesh, the power and Presence of Adonai, comes out of the Temple and overcomes the Jewish and Proselyte believers who were there that day worshipping on this special Shavuot. From there we see the Ruach is brought from the Jewish believers to those of the nations, and the nations experience His Presence and power and are affected by it. Cornelius' house was filled with his family and friends who were all gentiles that all of a sudden found the Jewish Messiah and were filled with the power and presence of the Ruach HaKodesh. We see this concept discussed by Paul in Romans 1 where Paul says salvation came to the Jew first and likewise to the nations. Salvation leads to the indwelling of the Spirit of God, the indwelling of the Spirit of God was also to the Jew first and likewise to the nations Which is exactly how we see things play out in Acts 2 followed by Acts 10. This is exactly how we see things play out throughout the Tanakh up to this point. We see Jews impacted by the Ruach HaKodesh to impact the nations, and in the exact same way, we see this revealed in Acts 10 as God sends Jews impacted by the Ruach to impact the nations.

CHAPTER 24

Now that we've looked at the outpouring of the Ruach in both Acts 2 and Acts 10, we are going to turn in a slightly different, but a necessary direction. There is a very important word used in the Greek in regards to the Holy Spirit, it is the word "dunamis" from the root word "dunami" (from which we get the English word dynamite) and means "power" as in miraculous power, and is from the root word Dunami meaning to be able or possible. It is seen in the book of Acts 10 times, the first of which is in Acts 1:8. We see some form of this exact same Greek word used throughout the Brit Chadashah (New Testament) 120 different times, which tells us this is a pretty important word. (For your own record of where this word is used all 10 times in Acts—1:8; 2:22; 3:12; 4:7, 33; 6:8; 8:10, 13; 10:38; and 19:11.)

The word dunamis, when used throughout Acts (and the Brit Chadashah), is talking of the power of the mantle of the Ruach HaKodesh. In Acts 1:8 we read, *8 But you will receive POWER when the Ruach ha-Kodesh has come upon you...* Here, this word in Greek that is translated as power is the word Dunamis as we mentioned. Throughout the Brit Chadashah, it is always used in reference to God's power, miracles, signs, and wonders. So, when we read in Acts 1:8 and it says you will receive the DUNAMIS (power) when the Holy Spirit comes upon you, it is referencing the signs, wonders, miracles, and literal divine power of God that will flow through us. Think about it this way, have you ever stuck your finger in an electrical socket? When you put your finger in one, you feel a flow of power. It's not going to feel like a good power... It is going to hurt (or worse) and it will most assuredly get your attention. But, it is power. This image is the same for us as believers with the

Ruach HaKodesh. We are plugged into the electrical socket of the power of God, the presence of the divine mantle of the Holy Spirit. There is a divine power (quite literally) that is given to us.

We discussed Elijah and Elisha previously in this book. They both performed miracles, signs, and wonders, they didn't just prophesy. They proved that God sent them and was speaking through them by the signs and wonders that He did through them. We see the same is true with Moses, Joshua, Samuel, David, and so on... We see signs and wonders through each and every one of them from the mantle of the Ruach upon them. Yeshua proved His Messiahship through signs and wonders. In the Gospel, it says the Jew requires a sign... Why? Because the Jewish people are looking for signs and wonders to know that the Presence of God is among them. We see Yeshua performed signs and wonders as was expected because Yeshua is God Himself robed in flesh. And now that same Dunamis power of God is a part of who we are as believers in Messiah through the mantle of the Holy Spirit upon us.

As believers, far too often, we don't walk in that power. Do you know why? If I go to the breaker box in my house and turn off the breaker for the outlets in my living room, you can stick your finger in the outlets and you won't feel anything. When we let sin creep into our lives, in essence, what we are doing is turning off a breaker in the spiritual breaker box of the Power of God in our lives. Sin is a barrier between the Power of God and what God has called and restored us to be. Sin is a barrier between what God wants to do in and through our lives and what we are allowing Him to do in and through our lives. Every time we allow sin in, we are damaging what God can and will do through us.

We nee\ to realize that God wants to use us for His purposes, for His Kingdom. He gave us the mantle of His Holy Spirit for this reason. As we read in Acts 1:8, *8*

But you will receive power when the Ruach ha-Kodesh has come upon you; and you will be My witnesses in Jerusalem, and through all Judah, and Samaria, and to the end of the earth. He hasn't given us the Dunamis power of the Ruach for us to sit on our hands lazily. He hasn't given it to us for us to try and gain anything for ourselves or to get rich off of parlor tricks. He hasn't given it to us so we can slap and kick people or blow really hard across a crowd for people to hope they can get healed. He hasn't given us His Holy Spirit for us to make a laughing stock of Him or for us to make a circus of the Body of Messiah. He gave it to us for His purposes, He gave us the Holy Spirit so we could be *HIS witness to Jerusalem, and through all Judah, and Samaria, and to the end of the earth.*

The whole reason the Body of Messiah has been endowed with the Ruach HaKodesh is to impact the world around us for Adonai's purposes. The dunamis power, the exponential power of the Ruach HaKodesh is what the disciples and early believers walked in every single day of their lives from Acts 2 and on. We can read about it all over the first half of the book of Acts, which is all about the talmidim walking in this newfound power and presence of God. We see that the talmidim live their lives in complete submission to let the Ruach HaKodesh lead them, and in turn, we see the signs and wonders that flowed through that.

We see these types of signs and wonders throughout the book of Acts 1. As a prime example, let's take a look at Acts 3— *1 Now Peter and John were going up to the Temple at the ninth hour, the time of prayer. 2 A man lame from birth was being carried— every day they used to put him at the Temple gate called Beautiful, so he could beg for tzadakah from those entering the Temple. 3 When he saw Peter and John about to go into the Temple, he began asking to receive tzadakah. 4 But Peter, along with John, looked straight at him and said, "Look at us!" 5 So he gave them his attention, expecting to receive something from them.*

The dunamis power of the Ruach HaKodesh was upon Peter and John, they walked, spoke, and operated with the authority of the Holy Spirit, just as Yeshua did. It was this power which grabbed ahold of this man's attention and he locked on, with complete focus, the two men of God standing in front of him. He could sense something was different about them.

5 So he gave them his attention, expecting to receive something from them. 6 But Peter said, "Silver and gold I do not have, but what I do have I give to you—in the name of Yeshua ha-Mashiach ha-Natzrati, get up and walk!" 7 Then grabbing him by the right hand, he raised him up; and immediately the man's feet and ankles were made strong. 8 Jumping up, he stood and began walking; and he went with them into the Temple, walking and leaping and praising God! 9 Now all the people saw him walking and praising God. 10 They began to realize he was the one who used to sit begging for tzadakah at the Beautiful Gate of the Temple, and they were filled with wonder and astonishment over what had happened to him.

Peter then began to preach to the crowd about exactly what happened. He begins to tell them about the power and presence of the Lord. There were those that were added that day that were saved because they saw the tangible Presence of God in their midst. Do you want to know the truth about why we don't often see people come to faith today in the same manner we read about in the Brit Chadashah? It's because we, the Body of Messiah, have lost focus on what it means to walk in the power of the mantle of the Holy Spirit. Every time we see people come to faith in Yeshua in the book of Acts it is specifically because they saw the Presence of God at work in the lives of Yeshua's followers. They saw the power, the signs, and the wonders that proved that God was, in fact, walking among them in their midst.

Do we as believers in Messiah Yeshua truly walk in the Power of God today as we read about in the lives of the early believers? Honestly, half the time most believers are entirely skeptical of the Power of God today. If what we read about in Acts began to occur to and/or through some of us today, I think many believers would denounce it themselves just out of fear. Earlier in the book, I mentioned that certain denominations believe in a theological principle called cessationism and means that the Holy Spirit has ceased to operate in our midst entirely, that it was solely a 1st Century thing and never meant for us in the 21st Century. If this is the camp you find yourself in, I hate to break it to you, but this is just not a biblical reality, it is completely contrary to the Word of God.

In the same sense, however, there are denominations that swing to the exact opposite end of the pendulum. There are denominations that are hyper-legalistic about the Holy Spirit, churches where Sunday night church starts at 6 pm and people aren't done jumping pews until 2 am. These denominations believe and teach that if you do not speak in tongues then you are not really filled with the Holy Spirit. If I can be perfectly honest here, I have grown up knowing a lot of the "super-spiritual-holy-rolling" types. I personally am very skeptical of that kind of stuff... I am not skeptical of a true move of God, I've experienced the power of God over and over again. I have seen countless lives changed because of the signs and wonders of God's miraculous hand. I am personally alive today because of the divine hand of God providing healing and protection in several situations throughout my life.

When I was little, I had some issues breathing and my parents took me to the doctor to try and figure out what was going on. They ran all sorts of tests and x-rays and so on. I ended up being diagnosed with extremely severe asthma and was also diagnosed with severe bronchitis at the same time. They were pretty confident that there was a hole in one of my lungs. We were scheduled to come back to the doctor for even more tests to try and figure out a treatment plan and find out a little more about what exactly was going on. In the meantime, we went to our home congregation and my parents had our community gather around me in prayer. They laid hands on me and prayed for healing. There was definitively something powerful that occurred when they prayed, and when I went back to the doctor they ran test after test, they ran x-rays on every x-ray machine they could get their hands on and they couldn't find anything... There was no asthma, no bronchitis, not spot on my lung, nothing. Everything that was documented as present a week or two before was now completely gone as if nothing had ever happened. I have legitimately seen the power of God in my life countless times. I have been in car accidents that should have killed me and walked away with nothing more than a bloody nose. I have had way too many near accidents while riding my motorcycle such as people pulling out in front of me or changing lanes on top of me with no warning.

We have had incidents in our synagogue where we have laid hands on people who were wheelchair stricken who then got up and walked. I have laid hands on people with massive growths on their backs and felt the growth recede under my hand. I have had people prophesy over me and my family, and then have seen those words come true. I have two beautiful children who are complete miracles, especially considering the doctors told my wife she'd likely never get pregnant, and with much prayer, our God proved the medical community wrong. I am, thankfully, well acquainted with the true move of God. Nothing excites me more than seeing God use His people bought by the blood of His only Son to reveal His Presence in this dark world.

What we have today is two vastly different slants on the Holy Spirit, and they are at odds with each other. This division is a work of the enemy to try and derail what God can and wants to do through His Bride. Some believers wholeheartedly believe that the Ruach is no longer active, and others are so spastic about it that in many ways they make a fool of the Ruach HaKodesh. I entirely believe that for the Body of Messiah to be as effective for the Kingdom of God as He desires for us to be, for us to see the vast salvation experiences that the early Body saw, we must dig into what the Bible actually says about the Holy Spirit. We must completely submit to the Holy Spirit, and we must live day in and day out in the dunamis power of the Holy Spirit in such a way that lives are changed and hearts are won just because people can sense the Presence of God among them.

Look, I'll admit, it would be way easier to just say that the Ruach doesn't work today. It is definitely easier to say the Ruach isn't active than to have to own up to the fact that the move of the Ruach can be weird and we don't necessarily understand it and it spooks us. Do you think people weren't spooked when Lazarus came out of the grave and started to talk with them…? When the masses saw the resurrected Yeshua on the Mount of Olives ascend into the sky do you think people weren't freaked out…? That's not normal… And that's the beauty of the power of the Ruach HaKodesh, it illuminates the discussion of normality because it takes us from what we think of as normal as finite humans to what God thinks of as normal. What is normality to God is restoration, redemption, renewal. His desire is for us to be restored to the Presence of God through the work of salvation in Yeshua HaMashiach, and these are things that do not make sense to us as humans.

We can look even further at the narrative of events of the Holy Spirit in Acts with chapter 4. We see Peter and the others begin to speak to the Sanhedrin and begin to preach and minister there. At the end of chapter 4, we read—*32 Now the whole group of those who believed was one in heart and mind. No one would say anything he owned was his own, but they had everything in common. 33 With great power the emissaries were giving witness to the resurrection of the Lord Yeshua, and abundant favor was upon them all. 34 No one among them was needy, for all who were owners of lands or houses would sell them and bring the proceeds 35 and set them at the feet of the emissaries. And the proceeds were distributed according to the need each one had.*

There are two key things to recognize here: First, In verse 33 the word "power" in the Greek is again the word dunamis. We continue to see this reality of the dunamis power of God upon His followers over and over again. The second, notice that the believers didn't just haphazardly sell everything they owned and hand the proceeds over to some central purse. Instead, they sold stuff as it was needed to take care of others. Especially in America, we look at things as though it is the government's responsibility to take care of the needy, but this is only because we the Body decided we didn't want to do our job. What is it Yeshua said? Take care of the widowed, the orphaned, the sick, the needy. He calls us to take care of those who can't take care of themselves. The Lord says it is our responsibility, the responsibility of the Body of Messiah.

Imagine how much greater an impact the Body of Messiah could make for the Kingdom if we began to live what Yeshua preached. We have relegated our responsibility to meet physical needs to the government, then we get upset because of "entitlement programs" that the government uses to do the very job we decided we were too good to do. But, what would it look like if believing congregations began to work together to provide food for the hungry, housing for the homeless, met the needs of the widowed and orphaned that society tends to forget about? The Holy Spirit isn't some magic show that we wait on to work some crazy miracles and move on, the Holy Spirit empowers us to be used by G-d to further His Kingdom. Perhaps instead of grumbling against government programs and those who are benefiting from them, we as the Bride of Messiah should swallow our arrogance and get our hands dirty doing the work of meeting physical needs as our Messiah did. As many as 9,000 lives were immediately impacted by the Gospel message because Yeshua simply fed them with fish and bread... How many more lives could we impact today considering there are way more believers today than just the 12 dudes Yeshua ran with...?

Skipping to Acts 5:12— *12 Meanwhile, through the hands of the emissaries many signs and wonders were happening among the people. And they were all together in Solomon's Portico. 13 But no one else dared to join them, though the people continued to think highly of them. 14 Yet more than ever those trusting in the Lord were added—large numbers of men and women. 15 They even carried the sick into the streets and laid them on stretchers and cots, so that when Peter passed by at least his shadow might fall on some of them. 16 Crowds were also gathering from the towns around Jerusalem, bringing those who were sick or tormented by unclean spirits, and they were all being healed.*

Folks, this is the Dunamis power of the Ruach we are talking about. The disciples operated faithfully and consistently in the Dunamis power, the mantle of the Ruach HaKodesh. They let the Holy Spirit lead their footsteps and guide their words and their actions. Often when we pray for healing today we feel the need to tell

God what exactly is happening, who's being affected, what the doctor says, what the prognosis is, what's going to happen if they have this procedure or that procedure, and what we really want to see happen, and what it could mean to the family if this or that happened, and so on and so forth... And all the time, I think, we're just trying to build our own faith in what God can actually do. We feel the need to explain to the God of all creation, the omnipotent, omnipresent, omniscient God information of which He is already well aware. Whereas what we read in the Gospels is, when the disciples came to Yeshua and said, "Hey, why couldn't we do this?" Yeshua's response was, "Because you didn't have enough faith..." He didn't say it was because the person your asking for healing for didn't have enough faith to get up and walk, He said because you with the Dunamis power of the Holy Spirit didn't have enough faith.

When we look at Yeshua and the disciples throughout the Gospels and Acts, as we saw with Peter who proclaimed, "Silver and gold I do not have but what I do have I give to you, get up and walk!" they operated in great faith in the Ruach. Peter didn't wait around to see what would happen after he declared healing over the guy, unsure of whether it would work or not. He picked the guy up and sent him into the Temple. Yeshua said when the Comforter (speaking of the Ruach HaKodesh) comes we'd be able to do even greater things than He did. Do you know what Yeshua did when people needed healing? He didn't ask for it or beg for it. He didn't attempt to "*mansplain*" it to God. He declared, "Get up and walk! Open your eyes and see! Lazarus, come out of the grave!" Yeshua also didn't need to show off His miraculous works either. When He healed people, He sent them on their way to do whatever was needed from there. When He healed the man with leprosy, He told them to go to the Temple and do what was needed from there, to report to the Priest for inspection.

People saw what God was doing through the mantle of the Ruach HaKodesh on them and, unlike with Elijah and Elisha, people were bringing all who were sick or tormented to the streets hoping that maybe even Peter's shadow might fall on them and they'd be healed. This wasn't because they thought Peter could perform some sort of magic, but rather people could see the Presence of God upon him. Later in the Brit Chadashah we read of similar occurrences with Paul as well. These are such powerful examples of walking fervently and faithfully in the mantle of the Ruach, and when we live like this people see the Shechinah, the divine presence of God in us, and lives will be changed.

Notice that in these situations, Paul didn't tell people to grab his coat or handkerchief, notice Peter didn't ask people to lay their sick at his feet. They saw God in these men and they wanted to see what God could do through these men in their lives. And the text here says, "**Crowds were also gathering from the towns around Jerusalem, bringing those who were sick or tormented by unclean spirits, and they were all being healed.**" Peter didn't tell God these folks' problems, or what the doctors said, or how many lives would be affected if they died... Peter simply let God work through him faithfully. In the same way, the Spirit of God flows in you and I as believers in Messiah for HIS purposes—the question is are we going to walk in faith in the power of the mantle of the Ruach HaKodesh that is upon us? Are we going to live faithfully in what the Lord says He can and will do in and through our lives?

In Acts 7 we read of another powerful example of operating in the Presence of the Lord in Stephen's martyrdom. This is one of my all-time favorite biblical narratives. Stephen was given a chance to testify on his own behalf while he was staring down guys who had stones in hand, ready to kill him. He had the opportunity to say or do whatever it took to get out of this situation...

However, the dunamis power was so intense upon him that when he began to speak, he started all the way back at the beginning of God's plan for redemption and he preached the message of Salvation—what Yeshua came to do and why. Stephen wasn't afraid to die, and in faithfulness to the mantle of the Holy Spirit upon him, he preached with might, with power, and with authority (just as he knew from the example of Yeshua). The outcome was that the man who gave the final approval for Stephen's stoning was none other than *Rav Sha'ul* (Paul). Two chapters later, we see Paul's miraculous encounter with the divine Presence of HaShem and his coming to faith in Yeshua as the promised Jewish Messiah. I believe that the authority of the Ruach that was upon Stephen as he preached his final Gospel message softened the stiff-necked heart of Paul in preparation for what God had planned two chapters later.

CHAPTER 25

As we read through the book of Acts, we see events like what happened at the Temple on Shavuot in Acts 2 when the Ruach HaKodesh was poured out in a huge event, or we see the similar circumstances of the outpouring of the Ruach at Cornelius' house in Acts 10. We presume this is the way it must always happen. We think it must be this major downpour, flood of the Spirit of God event. However, if we look at Scripture, everything we've looked at up to this point, the mantle of the Ruach is imparted primarily from person to person. Before Acts 2 it was imparted for specific individuals at specific times for specific purposes, but Acts 2 changed everything and that is no longer the case. But the Ruach is still transferred or imparted in the same way, but now made available for all, and it is our job to impart that mantle of the Ruach on others.

If we go to Acts 8 beginning with verse 4: *4 Now those who had been scattered went around proclaiming the Word. 5 Philip went down to the main city of Samaria and proclaimed the Messiah to them. 6 The crowds were paying close attention to what Philip was saying—as they both heard and saw the signs that he was doing. 7 For unclean spirits were coming out of many who were plagued, shrieking with a loud voice. Many paralyzed and crippled were healed also. 8 So there was great joy in that city. 9 Now a man named Simon had been practicing magic in the city and astonishing the people of Samaria, saying he was someone great. 10 They all were paying special attention to him, saying, "This man is the power of God that is called 'Great.'"*

Notice how, unlike with everyone else, the people around Simon see what he is doing and they say, "This man is the power of God that is called 'Great.'" They didn't simply give glory to God. They didn't say God's great glory is in this man. They immediately idolized the man.

We continue with verse 11: *11 And they kept paying attention to him, because for a long time he had astonished them with his magical arts. 12 But when they believed Philip proclaiming the Good News about the kingdom of God and the name of Messiah Yeshua, both men and women were immersed. 13 Even Simon himself believed; and after being immersed, he continued with Philip. And when he saw signs and great miracles happening, he was continually amazed. 14 Now when the emissaries in Jerusalem heard that Samaria had accepted the message of God, they sent Peter and John to them. 15 They came down and prayed for them to receive the Ruach ha-Kodesh. 16 For He had not yet come upon them; they had only been immersed in the name of the Lord Yeshua. 17 Then they began laying their hands on them, and they were receiving the Ruach ha-Kodesh.*

It wasn't a repeat of this mass outpouring as seen in Acts 2 and Acts 10. Instead, the disciples came down and laid hands on them and there was a transference of the mantle of the Ruach HaKodesh that was placed upon them. There was a literal immersion of the Ruach that they experienced through the laying on of hands.

We move forward to Act 9:17 after Paul becomes a believer: *17 So Ananias left and entered into the house. Laying hands on Saul, he said, "Brother Saul, the Lord—Yeshua, the One who appeared to you on the road by which you were coming—has sent me, so that you might regain your sight and be filled with the Ruach ha-Kodesh."* He imparted the Ruach HaKodesh upon Paul through the laying on of hands. Paul just had this massive experience, this intense encounter with

Yeshua. If it were God's intention for the Ruach to always fall in an Acts 2 sort of event, do you not think God could have done so for Paul already? But instead, the Ruach was imparted to Paul by Ananias with the laying on of hands.

Acts 18:24: *24 Now a Jewish man named Apollos, a native of Alexandria, came to Ephesus. He was a learned man, well versed in the Scriptures. 25 He had been instructed in the way of the Lord. With a fervent spirit, he was speaking and teaching accurately the facts about Yeshua—while only being acquainted with the immersion of John. 26 This man began speaking out boldly in the synagogue. But when Priscilla and Aquila heard him, they took him aside and explained the way of God more accurately. 27 When Apollos wanted to cross over to Achaia, the brothers encouraged him and wrote to the disciples to welcome him. Upon arrival, he greatly helped those who by grace had believed. 28 For he powerfully refuted the Jewish people in public, demonstrating through the Scriptures that the Messiah was Yeshua.*

19:1 While Apollos was at Corinth, Paul traveled through the upper region and came to Ephesus. He found some disciples 2 and said to them, "Did you receive the Ruach ha-Kodesh when you believed?" They replied to him, "No, we've never even heard that there is a Ruach ha-Kodesh. 3 He said, "Into what were you immersed?" They said, "Into John's immersion." 4 Paul said, "John immersed with an immersion of repentance, telling the people that they should believe in the One coming after him—that is, in Yeshua." 5 When they heard this, they were immersed in the name of the Lord Yeshua. And when Paul laid hands upon them, the Ruach ha-Kodesh came upon them, and they began speaking in tongues and prophesying. In all, there were about twelve men.

We see that there is this biblical precedence in the New Covenant writings of the impartation of the Ruach through the laying on of hands. This is something that can be seen throughout Scriptures. This idea in Hebrew is called *s'micha*, the laying on of hands to impart authority and anointing. I was ordained as a Messianic Jewish rabbi and there was s'micha of anointing and authority that was given in that. In the same way, the impartation of the Ruach HaKodesh should be imparted, it should be a part of the process of making disciples as Yeshua commands us to do in Matthew 28:18-20: *18 And Yeshua came up to them and spoke to them, saying, "All authority in heaven and on earth has been given to Me. 19 Go therefore and make disciples of all nations, immersing them in the name of the Father and the Son and the Ruach ha-Kodesh, 20 teaching them to observe all I have commanded you. And remember! I am with you always, even to the end of the age."* This doesn't mean there are not circumstances and opportunities in which God moves powerfully and the outpouring of His Ruach overcomes a crowd at once. I'm not saying that that is no longer possible. What I am saying, is there is an overwhelming amount of support in Scripture that names impartation through laying on of hands as the way we are supposed to be doing things.

As I said, it should be a part of making disciples, and I'd encourage you, if you feel ill-equipped to lay hands on people and see them filled with the Ruach, then it is time to seek a fresh infilling for yourself so you can impart in others. As followers of Yeshua, we are His representation here on earth to further His Kingdom, and as such, He has told us that we could do even greater things than He did through the Ruach. Part of that "even greater" is not just signs and wonders, but impartation to others. If each and every follower of Messiah were to operate in the fullness of the Ruach at all times, we could truly transform the world. However, I believe far too many are either unsure of the Ruach, afraid of the Ruach or what others may think, or are just closed off to what God wants to do through His Ruach in us. Imagine how much of an impact we could have if we wholeheartedly submitted to the power of the Holy Spirit each and every day!

On the other hand, there are many who make a fool of the Spirit of God by trying to be showmen with it. Ministers swinging their sport coat around overhead and telling people the wind blowing off the coat is the wind of the Spirit coming upon them. Ministers kicking people in the face from the stage to "impart the Holy Spirit" or "to bring healing" and so on. As with most things, something good can easily be taken advantage of and made to seem bad. These are great extremes that I am mentioning here and are by no means the norm, but they do exist. The overwhelming majority of the Body of Messiah has an unhealthy and unbiblical view of the Holy Spirit, are afraid of submitting to the Spirit, or just do not have a solid foundation of what a move of the Holy Spirit looks like, so we don't operate fully in the Spirit and we allow for the extremes to appear as the norm.

God is grace, love, and mercy. He is not vindictive, angry, harsh, or mean (and He never has been, so toss out the false-juxtaposition of the Old Testament God versus the New Testament God). Who do we think we are to go and make a fool of God? Look through the Bible and see if anyone who ever made a fool of God made it out unscathed... We have been given the empowerment of the Holy Spirit, the Dunamis power of the Presence of God in our lives so we can impact the world around us for His Kingdom, not for ours, and certainly not to make a fool of Him. Just like the apostles we read about in the Book of Acts, we are expected by God to fully submit our lives to the leading of the Ruach HaKodesh. The people that wrote the Bible did so at the leading of the Ruach HaKodesh, they laid their lives down to follow His leading. The people who came to the emissaries in the Book of Acts to be healed did so because they could see that the emissaries were completely submitted to the Holy Spirit, they could see the tangible Presence of God upon them, and they came to find Salvation because of it.

As I've mentioned several times in this book already, we now live in what is being called the Post-Truth Era. This is why we have guys pretending to be girls and girls pretending to be guys and no one seems to question it because who are we to tell someone else what their "truth" is? We live in a Post-Truth Era which means I can preach the Gospel all day long, with conviction, gusto and the power of the Ruach HaKodesh speaking through me, but until the people around me see God in me before they hear me speak His Word, they will never be changed. Because as believers, we often don't align our lives with the impartation of the mantle of the Ruach that we've received. So we speak in the Power but we don't live in the Power, and when we don't live in the Power, people are skeptical of our words because they don't see our lives aligning with what we're saying. If we preach against sin while walking in sin, no one around is us going to want to hear what we have to say. If we preach against sin while hiding sin, then we're allowing the darkness to take over. However, John 1 says Yeshua is the Light and the darkness cannot overcome it. So, if there is darkness overcoming in our lives, then maybe we are not as completely devoted to the Light as we think we are.

The real problem in this Post-Truth Era for the Body of Messiah is that, much like the Pharisees, Yeshua verbally wrestled within the Gospels, we try to make sure our external lives are clean-cut "righteous," but we leave our internal lives a complete and total wreck. However, those around us can see right through us... We don't live in a world where just putting on a good show is enough... If we want to see people come to faith in Messiah Yeshua through our lives, we must make sure He is the only thing that is seen when they look at us. We must make sure we are readily and regularly on our knees in repentance and restoration, we must make sure we are allowing the Ruach to continue to hack away areas of our life that are not up to par with the image and likeness in which we are created in, and through the Blood of Messiah, we are recreated in. Because the world around us is hopeless and lost and when they see us talking about godliness through our mouths but living something completely different in our day-to-day lives, then they are not going to truly see God in us. But, if we fully submit to the impartation of the Ruach HaKodesh and walk in the fullness of the Power of God available to us then they will see His tangible Presence in us and they will want His transformative Presence that we have. See, it isn't and shouldn't be about trying to give a Gospel sales pitch to get people to accept Yeshua, they should see that there is something dramatically different about our lives, something they can't help but want in their own lives. And much like Paul after hearing Stephen's bold and faithful proclamation of the Gospel in the face of death itself, when they see the revelation of Yeshua in our lives before them they will be softened in the heart and be open to His Salvation and transformation. But first, we must walk in transformation ourselves.

It doesn't matter how much we speak the Good Word if our lives are not in alignment with it, then in this Post-Truth Era people are going to say, "You talk it, but you're not walking it, and if you're not walking it why should I care? If you don't believe enough in this product you're selling to live by it and use it, then why should I believe in it?" We are sh'lichim (emissaries) and talmidim (disciples) of Yeshua, the sh'lichim and talmidim in Acts operated fully in the Dunamis power of God, even to their death in many cases. But we as believers today, more often than not, are afraid. We don't want to look different. We don't want the world to think we're weird. But guess what, you're weird with or without the Presence of God. Get over it. We all are, which means we have nothing to lose. However, the Kingdom of Messiah has everything to gain if we truly allow the Power of the Holy Spirit to fully and completely overtake our lives.

Let me ask you a question, as a believer filled with the Holy Spirit who has received the promise of Messiah that we could do even greater things than He did when we receive the Holy Spirit, when was the last time you've had people lay their sick at your feet, hoping maybe your shadow might fall on them and they'd be healed? When was the last time that you called someone forth from the grave? When was the last time you proclaimed sight to the blind, hearing to the deaf, or the ability to walk to the lame? When was the last time that we, with every ounce of faith, prayed for someone knowing (not hoping, but knowing) that they were going to be healed? We spend way too much time trying to build up our own faith (which is why Yeshua said, "you of little faith" over and over again). We shouldn't still be simply of little faith 2000 years after the events of the Gospels and Acts.

This is why we don't talk it up anymore when we're asked to pray for healing in our congregation. We don't try to convince ourselves or God of what He is capable of. We don't feel the need to over-communicate to God things He already knows. We simply declare healing in the Name of Yeshua our Messiah. I am trying to walk out what I preach, and I'll admit that (like most of you) I am still not 100% perfect in this area yet, but I am trying to be fully submitted to the Ruach in every circumstance and every situation in my life and ministry. I am willing, and desire greatly, to walk in the Dunamis power of the mantle of the Ruach HaKodesh. I am willing to walk in the indwelling of His Holy Spirit and to allow Him to lead me at all times, to allow Him to speak through me, to allow Him to be seen before me.

One thing to pay attention to in the Book of Acts is that the events we read about, the works of the Ruach didn't necessarily always occur at the Temple or in the synagogue. Do you know where most of them took place? In the streets, in peoples' homes, in the marketplace, in the real world... People were brought into the synagogue for shepherding, to be lead from milk to meat. People come to Salvation because they see and feel the tangible Presence of God in their midst, not because we can present the Roman Road to Salvation. People don't come to faith simply because someone led them in a repeat-after-me prayer while every head was bowed and every eye was closed. This isn't to say that these things can't happen, but we shouldn't rely solely on them, especially considering that if we do, then we aren't being disciples making disciples, we're waiting on our rabbis and pastors to make more disciples. This isn't how it happened in Acts, and it isn't the way it will happen now in the Post-Truth Era. People have to see the Presence of God in us again, we as followers of Yeshua have to know that there is truth in the Dunamis power. We must walk in the mantle of the Holy Spirit in our lives. We have to be overcome by His presence so that people will come to us looking for Messiah. I love when people walk up to me and say, "I knew there was something different about you, I could sense it and I really felt like I had to talk with you." This means they see God in me first, and that's what it's all about.

CHAPTER 26

We have spent a good deal of time in this book leading up to this point discussing a biblical foundation of understanding for the mantle of the Ruach HaKodesh. Now we are going to shift gears a little bit and move from the examples throughout the Tanakh and Brit Chadashah to the application of what we've learned for our lives as believers today. There are few tools for the Body of Messiah more powerful and effective than the Holy Spirit, and truthfully everything we do should be done solely by His leading. So, what exactly would it look like if we walked in the Dunamis power of the Holy Spirit today? Is it possible to see signs and wonders of biblical proportions in our day and age? How would it transform our impact on this world for the Kingdom of Messiah and the reality of *Tikkun Olam* (Healing of the World) if we operated in the Ruach as our spiritual predecessors did in the Bible? Let's find out...

Romans 8:1—*1 Therefore, there is now no condemnation for those who are in Messiah Yeshua. 2 For the law of the Spirit of life in Messiah Yeshua has set you free from the law of sin and death. 3 For what was impossible for the Torah—since it was weakened on account of the flesh—God has done. Sending His own Son in the likeness of sinful flesh and as a sin offering, He condemned sin in the flesh —4 so that the requirement of the Torah might be fulfilled in us, who do not walk according to the flesh but according to the Ruach. 5 For those who live according to the flesh set their minds on the things of the flesh, but those who live according to the Ruach set their minds on the things of the Ruach. 6 For the mindset of the flesh is death, but the mindset of the Ruach is life and shalom. 7 For the mindset of the flesh is hostile toward God, for it does not submit itself to the law of God—for it cannot. 8 So those who are in the flesh cannot please God.*

So here we're seeing that Paul is saying if we walk in the Spirit we will not fulfill the lusts of the flesh. There is a very strong argument, and biblically ample proof, that if we live our lives only in the flesh, then we can only do what the flesh does. We can strive to follow the Torah, we can strive to do what pastors and rabbis tell us is righteous, we can try to live a good believing life, but if it's not in the spirit man lead by the Ruach then we will not succeed. As a matter of fact, this is exactly what Yeshua was referring to in Matthew 5 in dealing with the discussion of murder/hatred and adultery/lust. All four things are dealt with in the Torah so He isn't presenting anything specifically new. However, what He does present is a fresh way to look at living it out as He tells us it is all about the heart. We can go out of our way to not commit murder or adultery, but if we still hate and lust in our hearts then we've done the same thing spiritually. He tells us for every external sin there's an internal sin, and if we allow Him through His Ruach to handle the internal, then the external will never be a problem. This is exactly what Paul is saying here, we must die to the flesh and live by the Ruach only. The Spirit is at war with the flesh, and vice verse. If our mind is set according to the things of the Ruach then we will walk according to the Ruach.

Continuing with verse 9—*9 However, you are not in the flesh but in the Ruach—if indeed the Ruach Elohim dwells in you. Now if anyone does not have the Ruach of Messiah, he does not belong to Him. 10 But if Messiah is in you, though the body is dead because of sin, yet the Spirit is alive because of righteousness. 11 And if the Ruach of the One who raised Yeshua from the dead dwells in you, the One who raised Messiah Yeshua from the dead will also give life to your mortal bodies through His Ruach who dwells in you.*

Think about the power of those words. The same Spirit that raised Yeshua from the dead, the same Spirit that both Yeshua and the disciples walked in and ministered through, is the same Spirit we have readily available to us every single day of our lives. We can emulate Yeshua and His disciples through the Holy Spirit, and this goes far beyond just signs and wonders and things of that nature, this is how we are to live our lives daily to avoid the things of the flesh and to be made continually righteous before the Lord.

Let's move now to Romans 12: *1 I urge you therefore, brothers and sisters, by the mercies of God, to present your bodies as a living sacrifice— holy, acceptable to God—which is your spiritual service. 2 Do not be conformed to this world but be transformed by the renewing of your mind, so that you may discern what is the will of God—what is good and acceptable and perfect.*

How do we discern what the will of God is? By our minds being renewed. How are our minds renewed? By reading the word of God. If you want a new mindset, if you want to walk in the Spirit and not in the lust of the flesh, if you're not reading the Word, it is not going to be possible. The Word brings life, the Word was inspired by the Spirit which brings life, and they come together to give us a Dunamis experience so that we can walk every single day overcoming our own flesh. In the natural, we are our own worst enemies, but if we walk in the Spirit and have the Word of God then we can walk in the mindset of the Kingdom of God and will not strive to fulfill what our flesh wants to do. The reality is, this is a daily choice, we must wake up every morning and decide that we are going to put the Kingdom of God first in our lives, that we are going to be completely submitted to the Ruach HaKodesh. We can't just think we can rely on getting fed enough on Shabbat at synagogue or Sunday morning at church, or a midweek service or Bible study. We must make it a priority to be fed in our daily life by His Word through His Ruach.

2 Do not be conformed to this world but be transformed by the renewing of your mind, so that you may discern what is the will of God—what is good and acceptable and perfect. 3 For through the grace given me, I say to everyone among you not to think more highly of yourself than you ought to think —but to use sound judgment, as God has assigned to each person a measure of faith. 4 For just as we have many parts in one body—and all the parts do not have the same function—5 so we, who are many, are one body in Messiah and everyone parts of one another. 6 We have gifts that differ according to the grace that was given to us—if prophecy, in proportion to our faith; 7 if service, in our serving; or the one who teaches, in his teaching; 8 or the one who exhorts, in his exhortation; the one who gives, in generosity; the one who leads, with diligence; the one who shows mercy, with cheerfulness. 9 Let love be without hypocrisy—detesting what is evil, holding fast to the good. 10 Be tenderly devoted to one another in brotherly love; outdo one another in giving honor. 11 Do not be lagging in zeal; be fervent in spirit. Keep serving the Lord, 12 rejoicing in hope, enduring in distress, persisting in prayer, 13 contributing to the needs of the kedoshim, extending hospitality.

That's going to henge on "*Do not be lagging in zeal, be fervent in the Spirit.*" If we don't live a life that allows the Ruach HaKodesh to lead, guide, and direct us then we will not be successful at following the Kingdom of God. Here's an enlightening way to think of it: we are created in the image and likeness of God and as such we have a body, soul, and spirit. When God breathed His breath into us, we became a living being in body, however, we cannot allow our body to lead our soul. Our body wants to do everything feel-good, our spirit man is like the Holy of Holies, if you will, that not just anyone can see, only God. When the Ruach HaKodesh comes into our lives He splits the veil to our internal Holy of Holies so that we no longer have to live based on the sin nature of the body/flesh. Yeshua bought back that dominion and freedom for us so that we can be lead by the Spirit of God and our soul (mind, will, and emotions) will follow after the Spirit. But if we only live for the flesh then our soul (mind, will, and emotions) will only want to follow after those things. Living our lives walking in the Holy Spirit leads our fullness to walk in righteousness because of the empowering of the Ruach HaKodesh.

When this book concept was developed, it was developed from a Bible study we did at the Messianic synagogue I am the rabbi of in Daphne, AL. The ultimate intention of the study, and the same with the book as a whole, was to bring us to this—application. From here on out, we will be dealing primarily with Pauline Epistles, with a little bit of Hebrews thrown in for fun, for the distinct purpose of application, how do we apply this study of life in the mantle of the Holy Spirit in the world that we live in today? The world around us appears to be completely contrary to what we read about in the Word of God. It is most certainly a different world than it used to be, it is most certainly a different world than it was when I was a kid in the '80s and '90s.

So, as we look at the world around us, we must cleave to a very specific reality: the Word of God says that the darkness cannot overcome the Light, that the Light will drive out the darkness. You and I have been given the empowerment of the Holy Spirit to carry the Light of Messiah in this world. As we spoke of previously, we see this reality of a calling from the Lord to love people, to impact their lives. Romans 12:20-21 says *21*

Rather, "If your enemy is hungry, feed him; if he is thirsty, give him a drink. For by doing so you will heap coals of fire upon his head." 21 Do not be overcome by evil, but overcome evil with good. This is a quote directly from Proverbs 25:21-22, and we can understand this verse in light of the words of John 1 like this, "Do not let the Light within you be overcome by the darkness of this world, but instead overcome the darkness of this world with the Light that is in you." This is the distinct purpose for our existence as followers of Messiah, to shine the Light of Messiah.

This is an overwhelming calling that is seen throughout the Bible. Let's take a moment to look at what Isaiah 42 says— *1 Behold My servant, whom I uphold. My Chosen One, in whom My soul delights. I have put My Ruach on Him, He will bring justice to the nations. 2 He will not cry out or raise His voice, or make His voice heard in the street. 3 A bruised reed He will not break. A smoldering wick He will not snuff out. He will faithfully bring forth justice. 4 He will not be disheartened or crushed until He establishes justice on earth. The islands will wait for His Torah. 5 Thus says God, Adonai, who created the heavens and stretched them out, who spread out the earth and what comes from it, who gives breath to the people on it, and Ruach to those who walk in it—6 "I, Adonai, called You in righteousness I will take hold of Your hand, I will keep You and give You as a covenant to the people, as a light to the nations, 7 by opening blind eyes, bringing prisoners out of the dungeon, and those sitting in darkness out of the prison house.*

Here we see the prophet Isaiah speaking of the future coming of Messiah who He says would be a light to the nations. He says through the Ruach upon Him He will bring justice to the nations, He will open the eyes of the blind, he will set free the prisoners, and give light to those in darkness. This is an amazing reality of the work of Mashiach, and it is exactly what He did and continues to do today for those who call upon His name. But, the idea goes even deeper as we take into consideration the fact that we are called to emulate Yeshua and His Light should dwell within us. As such, we should be continuing the work of the Kingdom of Mashiach by serving in His Ruach in the same fashion, carrying His Light to the nations. This is the exact purpose for His placing His Ruach within us.

CHAPTER 27

As we talk about how to apply the reality of the Holy Spirit biblically in our lives today, we must begin to look at how the Spirit works within us today. In other words, we are going to look at the Gifts of the Holy Spirit, so let's look at 1 Corinthians 12–*1 Now concerning spiritual gifts, brothers and sisters, I do not want you to be ignorant. 2 You know that when you were pagans, you were enticed by idols that cannot speak, and you got led astray. 3 Therefore I make known to you that no one speaking by the Ruach Elohim says, "Yeshua be cursed," and no one can say, "Yeshua is Lord," except by the Ruach ha-Kodesh. 4 Now there are various kinds of gifts, but the same Ruach. 5 There are various kinds of service, but the same Lord. 6 There are various kinds of working, but the same God who works all things in all people. 7 But to each person is given the manifestation of the Ruach for the benefit of all.*

In other words, there are numerous ways that the Ruach HaKodesh may operate in our lives, but there is only one Ruach. It doesn't matter how many different ways the Spirit uses us, or how many or what kind of gifts He bestows upon us, there is only ONE Spirit. Along with that, His Ruach in us is not for the benefit of simply us, or simply the Body of Messiah, but the benefit of ALL. It isn't about my kingdom, or your kingdom, or the kingdom of whatever televangelists... It is about Messiah's Kingdom, and Messiah's Kingdom alone, and when His Ruach operates within us it is for the furthering of His Kingdom (as we see in Acts 2 with thousands coming to faith in one day).

8 For to one is given through the Ruach a word of wisdom, to another a word of knowledge according to the same Ruach, 9 to another faith by the same Ruach, to another gifts of healings by the one Ruach, 10 to another workings of miracles, to another prophecy, to another discerning of spirits, to another different kinds of tongues, to another the interpretation of tongues. 11 But one and the same Ruach activates all these things, distributing to each person individually as He wills. 12 For just as the body is one and has many parts, and all the parts of the body—though many—are one body, so also is Messiah. 13 For in one Ruach we were all immersed into one body—whether Jewish or Greek, slave or free—and all were made to drink of one Ruach.

Again, we see Paul using the same imagery Yeshua speaks of when he talks about the Ruach HaKodesh being the Mayim Chayim (Living Waters). Yeshua says, "If you asked me to drink I would have given you the Waters of Life that will never run dry."

27 Now you are the body of Messiah, and members individually. 28 God has put into His community first emissaries, second prophets, third teachers, then miracles, then healings, helps, leadership, various kinds of tongues. 29 All are not emissaries, are they? All are not prophets, are they? All are not teachers, are they? All do not work miracles, do they? 30 All do not have gifts of healing, do they? All do not speak in tongues, do they? All do not interpret, do they? 31 But earnestly desire the greater gifts.

There's a whole segment of the Body of Messiah that says, "'If you are saved and filled with the Holy Spirit, then the Gift of Tongues is the absolute evidence. If you do not speak in tongues then you're not really saved or you're not really filled with the Holy Spirit." However, we see here in Paul's own words written by the inspiration of the Holy Spirit that this just isn't true or biblical. It doesn't matter how we try to make it work or how we try to force

236

it into our theology because that's what we've always been taught, it isn't in alignment with the Word of God. Paul is referencing Moses in the account of the 70 elders that we discussed early in this book when he says, "I wish that all could do this, but they don't, Paul is alluding to Moses' words here.

Paul says not all are going to speak in tongues, not all are going to prophesy, not all are going to heal, etc... But to each is given whatever manifestation for His purposes and together we all work united in the Ruach for the Kingdom of God. The problem is, we want to pick and choose what we think is best for us. But, are we really wanting to do the work of God if we're telling Him what we want Him to do through us? Is this following God's lead, or are we telling Him how we want Him to lead us? Humility is necessary for us to truly see the fullness of what the Ruach wants to do through us.

Now before we go any further I also want to take the time to say that I do not believe that the list we read here in 1 Corinthians 12 is a complete list. I think it is meant to be a concise list, a shortened list giving a lot of information. But, I don't think that this is an exhaustive list of all the gifts of the Ruach. I think it is a hint at some of the things God can and wants to do in us through His Ruach, but I have a feeling there are a lot more ways His Spirit might move upon us.

Let's look back again at Romans 12—*4 For just as we have many parts in one body—and all the parts do not have the same function— 5 so we, who are many, are one body in Messiah and everyone parts of one another. 6 We have gifts that differ according to the grace that was given to us—if prophecy, in proportion to our faith; 7 if service, in our serving; or the one who teaches, in his teaching; 8 or the one who exhorts, in his exhortation; the one who gives, in generosity; the one who leads, with diligence; the one who shows mercy, with cheerfulness.*

He then goes on in verse 9-16 to express how we are to live those out. But if you pay close attention, you'll notice Paul mentions things in Romans 12 that he calls gifts that he doesn't mention in 1 Corinthians 12. I think this shows us that neither of these lists are meant to be an end-all-be-all list of the Gifts of the Holy Spirit, but instead to be a little taste of something to get our brains working to recognize God's move in our lives. The reality is that if the Spirit of God is moving in our lives, He may lead us in several different directions. He may use us in one situation for a specific purpose in a specific time with the gift of interpretation of tongues, and later on, we may be moved upon with the gift of healing. I honestly believe that what Paul is getting at is that the Holy Spirit is going to do through us what the Holy Spirit needs to do in whatever situation He places us in. It is our responsibility to be humble enough to allow Him to move as He sees fit and not to try and tell Him what He's going to do. One of the main things I am trying to present here is an application of holy submission to the mantle of the Ruach HaKodesh. We have to be willing to follow His lead however He chooses to use us.

Back to 1 Corinthians we continue with the end of chapter 12 and move directly into 13–*31 But earnestly desire the greater gifts. And still I show you a far better way: 1 If I speak with the tongues of men and of angels but have not love, I have become a noisy gong or a clanging cymbal. 2 If I have the gift of prophecy and know all mysteries and all knowledge, and if I have all faith so as to remove mountains but have not love, I am nothing. 3 If I give away all that I own and if I hand over my body so I might boast but have not love, I gain nothing.*

Paul says the greatest of all the available gifts of the Ruach is love. I have been in environments where I've met people who try to speak in tongues like it's their job, but they are as mean and angry as anyone I've ever seen in my life. There's a certain point at which we've got to truly run our hearts and our lives as believers through a diagnostics check to determine if we are presenting the message of Messiah in the right way. The truth is, if we're honest with ourselves, we've all been that person in one way or another. We've all been the person who prays for healing or prophesies, or whatever, one minute and the next we're flipping off the driver who just cut us off on the freeway... But is this how God would want us to present Him? Is this the best revelation of His love we have to offer...?

4 Love is patient, love is kind, it does not envy, it does not brag, it is not puffed up, 5 it does not behave inappropriately, it does not seek its own way, it is not provoked, it keeps no account of wrong, 6 it does not rejoice over injustice but rejoices in the truth; 7 it bears all things, it believes all things, it hopes all things, it endures all things. 8 Love never fails—but where there are prophecies, they will pass away; where there are tongues, they will cease; where there is knowledge, it will pass away. 9 For we know in part and we prophesy in part; 10 but when that which is perfect has come, then that which is partial will pass away. 11 When I was a child, I spoke like a child, I thought like a child, I reasoned like a child. When I became a man, I put away childish things. 12 For now we see in a mirror dimly, but then face to face. Now I know in part, but then I will know fully, even as I have been fully known. 13 But now these three remain—faith, hope, and love. And the greatest of these is love.

So what is the ultimate gift of the Spirit? What is the only gift we know for a fact we should all be operating in? LOVE! How do we know this, aside from what we read here? Through Yeshua's response when asked what is the most important commandment, *"Love the Lord your God with all your heart, soul and strength, and love your neighbor as yourself.*" What is the greatest gift of the Spirit? LOVE! How should any of the other gifts be manifested in our lives? Through love first. Love predicates it all. If we're not operating in the gifts of the Spirit, if we're not operating in the leading of the Spirit, if we're not operating in the mantle of the Spirit with love predicating all gifts (prepare for a bold statement here) then we're not operating in the Ruach, at least not in the Ruach Elohim.

It is important that we understand that there must be love in our hearts and lives if the Ruach is moving in us. When His Ruach overcomes us it should be the love of God overcoming us and flowing through us and everything else flows from that. See, when we read through the Torah and the Gospels and we see the commands to take care of the sick, the orphaned, the widowed, the foreigner, and so on, these are works of love. These are things that should, in my opinion, far outweigh the gifts that are often more desired by believers. Acts and services of love should be something we all are led into through the Spirit of God, and it is through this love that we will find ourselves able to uphold these social justice commands. Not out of obligation, out of love, specifically the love of God flowing through us.

Let's move on now to 2 Corinthians 10—*1 Now I, Paul, appeal myself to you by the meekness and gentleness of Messiah—I who am humble when face to face with you, but bold toward you when far away. 2 I beg of you that when I am present I won't need to be bold with the courage I consider showing against some who judge us as walking in the flesh. 3 For though we walk in the flesh, we do not wage war according to the flesh. 4 For the weapons of our warfare are not fleshly but powerful through God for the tearing down of strongholds.*

Powerful through God for what...? Tearing down strongholds. Again we hover back around to power, dominion, and authority over things of this world. Strongholds of the enemy are things of this world, not things of God. "Your will be done on earth as it is in Heaven," that is what we are aiming for, God's will on earth, not the enemy's.

We are tearing down false arguments 5 and every high-minded thing that exalts itself against the knowledge of God. We are taking every thought captive to the obedience of Messiah— 6 ready to punish all disobedience, whenever your obedience is complete. 7 Look at what is before your eyes. If anyone is confident in himself that he belongs to Messiah, let him reconsider that just as he belongs to Messiah, so also do we. 8 For even if I boast a little more about our authority—which the Lord gave for building you up and not for tearing you down—I will not be put to shame. 9 Not that I would try to terrify you by my letters— 10 for they say, "His letters are weighty and strong, but his presence in person is weak and his speech of no account." 11 Let such a person consider this, that what we are in word through letters when we are absent, we also are in action when we are present. 12 For we do not dare to classify or compare ourselves with some of those who commend themselves. But when they measure themselves by themselves and compare themselves with themselves, they have no understanding. 13 But we will not boast beyond limits, but within the limits of the area that God has assigned to us—to reach even as far as you. 14 We are not extending ourselves too far, as if we did not reach you—for we did come even as far as to you with the Good News of Messiah. 15 Neither are we boasting beyond limits based on the labors of others, but we have hope while your faith is growing for our area among you to be greatly enlarged— 16 so that we may proclaim the Good News even to regions beyond you, not boasting about what has been accomplished in another's area. 17 But "let him who boasts boast in the Lord." 18 For it is not the one who commends himself who is approved, but the one whom the Lord commends.

Remember, there will be those who stand before the Judgement Throne of HaShem who will hear Him say, "Get away from me for I've never known you, you workers of iniquity..." And they'll say to Him, "But Lord, haven't I done this and that and the other in Your Name?" It's not about boasting of what we have done, it is about boasting in the Lord.

We live in a Post-Truth Era, I don't care how much you preach the Gospel if the Gospel is not alive in your life, then the words coming out of your mouth are useless. The power and authority of the Ruach HaKodesh is necessary for our lives, the Light of the Presence of Messiah is necessary for people to hear the Gospel coming from us and believe it. They must see the revelation of the Gospel in our lives before they ever hear us talking about it. The most important way for this to occur is through what Paul called the greatest gift— LOVE.

It begins with love... It's not about tearing people down or bashing people, it's not blowing up abortion clinics or beating up homosexuals. It is not trying to bash people over the head with our idea of morality or to shove them down someone's throat. It is about letting the love of God shine through our lives. It's about letting the mantle of the Ruach HaKodesh radiate so feverishly off of our hearts and lives that people are drawn to the work of God in our lives. Not to our words, or our actions, or our charisma, or whatever else... But to the tangible Presence of the Lord in our lives.

The truth is, part of fulfilling what Paul is saying here is to tear down the false arguments and teachings throughout the Body of Messiah about what a move of the Spirit of God looks like. For far too long we have allowed bad doctrine and theology to permeate the Body of Messiah, we've allowed it to divide and conquer the Body of Messiah. It is time we humble ourselves and allow the Ruach to regain the ground that is rightfully His and allow Him to bring back into the Body one thing that is so terribly missing... unity, particularly unity in the love of Messiah. And the reality is, we can read over and over again throughout Paul's writings, his efforts to clean up and rid the Body of Messiah of false teachings that cause division, false teachings that break down the love of Messiah among us. Maybe we should consider picking up where Paul left off...

Another important facet of what we see in 2 Corinthians that impacts how the Ruach can work in us is obedience. Obedience to humbly following the leading of the Ruach HaKodesh by faith. When talking about the gifts of the Spirit we recognize there will likely be predominate gifts in people's lives, so when Paul says one may speak in tongues while another may prophesy, we see this idea revealed. However, from time to time the Lord may use a gift that is not primary in our life, and if we're willing to be obedient in faith, then we can also be used in other ways. Some people may say, I only operate in tongues or prophecy, but we really cannot do this... In doing so we are limiting our God who is limitless. In attempting to limit God, we can unintentionally rob someone else of a blessing in their lives, and in turn (albeit it is not all about ourselves) we will rob ourselves of His blessing too.

CHAPTER 28

With that idea of unity prevailing nearly any discussion of the Body of Messiah, we're going to now take a look at Ephesians 4—*1 Therefore I, a prisoner for the Lord, urge you to walk in a manner worthy of the calling to which you were called— 2 with complete humility and gentleness, with patience, putting up with one another in love, 3 making every effort to keep the unity of the Ruach in the bond of shalom.*

Unity in the Spirit is not simply caught, it is kept. There may be people in the Body and in our own congregations whose personalities may not necessarily naturally mesh well with mine, however, if we strive for the unity of the Spirit and the bond of peace and we belong to Yeshua, then we belong together. God can use us mightily through the power of His Ruach HaKodesh together in ministry despite our differences. We may worship regularly with people who on any given day outside of the congregation we may not have gone out of our way to get to know, but there is a common denominator between us that is powerful—Yeshua and His Ruach—and that can and will unite us. Whereas division is not of the Lord but is solely of the enemy. Division is the enemy's greatest tool against the Body of Messiah. Yeshua said the world would know who sent Him through the unity of His followers, yet the Body is fractured and divided... If division is not of God, then who does the world see in our division?

4 There is one body and one Ruach, just as you also were called in one hope of your calling; 5 one Lord, one faith, one immersion; 6 one God and Father of all, who is over all and through all and in all. 7 But to each one of us grace was given in keeping with the measure of Messiah's gift. 8

Therefore it says, "When He went up on high, He led captive a troop of captives and gave gifts to his people."

Notice how consistent Paul is in his teaching... He continuously taught one God, one faith, one Ruach, one immersion. Notice how the good Jewish believer taught so regularly the very central foundation of Jewish faith from Deuteronomy 6:4–*Hear O Israel, the Lord your God the Lord is one.*

9 Now what does "He went up" mean, except that He first went down to the lower regions of the earth? 10 The One who came down is the same One who went up far above all the heavens, in order to fill all things.

Yeshua provided redemption for us! Let that sink in for a moment... The God of all creation came a little lower than the angels to redeem us! He went to hell and took the dominion and authority from the enemy that we had given over to him, and he brought those back to us. And once again Yeshua gave that dominion and authority back over to us through the Ruach HaKodesh. So as we walk in the power of the Ruach HaKodesh we can truly have the dominion and authority over things of this world and live in freedom. Where the Spirit of the Lord is there is FREEDOM!

He has given us the freedom to not be angry. He has given us the freedom to not be hateful. He has given us the freedom to not be lustful. He has given us the freedom to not be covetous. He has given us the freedom to not be bound to the ways of the flesh. He has given us the freedom to love as He has loved us. But, He has not given us the freedom to simply live our lives however we want with zero consequences.

11 He Himself gave some to be emissaries, some as prophets, some as proclaimers of the Good News, and some as shepherds and teachers— 12 to equip the kedoshim for the work of service, for building up the body of Messiah. 13 This will continue until we all come to the unity of the faith and of the knowledge of Ben-Elohim—to mature adulthood, to the measure of the stature of Messiah's fullness. 14 As a result, we are no longer to be like children, tossed around by the waves and blown all over by every wind of teaching, by the trickery of men with cunning in deceitful scheming. 15 Instead, speaking the truth in love, we are to grow up in all ways into Messiah, who is the Head. 16 From Him the whole body is fitted and held together by every supporting ligament. The proper working of each individual part produces the body's growth, for building itself up in love.

Paul is still talking about the works of the Holy Spirit. Why was the Ruach given? So we could live in unity and shalom. Why are these things important? So we can build one another up and through that build up the Kingdom of Messiah here on earth.

Yeshua calls us to emulate Him, He calls us to live like Him, to serve like Him, to love like Him. It is through the Ruach that we can mature into those areas of emulation of Messiah to bring us "to the measure of the stature of Messiah's fullness." We cannot truly emulate Messiah, we cannot truly live like Messiah if we are not truly filled with the same Holy Spirit that Messiah operated in. As believers in Messiah, the Body of Messiah as a whole is called to this very reality, how then are we to live up to this calling without humble submission to His Spirit? How are we to be truly united in the Spirit when so many either deny the modern activity of the Spirit or cleave to bad theology about how the Spirit works in our lives?

The Ruach is for all of us who are washed in the Blood of the Lamb. The Ruach overcame our predecessors like Moses and Joshua, Samuel and David, Elijah and Elisha, the mantle was passed down from person to person. Ultimately we are brought to the life of Yeshua through whom the mantle of the Holy Spirit was made available to all, not just one or two at a time, but to all who would believe and be made righteous by the Blood of the Lamb. He gave us His Ruach to come to a fullness of mature adulthood in the measure of stature in Messiah's fullness.

Ephesians 6:10–*10 Finally, be strong in the Lord and in His mighty power. 11 Put on the full armor of God, so that you are able to stand against the schemes of the devil. 12 For our struggle is not against flesh and blood, but against the rulers, against the powers, against the worldly forces of this darkness, and against the spiritual forces of wickedness in the heavenly places. 13 Therefore, take up the full armor of God, so that you may be able to resist when the times are evil, and after you have done everything, to stand firm. 14 Stand firm then! Buckle the belt of truth around your waist, and put on the breastplate of righteousness. 15 Strap up your feet in readiness with the Good News of shalom. 16 Above all, take up the shield of faith with which you will be able to extinguish all the flaming arrows of the evil one. 17 And take the helmet of salvation and the sword of the Spirit, which is the word of God. 18 Pray in the Ruach on every occasion, with all kinds of prayers and requests. With this in mind, keep alert with perseverance and supplication for all the kedoshim.*

We see here that we have been given weapons and defenses through the Ruach HaKodesh. The Word of God is one of the most important, most powerful, and most underused weapons we have against the wages of war thrust at us from the enemy. When Yeshua was tempted by the enemy in Matthew 4 and Luke 4, what was the weapon He used against the enemy? The Word of God. The Bible has got to be an integral part of our lives, day in and day out. I have often heard people ask how are they to know if they are hearing the voice of God and I ask them are they in the Bible regularly... If we aren't practicing listening and hearing His Word then how are we ever going to know His voice? Hebrews 4:12 says the Word of God is sharp, it is powerful, it divides between bone and marrow, between flesh and spirit. The Holy Spirit will guide us into all truth and He will teach us how to use the tools of warfare that have been given to us, because this war we are facing is a war of that is not of flesh and bone, but of powers and principalities. It is not a war we can wage, much less win, on our own.

Interestingly enough, this passage from Ephesians reminds me of the days of Ezra and Nehemiah. As they were rebuilding the walls of Jerusalem and the Temple, how were they working? They were building with one hand and had a sword in the other, at all times alert and prepared to defend what the Lord was doing in this work of restoration. They were following the leading of the Ruach HaKodesh. Think about it, they were rebuilding the Temple and the walls of the Holy City. Of course, the Spirit of God was upon them as it was with Bezalel and Oholiab as they were building the Tabernacle. The Spirit of God was upon them, and as they were following His lead in a work of great restoration, they had on the full armor of God literally and figuratively. And they were willing to do whatever was necessary, even laying down their own lives if it came down to it, to see the will of God become a reality. Are you willing to do whatever it takes? Are you willing to walk in the fullness of the mantle of the Ruach as our spiritual predecessors did?

Having a stone or trowel in one hand and a sword in the other is a perfect type and shadow, a picture of what we are to do today as believers in Messiah. We are to have the Sword of the Spirit in one hand while building up the walls with the other. I'm not talking about walls of separation or psychological walls and barriers that divide.

I'm talking about building the foundation of faith in the Body of Messiah, line upon line and precept upon precept of the Word of God that is going to build up the defenses against the enemy in our lives, in our families, in our congregations, and in the Body of Messiah. Because the enemy is always trying to come in to steal, kill, and destroy.

Moving forward now to 2 Timothy 1, this is written by Paul to a young Timothy who is fresh in ministry–*6 For this reason I remind you to fan into flame the gift of God, which is in you through the laying on of my hands. 7 For God has not given us a spirit of timidity but of power and love and self-discipline... 13 Keep the standard of sound words you have heard from me, in the faithfulness and love that are in Messiah Yeshua. 14 Guard the good that has been entrusted to you, through the Ruach ha-Kodesh who dwells in us.*

Paul reminds Timothy that we can encourage ourselves in the Lord. There are situations that arise in our lives and our ministries in which it is absolutely necessary that we learn to encourage ourselves, or else we may find ourselves spiraling out of control right into the enemy's trap of deceit, or unforgiveness, or anger, or disbelief, or any number of things. Notice here Paul says to continue to fan the flame of the gift of God which was imparted through the laying on of hands. What gift is he speaking of here? The Ruach HaKodesh! He is reminding Timothy, and you and I today, that we must continue to stoke the fires of the Holy Spirit in our lives. How do we do this? Through the consistent study of the Word, through continual prayer and worship, through fasting, through corporate worship.

I believe the New Testament command to not forsake the assembly is one of the most important things we can do outside of being in the Word daily. Why? Because we are called to be united in the Spirit. "There is a growing voice in the Body today that says that we don't need to gather corporately anymore because we can just worship whenever we want in our homes, in our cars or wherever. We don't need the building to be able to worship." There is truth in these sentiments and we should be in worship daily on our own, but it is in corporate worship that we grow in unity and that we see the fullness of the various parts of the Body come together as one. We also find great encouragement in corporate worship as well as opportunities to encourage others who may be in need.

I love the wording Paul uses in writing to Timothy here, *For God has not given us a spirit of timidity but of power and love and self-discipline...* Let us not become timid. The world around us is only growing darker and darker and it is more important now than ever before for us to shine the Light that can only be found in Messiah Yeshua. So we must continue to keep the fire of the Spirit of God stoked and burning no matter what is going on around us.

I think it's interesting how often we see the image of fire in Scripture as we see discussion of the Holy Spirit. Imagine you're kindling a fire and as it starts to ignite, you begin to fan that flame to make it grow larger and more stable. If you fan that flame long enough, it becomes an all-consuming fire and that is exactly what His Ruach is, an all-consuming fire, if you fan that flame we allow Him to become completely consuming of our lives. Paul says to fan the flame of the gift of God, to fan or stoke the fire of the Holy Spirit in our life. How exactly do we do that? Paul goes on to say that it is through power, love, and self-discipline, but what does that look like? It is through time in the Word, time in prayer, time in fellowship and communion with the Lord, it is through time in fellowship and communion with other believers, it is through fasting, it is through time of just shutting up and letting the Spirit of the Lord move and come over us.

He goes on to say, "which is in you through the laying on of hands." Again we see, as we discussed previously, the idea of the Ruach's impartation primarily through the laying on of hands. As said before, this is not to discount the reality that there absolutely can be a divine and miraculous outpouring like seen in Acts 2 and Acts 10 today if God so desires, but predominately in Scripture what we see is a literal laying on of hands for the impartation of the power and mantle of the Holy Spirit.

As we continue in this discussion let's take a look at Hebrews 12–*18 For you have not come to a mountain that can be touched, and to a blazing fire, and to darkness and gloom and storm, 19 and to the blast of a shofar and a voice whose words made those who heard it beg that not another word be spoken to them. 20 For they could not bear what was commanded: "If even an animal touches the mountain, it shall be stoned." 21 So terrifying was the sight that Moses said, "I am quaking with fear."*

In other words, you have not come to Mount Sinai with the heart of the first generation of Israel out of slavery in Egypt, timid and quaking in fear at the Presence and Voice of the Lord.

22 But you have come to Mount Zion—to the city of the living God, the heavenly Jerusalem, and to myriads of angels, a joyous gathering, 23 and to the assembly of the firstborn who are written in a scroll in heaven, and to God the Judge of all, and to the spirits of the righteous ones made perfect, 24 and to Yeshua, the Mediator of a new covenant, and to the sprinkled blood that speaks of something better than the blood of Abel. 25 See to it that you do not refuse the One who is speaking! For if they did not escape when they refused the One who was warning them on earth, much less will we escape if we reject the One who warns us from heaven. 26 His voice shook the earth then, but now He has promised, saying, "Yet once more I will shake not only the earth, but also the heavens." 27 Now this phrase, "Yet once more," shows the removal of those things that are shaken—that is, created things—so that what cannot be shaken may remain. 28 Therefore, since we are receiving a kingdom that cannot be shaken, let us show gratitude—through this we may offer worship in a manner pleasing to God, with reverence and awe. 29 For our God is a consuming fire.

I want you to understand something, when we brought sacrifices to the Tabernacle and Temple there was reverence and awe. Think about it, the nation of Israel saw the tangible Presence of the Lord resting upon the mountain, later on, they saw the flame consumer Aaron's sons Nadav and Avihu, they saw the fire come forth from the Face of God and consume the sacrifice upon the altar and ignite the fire which they were commanded to stoke in continuum. The entire nation saw these things occur and they were awestruck. When they approached the Tabernacle or the Temple with their sacrifices there was a reverence and fear in their heart.

Then we recognize a similar reality in Acts 2 as the same all-consuming Fire of the Ruach was witnessed upon those filled with the indwelling of the Ruach HaKodesh. A fire that made it possible for us to recognize that we have not come to a mountain where we are to be timid and afraid, but rather we are at Mount Zion in the Presence of the Lord residing in the Holy Place. And by the all-consuming fire of His Holy Spirit within us, we can boldly enter into His throne room. We no longer have to stand a safe distance away from Mount Sinai, we no longer have to have a barrier of priest camp between us and the Presence of God. We are fully capable, washed in the Blood of the Lamb and empowered by the Fire of the Holy Spirit, to stand before the Lord and speak to Him

252

panim el panim (face to face) as Adonai says He spoke with Moses.

This passage brings my mind back to Paul's words in Romans 12–*1 I urge you therefore, brothers and sisters, by the mercies of God, to present your bodies as a living sacrifice—holy, acceptable to God—which is your spiritual service. 2 Do not be conformed to this world but be transformed by the renewing of your mind, so that you may discern what is the will of God—what is good and acceptable and perfect.*

The author of Hebrews says, "for our God is a consuming fire." I don't know about you, but I think there's something powerful to that concept of an all-consuming fire of the Presence of the Lord. We tend to get this mentality in the Body of Messiah after all these years of us trying to pick apart the Scriptures that we don't like and make it fit into what we want it to say and we make this nice cohesion of whatever we want the Word of God to say to make our lives easier, rather than just digging into the Word of the Lord and seeing what it says for ourselves and living it out fervently. The idea of God being an all-consuming fire is mentioned several times throughout the Bible and it is a concept that is so powerful and necessary for us to walk in. The Presence of God should be, must be, an all-consuming fire in our lives, the Ruach HaKodesh must be at the core of everything we do.

I've been in environments where people say if you don't speak in tongues, or if you don't prophesy, or if you don't heal, or whatever, then you're not really filled with the Ruach. But that is not what the Word of God says... It gets even more complicated when we do see the Lord do things like healing through us and we see things like people getting up and walking, then you go to pray for the next person and they don't get healed. Then we're going to wrestle with thoughts like, "well, was the gift of healing really upon me then..." Of course, it was, because the Lord healed that person. But, what happened to the other? Well, the Lord never says He will heal everyone here on earth. You know why? Because He tells us that (short of Messiah's return beforehand) we are all going to die. We are going to die here on earth because we chose sin over the eternal Presence of God. Just because we've been redeemed for eternity doesn't mean it eliminates the consequences of the actions that we chose to walk in here on earth. But, what it does mean is through that redemption we have eternal life. And through that redemption, we will see the eternal reality of Isaiah 53's Words, "by His stripes we are healed."

So, there may be someone we pray for who doesn't get healed, but we have to rejoice just the same. Because it's not our will be done, it is our desire to see His will be done. It is for His glory and His Kingdom. Who are we to say that the Lord doesn't want to take that person home? Who are we to say that the Lord doesn't have something better for them where they are no longer suffering, not in pain, not getting stabbed with needles or popping pills day in and day out just to "survive"?

Along with that, I've seen people pray for healing, and when it didn't come to pass they accused the person being prayed for of not having enough faith... Who are we to make such judgments and accusations? There's already one accuser of the brethren, the last thing we need is more, or to give him even more ground... But, wake-up call, as we said before, Yeshua said when His disciples weren't able to do something like this it was because *they* didn't have enough faith, not because the person receiving prayer didn't.

CHAPTER 29

The Word of the Lord says His Presence is an all-consuming fire. As we've gone through the Tanakh and the Brit Chadashah looking in-depth at the study of the Holy Spirit, what we see is that everyone who receives the mantle of the Holy Spirit is entirely overcome, overtaken. The Holy Spirit consumes them, it consumes their life, it consumes their hearts, it consumes their thoughts. Look back at Elijah and Elisha, look at David, Look at Jeremiah and Isaiah, it consumed their entire being. Look at Peter and Paul, look at how the Spirit of God moved upon Stephen in such a way that he wasn't even afraid of death. He stared his would be, soon to be killers in the eyes filled with rage and hate and he still shared the truth of the power of the Gospel. Adonai's Ruach, His Presence is all-consuming!

There may come times in our lives where we may be gifted with different manifestations of the Ruach for this purpose or that. We seem to get the idea that there is a necessary separation of gifts of the Spirit and offices of the Spirit (shepherd, teacher, evangelist, etc...). I am, by the gifting of the Ruach HaKodesh, a teacher and shepherd, this is precisely what the Lord has placed me here to do and I give Him my all to do just that by His leading, and I pray that He speaks through me. But, there are also times when He has used me to lay hands on someone for healing and they were healed, there are times when He's used me to speak words of wisdom and knowledge in peoples lives, there are times where He's used me just to be there for someone so they had the Light in their midst so they wouldn't be completely consumed by darkness, just to sit there and carry the suffering with them. There are times when He has used me to (figuratively) smack someone in the back of the head with a wake-up call to their stupidity and selfishness, or to their being completely outside the will of the Lord.

I want to take a moment to bring things back around again to where we began. When we first began this study we were taking a look at Genesis and the fact that God gave mankind dominion, power and authority over things of this world. We know Scripturally that death, despair, sickness, anger, oppression, etc. are all things of this world. They are all things that the enemy brought in, they are not things of heaven. God has dominion over Heaven and has everything under control there and it should be His will be done on earth as it is in heaven. So our purpose is to align heaven and earth, to be submitted to Him so that heaven and earth can be aligned. It is important to realize that when we are filled with the power of the Ruach HaKodesh, as I pray it is upon you as you read through this book, it is for a restoration of our dominion, power, and authority over things of this earth to be restored. That the dunamis power of the Holy Spirit will flow through our lives and unite with others empowered with the Spirit of God to make the Kingdom of God known here on earth.

I have spent most of my life as a believer, I came to faith when I was seven years old, and I have spent most of my life just watching people in the Body of Messiah. I have seen people that feel it necessary to put on a show because they see everyone else, as they perceive it, being moved in the Spirit. When you are moving in the Spirit you know, you don't have to put on a show, and the world around us knows the difference between the real deal and the show, even if they don't personally know the Ruach themselves.

As mentioned before, I do not think the gifts of the Spirit mentioned in 1 Corinthians 12 is an exhaustive list, and I'd hate to be one to limit God's move just because I don't see it listed there. I personally am one that, generally speaking, when the Spirit of God is really moving I find myself mouth shut, quiet, solemn, and overcome by His Presence. When that happens there is nothing I can do but revel in His glory... But, at the same time, I've also seen the Lord use the gift of healing through me, and words of knowledge, among others. I know others who, when the Spirit moves upon them they predominately speak in tongues. I believe our testimony in the Ruach is way more powerful when we give Him the freedom to do whatever He wants in us, after all that is exactly what we were given freedom for in the first place.

Let's take a moment also to discuss the idea of the Gifts of Tongues. There are two different types of tongues that we see biblically. One is for personal edification, and it is between us and God, some might call it their love language or prayer language. And that is not meant for everyone to hear, it is meant for you as the Lord is saying something specifically to you. There are also tongues for the edification of the Body, and that requires interpretation, and if it is spoken aloud and no interpretation occurs, then you are outside the will of God. How do we know which is which? Simple, we submit to the will of the Lord. I truly believe if we wholeheartedly submit ourselves to the Ruach HaKodesh we will not and cannot be outside of the will of the Lord. The same litmus test can be given to all of the gifts of the Spirit. How do we know if a prophecy is from God? The Torah tells us that if it comes true then it was from God. How do we know if it is the Spirit of the Lord moving? If it is in order with how the Bible tells us His Spirit moves then it is the Spirit of the Lord. If it is outside that order, then "get away from Me you workers of iniquity for I have never known you..." "But, haven't we done all these things in Your Name?" "You may have thought you were, but you did it all outside of My will..."

There are a lot of good things that have happened for the wrong reasons. We need to understand as believers empowered by the Ruach HaKodesh that it is our duty to entirely submit our lives to the mantle of the Ruach HaKodesh. That every thought, every word, every action that comes forth from us is solely lead by the will of the Lord. When our lives are lived in such a fashion, then we will know without a doubt that we are moving in the Ruach HaKodesh faithfully.

I truly believe that we are living in the latter days, in the days of the outpouring of the latter rains. I believe it will come forth from the modern Messianic Jewish revival and will impact the Body of Messiah as a whole. Why do I believe that? Because the Bible says that it will return to those it initially started with, that it will return to the Jewish people. And that is exactly what happens in a Messianic Jewish synagogue. As Paul says in Romans 11:15—*15 For if their rejection leads to the reconciliation of the world, what will their acceptance be but life from the dead?* I believe we are a part of this massive end-time revival, and I will point out that there has only ever been one revival and it began in Acts 2 and we're either in it or we're not. I believe that we are part of this, and if we are going to be effective with what God wants to do in our lives, in our communities, in the congregations that He has us in, it is of the utmost importance that we look through the Bible and see the patterns and order in which His Ruach HaKodesh moves and that we live our lives completely submitted to His will in that order. In this, the Light will overcome the darkness, good will overcome evil. Through this, the greatest gift of the Spirit, which is Love, can permeate our very being and impact the lives of those around us every single moment that we breathe the Breath of Life. Because the breath that is in our lungs is not ours to waste and it is important that we are overcome by the all-consuming power of His Ruach HaKodesh so that His breath is used to the fullest in our lives every single day.

DISCUSSION QUESTIONS

Creation is the Foundation (Chapters 1-3)

1. How does the reality that God was already aware of Adam and Eve's sin yet still came to meet with them in the Garden impact your receptivity to grace in your own faith life?
2. How does the idea of Yeshua not being "plan B" due to our sins, but instead being the only plan and all creation being made and restored through Him deepen your faith?
3. Looking at the world around us in the 21st century, discuss ways in which humanity is still falling prey to the enemy's efforts to demolish the image and likeness of God in our lives today?
4. What does Yeshua's interaction with the enemy as seen in Matthew and Luke 3 reveal to us about our ability to overcome temptation? And how does this connect to His lesson to us on prayer in Matthew 6?
5. If dominion and authority over thing of this world has been restored to us in the Holy Spirit, why do we as believers tend to be timid in our prayers for healing and deliverance?

Moses Walking in the Mantle (Chapters 4-5)

1. What are the differences between the individual and corporate experience with the Presence of God in Exodus 3-4 and 19-20? Discuss how these types and shadows can be applied to our experience with HIs Presence as followers of Messiah?
2. Notice how every part of Moses life and past uniquely qualified him for the calling Adonai had placed on his

life. In what ways do you see your life experiences combined with the Holy Spirit empowerment has uniquely qualified you for the calling on your life?

3. Moses' response to the voice of Adonai was a cry from his heart, "*Hineini!* Here I am!" Israel's response to the voice of Adonai was a cry from their heart, "*Kol d'ber Adonai na'aseh.* Everything that Adonai has spoken we will do." How can we model such responses in our own lives in the Body of Messiah today?

4. Moses faced a lot of challenges both before and after God called him to lead Israel, but when he submitted to the anointing of the Holy Spirit he was able to walk faithfully in that calling. The Body of Messiah has a similar calling to Moses, to lead people in the freedom that can only be found in Messiah, as such what do you think are the major hinderances to the Body experiencing and displaying the Power of God today?

The Mantle of the Spirit is Expanded (Chapters 6-8)

1. How often do we find ourselves in a situation where, rather than fully relying on God, we are returning back to our ways, habits, and mindsets of old just as we see with Israel longing for the "ease of life in Egypt" as seen in Numbers 11?

2. Consider the intentional request of Adonai for Moses to bring forth 70 qualified leaders of Israel to serve as under-shepherds in light of Paul's discussion of qualified leaders in the Body of Messiah in 1 Timothy 3. Notice that the most important qualification of these leaders appears to come after their calling, and that is the empowerment of the Mantle of the Holy Spirit. What are your thoughts on the value of not only waiting on the Lord's call for your life, but also on the empowering of the Spirit to move forward in it? And have you modeled this in your own walk with God?

3. Considering the purpose of prophecy is to call people to repentance, do you feel that the role of a prophet has been misused and abused in the Body of Messiah? And if so, what steps do you believe we can take individually and corporately to recalibrate our view and use of prophecy?
4. Look back at Joshua's response of fear and concern when Eldad and Medad began to prophecy in the camps. Was Joshua's fear and concern legitimate and healthy? Do you see similar responses in the Body today when God moves in a dynamic way?
5. Moses says he wished that all would prophecy, Paul says he wished all would speak in tongues, Paul also discusses the gifts of the Spirit and those operating them as different parts of the same body, but that not all are the same part of the body. With these biblical realities in mind, is it healthy for us to assume today that all filled with the Spirit will have the same gift/gifts? Or is there a healthier, more unifying approach?

The Ruach and the Next Generation (Chapters 9-10)

1. How important is the concept of l'dor v'dor (from generation to generation) in sparking a lasting and impacting revival? What role do you see discipleship playing in making that a reality today?
2. How important do you feel faithfulness to the Word of God is in experiencing and walking in the power of the Holy Spirit?
3. The world today is vastly different than that of the days we read of in the Bible, and that we have a much more visible life now with social media and such, and this means a great deal more eyes on the Body of Messiah both corporately and as individuals. Discuss your thoughts on how important it is to maintain a continuity of witness in our discipleship in

the world we live in today? And how do we do this at all times?

4. I'd pose that perhaps one of the biggest reasons we don't see the Power of God in our midst today as we should is because we don't take repentance as serious as we should. Discuss how we can adjust our hearts and mindsets to recognize not only the vital importance of repentance, but also to make it a regular part of our discipleship.

Dos and Don'ts of the Anointing (Chapters 11-13)

1. Considering the circumstances we find Israel in when the prophet Samuel comes into the picture, discuss what you feel caused a lack of vision from God?
2. Discuss the concept of the impartation of the Holy Spirit from one to another through the laying on of hands, as we see with Samuel to Saul and David, and is this something that can and should be modeled in the Body of Messiah today?
3. Notice the drastic difference between man's perspective of what a king should be (Saul) and God's (David). With that in mind, what lesson can we extrapolate from this in our own lives in regards to what we want to do verses aligning ourselves with God's perspective for direction?
4. Also, notice how God makes it a point in Deuteronomy 17 to that Israel would ask for a king so they could be like all the nations around them, and this is exactly what they asked for in 1 Samuel. What does it do to our witness for Yeshua when we are more concerned about looking like the world around us rather than focusing on being led by the Holy Spirit to see heaven and earth align?
5. It is absolutely possible, as we see with Saul and David, for there to be two people with the anointing for the ministry, yet one is the current anointed and

the other is the future anointed. Yet, often we see congregational and ministry splits because the future anointed wants the role sooner than God's timing. How important do you think it is to not only wait on God's timing in His anointing, but also to support the one who is currently operating in the anointing now? In what way do you see humility playing a vital role in this process?

Foreshadowing of Yeshua and His Disciples (Chapters 14-15)

1. Considering we enter the narrative of Elijah and Elisha with the nation of Israel divided into two separate kingdoms, and we are living currently in a time in which the Body of Messiah is divided beyond fragmentation, and Yeshua makes unity a primary focal point of His prayer in 17: How important do you think unity in the Holy Spirit is to the Body experiencing the fullness of revival we are desiring in these last days?

2. One dynamic difference we see between Elijah operating in the Holy Spirit and the Body of Messiah today is that Elijah had absolutely no concern at all about what others may think of him if God moved through him. However, often in the Body today we are scared to death by the thought that other people may think we are weird. How much more impactful for the Kingdom of God could we be if believers stopped worrying about what the world thought of us and only focused on what God thinks of us?

3. Consider Elijah standing in opposition to the prophets of Baal. What can we, as believers in the 21st century, learn from Elijah's boldness in faith and his relentless unwillingness to give the enemy any ground?

4. Notice, as we see with Moses and Joshua, Elijah invested time and energy into mentoring Elisha to follow the call of God in the Holy Spirit. How much more effective do you think the Body could be if we truly took the time to disciple and mentor young believers into their calling, whether that be vocational ministry or marketplace ministry?
5. Elisha ultimately received a double portion of the mantle of the Holy Spirit that was on Elijah, this is a foreshadowing of Yeshua saying through the Holy Spirit we would be able to do even greater things than He did. Do you believe that the Body of Messiah is truly operating in the "double portion" of the Holy Spirit as we see with Elisha? If so, how? And if not, what do you think we could be doing differently individually and corporately?

Yeshua Receives the Impartation (Chapters 16-18)

1. Do you believe it is important for us necessary for us, as believers, to emulate Yeshua in our lives today? And if so, why is it then so foundational for us to grasp Yeshua's walk in the mantle of the Holy Spirit?
2. Notice that a precursor to Yeshua's ministry was the appearance of John the Immerser, his entire ministry was exactly what we have previously discussed as the core calling of a prophet. Why do you think we see a prophet come forth calling Israel to t'shuvah before we see Yeshua, the soon-to-be Salvation of the world, begin His ministry?
3. The enemy is really good at contorting the truth just enough to make us question things. This is, in a lot of ways, one of the primary roots of temptation. In ways do you feel you see the enemy twisting the truth and causing issues in the Body of Messiah? What are some steps we can take to defend ourselves, individually and corporately, against such plots?

4. Yeshua said He came to set the captive free, yet so many believers still live in captivity. What kind of impact do you think it could have on the Body of Messiah of we lived in the freedom He has given?
5. We are called to emulate Yeshua, He was able to overcome temptation and live a spotless life. If we walk in the power of the Ruach HaKodesh we have the ability to avoid temptation following the example He laid out for us. How much more effective do you think we could be for Kingdom of Messiah if we strived in the Ruach to avoid temptation and live in His renewed image and likeness?

Yeshua Models Ruach Ministry (Chapters 19-21)

1. When Moses saw the Burning Bush his immediately reaction was to draw closer. The same Consuming Fire should be raging within us drawing others in. Why is it that, if the Ruach is in us, the world typically doesn't draw closer to us with the same yearning of Moses on Sinai?
2. If our example is to model a Yeshua-like life in the Holy Spirit, why is it we do not call people to turn from their sins with the same boldness and conviction we see from Yeshua in the Gospels?
3. What role do you think unforgiveness plays in hindering the work of the Ruach HaKodesh in the Body of Messiah today?
4. Matthew 10 says that Yeshua gave his disciples authority over unclean spirits in order to drive them and our to heal every kind of disease and sickness. Do you believe this authority was solely for the disciples in the first century? And if not, why do you think that as believers we do not tend to operate in faith in this authority today?

5. Discuss Yeshua's heart for restoration as seen in Matthew 18. Do you believe restoration of relationships is a vital piece of the puzzle for revival?

The Mantle on the Masses (Chapters 22-25)

1. What do you think of the correlation between the move of the Holy Spirit and the revelation of new salvations throughout the Book of Acts? And why do you think the Body of Messiah falls short on the fullness of the reality of both today?
2. Considering all of the biblical Feast Days, as found in Leviticus 23, have prophetic implications, how important do you believe it is for the Body to recognize that what is known as Pentecost was the biblical Feast of Shavuot? And that it was the same day as the events of Exodus 19 and 20 and that these events are mirrored in Acts 2?
3. How much does it change the perspective of the events of Acts 10 when we focus on the fact that Peter's vision is solely in relation to Gentiles coming to salvation and not about food?
4. Discuss the implications of the powerful image of the Holy Spirit falling on the Gentile household of Cornelius in the Acts 10 in the same exact manner in which it did upon the Jewish believers in Acts 2?
5. Do you think the Body of Messiah is tapped into the full reality of the Dunamis power of the Holy Spirit today as our predecessors were in the Book of Acts? Why or why not? If you believer we are not, then what can we do to better experience the Dunamis power?
6. Notice that it is rather common today for believers to cry out for an outpouring of the Holy Spirit as seen in Acts 2 and 10, however it is uncommon to see believers going out of their way to lay hands on new believers for the impartation of the Ruach as seen in Acts 8 and 9. Why do you think this is?

What now...? (Chapters 26-29)

1. If the Spirit is at war with the flesh and living in the flesh impedes the Spirits work in us, what efforts do you believe we can take to strive to walk in the Spirit and not in the flesh?
2. Paul says the same Spirit that raised Yeshua from the dead dwells in us, this is the same Holy Spirit that dwelled in Yeshua and the disciples. Why do we tend to not rely on the Holy Spirit to avoid and overcome temptation and sin today?
3. If Paul says that each person is given specific gifts of the Spirit the Lord's purpose and not all are given the same gifts, that each gift is equal and that together empowered by our gifts we make up one body which must work in unity, why do you think it is that some in the Body of Messiah have put a heavy focus on some gifts versus others?
4. What do you think of the correlation between Yeshua saying that the most important commandments are to "love the Lord your God" and to "love your neighbor as yourself" and Paul says that the greatest gift of the Spirit, and the one we should all seek after, is love?
5. How necessary do you believe unity in the Body of Messiah is in order to see true revival? And if you believe it is important then why do you think we allow ourselves to be so easily divided instead?
6. If through the power of the Ruach HaKodesh authority and dominion over things of this world have been restored to us, then why is it we allow fear to control us rather than working in the Ruach in faith?

ACKNOWLEDGEMENTS

Spirit + Truth was birthed from an in-depth study that we did several years ago at Congregation Mayim Chayim in Daphne, AL. The study along with this book would have never been what it is today had it not been for the help and co-teaching of my good friend and our synagogue's worship director, Lynn Huey.

I also want to thank my good friend Brooke Manolis who tirelessly edited Spirit + Truth for me. She helped take my work and make it a little easier to read for you, and I can't thank her enough for all the help she has been, not to mention the great encouragement she has given me through this process.

I'd like to acknowledge the awesome *mishpacha* (family) at Congregation Mayim Chayim who has encouraged me along the way as I've been working on writing this book.

I'd be beyond remiss if I didn't thank my friends at Soul Caffeine Coffee House in Daphne, AL for allowing me to spend countless hours there over the past several years working on Spirit + Truth. Plus, they provided ample fuel for thought through the endless cups of coffee I would drink while writing.

Last, but not least, I'd like to thank my wife (Danielle), our amazing children, as well as my parents for supporting me through this process. I would not be the man, father, and rabbi I am today if it weren't you guys, and especially for your prayers over the years.

ABOUT THE AUTHOR

David Tokajer is the founding rabbi of Congregation Mayim Chayim, a Messianic Jewish Synagogue in Daphne, AL. Both he and his wife, Danielle, are children of Messianic Jewish rabbis as well, and both have dedicated their lives to following the Promised Jewish Messiah.

David attended Nyack College in Nyack, NY. He has helped plant Messianic synagogues all along the Gulf Coast as well as in Manhattan, NY. He has served in synagogues and trained under Messianic rabbis in Alabama, Florida, Georgia, and New York. He is a sought after speaker and teacher.

David and Danielle have been married for 18 years and have enjoyed their ride following the call of Adonai on their lives. They love living on the Gulf Coast with their two beautiful children and two cuddle-loving dogs.

David is an avid motorcyclist, a vocal and passionate baseball fan, and Crossfit enthusiast.

Made in the USA
Monee, IL
02 February 2021